Praise for

"I really enjoyed it, It's the best book I've read on prayer."
~Carl D'Amico, Artist, Kansas City

*"I was deeply moved to think again about what I know about prayer
and consider how important it is in my every day life."*
~Marcia Streepy, Artist, Shawnee, Kansas

*"This book isn't a how-to. It's a warm hug. Reading it reminded me
that prayer is, essentially, an act of love....rather than shaming me about
how I should or should not be praying, this book embraced me with the
possibility of all that is, connecting me with women from thousands of
years ago and from down the street in a shared purpose and love."*
~Sally Nusbaum, Speaker/ Adoptive Mom, Colorado Springs

*"Oh, my... This is so beautiful. I just finished reading
it all in one sitting...a wonder and an inspiration."*
Debbie Kirchner, Organist, Kansas City, Missouri

*"There were some bits that I wrote down for myself
because I was like, 'I need to remember this.'"*
~M.Cordell, Author, Nodaway, Missouri

"Someone, somewhere should be hearing Polly tell a story."
~Sara Pike, Librarian, Cape Cod, Massachusetts

*"This is beautiful...I felt that....And really, I am all for 'praying like
a woman.' The strongest prayer warriors that I have ever met
are women."*
~Poet t.l. Sanders, Filmmaker, Chicago, Illinois

*"I've taught at two seminaries, led six congregations, and have one of
Polly's beautiful paintings. This book is an amazing scope of gifts,
calling, and inspiration."*
~Rev. Dr. Penny Zettler, Minneapolis, Minnesota

Pray
Like a
Woman

Polly Alice McCann

est. 1974

Light Shine Books

AN IMPRINT OF
FLYING KETCHUP PRESS ®
KANSAS CITY, MISSOURI

Fying Ketchup Press
11608 N. Charlotte Street,
Kansas City, MO 64115

Library of Congress Cataloging-Publication Data
Pray Like a Woman / McCann, Polly Alice
Library of Congress Control Number:

2 0 2 2 9 4 3 5 7 9

Softcover ISBN 13: 978-1-970151-22-0
Hardback ISBN-13: 9781970151-32-2
ePub ISBN-13: 9781970151-32-2

Other Books by Polly Alice McCann

✳

Puss' N Boötes: Dark Poems
Tea with Alice: Heirloom Poems
Kinlight: Homegrown Poems
Night Blooming Poems
Tomie Q. Barbeque: a folktale

Anthologies with Work by the Author

✳

Tales from the Goldilocks Zone
The Very Edge: Poems
Blue City Poets: Kansas City
Night Forest: Folk Art, Stories, Poetry
Tales from the Deep
Dreams that Changed our Lives, IASD, Hoss
365 Days: A Poetry Anthology, Vol. 3, 4, Benger
arc24, IAWE

✻

To Alyssa, Andrea, Dianna, Amy, Rebecca, Denise, and Christa, my cousins, and sister, to all my family and friends who inspired me to live a courageous life and hold onto faith. And to my son and daughter, nieces, and nephews, I wrote this book for you.

Pray Like a Woman

By Polly Alice McCann

�֍

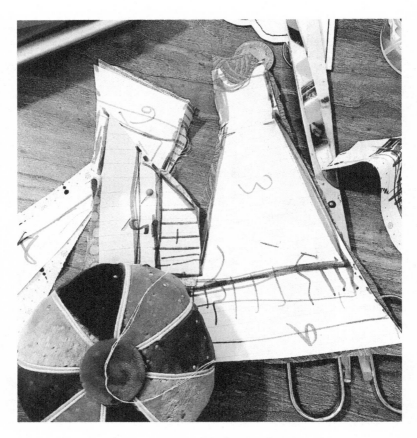

Battle Dress Pattern Mock up in Process, 2017

Preface

Have you ever heard the song "Jesus Take the Wheel" sung by Carrie Underwood? In the lyrics, a woman driving in a storm, spinning out of control, takes her hands off the wheel of her car. She gives over her future to God in faith he will drive better than she ever could.

You might have heard other stories where people share experiences like this—where they are miraculously saved. I have one or two. Maybe you do too. The idea of an invisible God immediately answering prayer is hard for a lot of us, but maybe not as foreign as we think. The song was on top of the charts for six weeks and won a Grammy or two. No matter what religion or culture we were born into, an emergency can cause a visceral reaction to pray. The idea of a living, present God, invisible but alive, tackling impossible problems with us and entering our fast-paced twenty-first century life, is hard for many of us to swallow. Setting aside differing beliefs, there are a lot of myths about prayer that keep us from trying it.

I first came across a "Jesus Take the Wheel" story when I was twelve years old. I found it in a faded book in my grandmother's kitchen. First you have to know, visiting my grandparent's house in a rather run-down neighborhood in Kansas City, Kansas, there wasn't much to do. My grandfather was a retired minister who sold Christian books in grocery store racks. My grandmother, a former Red Cross worker, tirelessly volunteered. The only things I found to do were digging around the flower beds, reading books in the attic, checking the snack drawer for cookies, or watching public television. The T.V. and cookies being limited, you can imagine that over the course of my childhood, I read an entire houseful of books.

One excruciatingly hot summer day, desperate for anything to do, I abandoned the dusty attic and prowled around the house for something to read. I found an undiscovered book stash above my grandmother's desk near the kitchen. *Mama's Way* by Thyra Ferré Björn stood out in faded gold letters. Fourth in a series published by Rinehart in 1959, the first three books were just sweet little stories of a family who immigrated to America from Lapland, i.e, Finland. The funny antics of an exasperated pastor, his young exuberant wife, and their nine children is much like parts of the memoirs written by Maria Von Trapp ("The Sound of Music") published a decade earlier. I adored the stories of Thyra's mother and her hysterical antics.

When it came to reading about Thyra as an adult, her book *Mama's Way* shared adventures with prayer. I couldn't get over her everyday kind of talking with God. The way she spoke to and about God made me ponder. How easy life must be if God were really listening and available to help at a moment's notice.

As I closed the book, finishing it to the end, I stopped to see my grandmother's name written carefully in the front page. Decades in the past, Thyra felt like someone I had just met. What if she were right? Could it be true that I was never alone? Could it be true that I always had help for big things, little things—everything? So right there, I prayed, "God, help me to be a person like this. Someone who prays and believes in you and gets help when I need it."

Sure, in one sense, I was a kid who wanted a magic charm, an easier life. I didn't know then that what I was really asking for was the ability to be a willing listener and to respond to those gentle promptings of something I would later learn to call the Spirit.

As I grew older, I read more and more books on prayer: biographies that were easily accessible to me like C.S. Lewis, Rees Howells, Brother Andrew, John Wesley, Hildegard of Bingen, Julian of Norwich, Mother Teresa, Watchman Nee, and more. Truthfully, finding books on prayer or people that wanted to talk about it was hard before the internet. However, I studied any workbook I could find like Neil Anderson's *Bondage Breaker*, Dutch Sheets' *Intercessory Prayer,* and St. Ignatius's *Spiritual Exercises.* I read the obligatory works by Richard Foster. I pored over Charles Spurgeon and everything from Carl Jung's completed works to Lao Tzu's Tao Te Ching on the Spirit. I took classes in Judaism and Islam and visited inner-city churches, gospel churches, Mennonite churches, missionary churches, even

Korean churches with kimchee afterwards! The more I studied, the more I discovered that what I learned about prayer, I didn't learn in books—I learned by praying.

I guess I was searching for something. Or maybe for other people who felt the same way as I did about prayer. I did over seven years of church internships—one at a Baptist seminary, one at an Episcopal church, and one at a Methodist church, to name a few. I taught Sunday school, youth group, VBS, children's church, college ministry, and took discipleship classes, Bible studies, and small group studies. I wasn't only a Bible nerd; I also took college Bible courses, traveled to Jerusalem, and did countless other religious activities.

None of those things taught me to pray either.

A few years ago, my cousin asked me how I pray. She wanted some advice. She had a handful of kids (six) and a husband serving as a policeman, and she wasn't sleeping much at night. She said she felt guilty asking for anything in prayer. Prayer might be selfish, she reasoned. Surely other people had more important needs that God should be listening to.

"Oh no, it's the opposite," I said. But I needed proof, an explanation.

I pored over my bookshelf for something that would easily answer her questions, but I couldn't find the right book to share with her. One book was very old. One book had examples buried in an obscure biography. One was about Jewish prayer. One was practically in old English. Often, they were by men. I knew none of these would help. I found one written for women but was from a Pentecostal point of view with a lot of special terminology someone outside that denomination might need a dictionary to understand.

Many of the books simply didn't address the issues my cousin faced because they were written by men. More accurately, gender aside, a lot of those books on prayer did not address the mindset of a helper/supporter role. Those books were not written by someone responsible for parenting, family outreach, or someone who had to help a spouse with a stressful job. Those books were written by someone who went to God in prayer about their work—and usually that work was some type of ministry—while their other needs, their support system, was taken care of by a spouse or partner. Their need for a hot meal on the table; someone to listen and care for them; someone to bounce ideas off of; someone to type their notes; someone to raise their children; someone to clean their house and buy their clothes, someone to make sure their home and family ran smoothly; someone to iron their suits and their handkerchiefs and drop their shoes off to be reheeled. All of their everyday matters were taken care of by someone else.

Now, to be blessed with an amazing partner or an army of helpers, didn't hamper these authors ability to pray or to write about prayer. However, to me, that meant their perspective on prayer was limited to a life experienced by a very small percentage of the general population.

I didn't need a book written by someone of privilege, I wanted a book about how to pray while standing up—while serving, while juggling, while parenting, while not having help, while having little income, and fewer resources. There weren't any books like this. Not a single book I owned on prayer could help my cousin.

So, naturally, I prayed about it.

Then I sat down and tried to write some of my own ideas in a letter, but I knew I was only scratching the surface. How could I share a lifetime of studying prayer in just a few pages?

You know what happened next? I felt a nudge. I would call it a deep inner question—deeper and smarter than my normal intuition. Some of us call that God speaking to us. And the question was this:

What would the loss be if I spent forty years learning how to pray, but never passed on my experiences?

I kept pushing that thought away. I told God that I wasn't spiritual enough to write a book on prayer, that I didn't have the right degrees. The next nudge reminded me that my favorite writers about prayer didn't have theology degrees.

I suddenly remembered Thyra. How unique her perspective! Her book was a memoir and not in the "spiritual" section. Her prayer was simple, creative, conversational, relational, and could be done quickly—or while doing ten other things. You didn't need to be a saint, or have a special ministry to save the world, she didn't ask her readers to do anything, she just told her story. That's what I wanted to do.

In a time when women were fighting to be allowed to be ordained ministers (something that continues to this day), Thyra became famous enough to do full-time speaking and writing on the topic of prayer all over the United States. It was her story of letting go of the wheel of her car on a slippery patch of ice that probably inspired the saying "Jesus, take the wheel." To her prayer was personal and immediate, as easy as making a phone call. I wrote a few pages about prayer for my cousin and then like all things, the idea lay somewhat forgotten.

Then one day wintery day, I went exploring. I found a little bookshop down by the river. It was so full of books, I could barely walk through the tiny aisles. *Steel's Used Books* had been around since my parents and grandpa had sold Christian books in Kansas City in the 1970s. It had once been a Christian bookstore, but now it looked like a mix between Diagon Alley and the end of the line for all Western thought. It was like my grandparents' house and more!

I walked to the back of the store, which was no small feat considering how crowded and twisted the path. After all the shelves of books on every kind of spiritual writing, poetry, folk tales, classics, cookbooks, there were a dozen shelves of Bibles and devotional books. In the back row (I say this figuratively as they went in every direction like a maze), I saw an entire shelf of the same book, each with the title "Miracles" in gold letters.

I pushed past more books and twisted around to a small nook created by shelves on four sides. I slipped in and sat down on a comfy chair and grabbed one of the books on the shelf.

Inside was a dedication. "Dear George," it read, "I thought you might like this book. It meant a lot to me, and it's been so wonderful to have you every week in our small group. Blessings as you go off to college. We will miss you! Love, D.A. Mears." Inside the book were just simple devotions and stories. Nothing to write home about—just someone's life, someone's spiritual experience.

That's when it hit me. All around me were hundreds of voices from the past. People's lives they shared. Each generation had people who felt it was important to share their stories. If other people had never shared their stories of faith and hope with me, where would I be? A flood of memories came to me. At a dry time, when I was worried I felt my faith slipping away, the chair in the bookstore became a life preserver, a sea of memories came pouring in of God's miraculous daily intervention in my life. This book began in that bookshop.

⊗⊗⊗

You will notice right away that each chapter in this book addresses a myth about prayer. For example, that it's silent, that it's about holding still, folding hands, or saying the right magic words—that prayer is selfish, that it can run out, or that it doesn't work. I debunk those myths using stories from my own life, and meditations or creative re-imaginings of the prayer life of women in scripture.

I've worked to make this book ecumenical. Each meditation on a Jewish or Christian women is careful to show their creative attitude toward a loving God–one that inspires both inside and outside the Western church. Everyone is invited here!

Although I address this book to women, these meditations can be read by anyone of any faith, age, or gender. To me, the "feminine" aspect is not about gender literally. Instead, it is about putting relationship, journey, creativity, intuition, and Spirit overall. These feminine values have often gotten people in trouble in a world that only looks to those masculine ideals of power and control.

At the end of each chapter, you'll find a short prayer based on that meditation—one you are welcome to use or rewrite as your own. If you have a blank journal that you want to write in as you read this book, go ahead. You don't need one unless you want one. These meditations are easy, something to borrow when you can't find the words. No homework. No blank spaces. No judgment. This isn't a Bible study with questions for you to fill in. It's a conversation between me and you. Imagine we are sitting together at a kitchen table. It's a way for me to introduce different ways I've found to connect with God through prayer; a sampling of situations you may not have known prayer was built for. I hope you too will find ways to relate to God, as a friend. I've provided a lot of scripture in the notes for you, and a few prayers in the back for quick reference.

These twelve women's stories have helped me understand my own.

Their prayers have helped me learn to pray. We won't have time to go into the Greek and the Hebrew language studies. We won't have time in this book to explore excellent prayer traditions of diverse faiths. We aren't going to parse grammar or debate theology. What I will do, however, is push to show the perspectives and values women have always held about prayer and how they pray. Not because they are the most true, or right, but to add balance; to provide an alternative feminine emphasis where it may have been overlooked or marginalized previously.

It's hard to remember for some that the name of God is neither masculine or feminine, but that God created us all with different perspectives, energies, attitudes, and gifts that represent all of God's amazing attributes. I use the masculine pronoun for God because of the English language tradition. For some people, this feels uncomfortable. If that is you, you are correct that "he" isn't the most accurate translation. For a long time, it wasn't comfortable for me to use the masculine pronoun for God. Feel free to change or remove unhelpful pronouns about God in this book to make it work for you.

Despite all my experiences, I'm not a theologian. I'm offering just a single layperson's testimony to faith. However, I know a testimony to faith in God through prayer changed my life for the better, even for the best. I can humbly hope that somewhere these stories might encourage someone on their faith journey. I know in the end, a testimony and an understanding of how we connect with God is one of the strongest ways to share a simple faith. What I hope will happen is that you will recognize these prayers as your own. I've gathered experiences to share openly with you what I hope will demonstrate that praying is how families are repaired, foundations built, and relationships restored. You can "pray like a woman," you can pray while busy, while serving, while poor, while confused, while needy—and you can see your life and the lives of others change. ✳

Introduction

We keep adding to that prayer, drop by drop, and then when it's full it's like a 'dam breaking.' I set down the letter translated from the curly Amharic script mailed from the other side of the world in Ethiopia. Glancing up from the letter, I watched snow fall in drifts outside my apartment window, and I wondered when I would see answers to my prayers.

❀ ❀ ❀

At twenty-three years old, my prayers seemed stuck at the ceiling. I was constantly underemployed and far from home. I often wondered if I was in the right place and what I could do to make things better.

My letters from a little girl named Mulu began shortly after I began sponsoring her through *Compassion International* when she was only four years old. As a student worker at my college, I made only a hundred dollars a month. I decided to trust God. For some reason, I felt compelled to be Mulu's sponsor even though one-third of my income would go toward her education and care.

Eighteen years later, I was still sponsoring Mulu. Despite many years of uncertainty, and even times of unemployment, I'd never missed a payment. My favorite letter from Mulu was the one where she explained learning the story of Jonah and how he was "saved" by a big fish. Jonah spent three days praying inside its belly before that fish coughed him up on dry land. I was stunned. Mulu's letter explained her understanding of prayer building up like a reservoir to overflowing; how prayer rescued a runaway missionary like Jonah. Reading Jonah's story again, I realized I had never imagined that big fish as a way to "save" him from a great storm. I'd seen the whale as punishment.

Mulu's insightful perspective kept me thinking. Did I think of prayer as punishment? How was I to figure out where to go in life, or know if I'd made a whale-sized mistake, without prayer? How much prayer would it take to fix my life, I wondered desperately. Prayer sometimes felt like a waste of time. Was it even getting me anywhere? Mulu's word pictures gave me hope. How could a small child on the other side of the world teach me so much about faith and prayer?

⊗⊗⊗

Thirteen years later, I got a letter that Mulu would graduate. She'd be on her own in just two months. I was living in a house back in my old hometown. Mulu was now older than I had been when I began sponsoring her!

I wanted to send her a graduation gift, but I couldn't. I couldn't even make the last monthly payment. My spouse had left our family suddenly, and for good, overnight. Now with only less than a third of an already scant income for myself and my two kids. I had little hope—and I was scared about where we might end up.

It had only been a few days in shock at our situation, but I had to snap out of it quickly and cancel as many payments as I could from our monthly bills. *Compassion International* was second on my list. I picked up the phone. A kind, older sounding man with a Swahili accent answered—I think he said his name was Francis—I told him my story.

"I've sponsored Mulu her whole life," I said, "since I was in college. And now–," I paused with tears in my eyes, "for the first time, I can't make the payment. I have to cancel with only two payments left. I won't be able to keep supporting her through her graduation."

The man said something completely unexpected. His words threw me off the rails of my grief. "First, I want to say, you've helped this child through her whole life. Thank you."

Stunned, I became simply undone as he continued to express thankfulness.

"Now God is going to support you." He thanked me for my faith and my support. Then he prayed for me while I was still there on the phone.

This stranger praying, with me, thanking me, shook me to my very core. Even more unexpectedly, he said he wouldn't cancel my account.

"You will skip this one payment," he said, "but you will be able to make the last payment. God will change your situation. He will provide."

I couldn't believe this man. Here I was about to be homeless. My job was new, and it consisted of teaching people to paint for slightly above minimum wage. I had a few hours, no benefits, and the job would end any day. Here I was, afraid for my sanity, even for my safety, but Francis wanted me to believe that in only one month I would be in a different situation. A situation expansive enough to make my last contribution to Mulu's education, her graduation day.

I had trouble accepting any of it, but what if he could be right? I had sponsored Mulu for her whole life. Those little payments added up to school income, extra food, and clothing for her. Surely God could sponsor me.

If one person had faith for me, maybe my situation could change. I was drowning, but didn't God promise to help us when we needed it? Faith was hard. What if I prayed backwards like Francis? What if I prayed looking backwards from a future where God had already answered—It was just enough to kick my imagination into high gear, just enough to find a smidgen of faith during crisis. Right then and there, I prayed for God to rescue me. And I said a big prayer:

"Lord, you are going to take care of us. You have a plan for us. You are going to bring something good out of this terrible situation. I'm ready to go anywhere you want, do whatever you want. Please rescue me."

Then I added the strongest prayer I know. "I know you are going to take care of this, you have taken care of this. It's already done. Praise the Lord."

I did feel better. I thanked God for hearing and for providing as though he'd already done it. God's outside of time, I reasoned, so it couldn't hurt.

After that day, admitting on the phone my inability to keep my promises or pay my bills, I washed my face and took care of the kids and the house. I went to work at my part-time job and waited for God to rescue me. I had about six or eight weeks to find a place for us to live, and a new life. I had no idea where to start.

One day, I took a wrong turn while driving to my cousin's house who had been watching my kids for me. I'd been on the road a few times and it was one that always brought me peace.

Courage suddenly made me begin praying that I'd find somewhere to live on that beautiful straight road north of the city. It was out in the country where cows still roamed, and hay bales shone in the sun. For the first time in a long time, I felt a strong sense of excitement for my future. It suddenly seemed a new and different view of my situation came to me in prayer. It was more like a conversation than anything else.

Almost immediately, I started remembering what it felt like to be close to God. During the past few months, I had almost stopped believing in God altogether because life seemed so gray and dim and heartless. Despite poring over devotionals and trying everything I could to stay sane, I remember one particular moment where I said to myself, "If love doesn't exist, maybe God doesn't either." That scared me because God had always been my anchor, my friend. I knew something was wrong, but I didn't know what. I had immediately buckled down and read scripture after scripture, but I felt like one of those dried-out plants that couldn't even absorb water.

That day in the car, on the beautiful country road, I gave God my future, hoping for miracles changed me. I felt secure, strong, and beautiful. As though I felt it for the first time: I felt God loved me. A quiet, peaceful feeling in my heart reminded me of all the times I enjoyed prayer when I was young.

Don't you remember all the dreams you had? All the things we were going to do together. I felt a still small question in my heart.

I did remember. Those thoughts felt deeper than my own; invitational, full of promise.

"I'm too afraid, too lost, too alone," I prayed. "Can anything good happen now?"

It's not like I heard a voice aloud. It was just that those inner thoughts felt deeper, warmer, and had a different tone than my own inner voice, as if someone held a gong up to my ear and hit it. Those thoughts vibrated at a different frequency. I felt truly awake for the first time in a long time. The whole rest of the world seemed quiet and faded. This voice was the one from my childhood prayers, a voice I knew—a voice that was hard to ignore.

What about all the places you wanted to go, and things you wanted to do?

I remembered my childhood dreams of being an artist, of having a big family, teaching Bible studies, teaching classes, serving people, writing books. None of those dreams had been fulfilled yet, but maybe they still could be. I remembered my dreams to travel the world, to study painting in France, to explore ancient ruins and old libraries, see big forests, walk quiet paths. I had a lot of dreams. God knew me better than I knew myself.

"Yes," I finally said. "Let's go with your plan. I don't have one anymore." I felt like I was losing an argument. God's case was convincing. I had two choices: I could stay drowning in sorrow at my losses and attempt to try to maintain my life as it was, staring at the closed doors—or I could accept my situation. I could turn around and look at the whole world open in front of me; listen to God's heart just calling me to come out and enjoy life with him at the helm again.

My friend Mulu was right about prayer. All those prayers I had prayed about those dreams over my whole life, the dreams to make art and books. Those dreams to share my love of God and prayer with other people. Those dreams of having family around me. Of finding a home where I belonged. Suddenly, they just seemed to fill and overflow. My yes to God that day must have been that last drop because, like a broken dam, the answers to my prayers began to overflow.

Within three days, my baby brother, Mike, drove all night from Georgia, making it to my house in an impossibly short time. God made sure I wasn't alone for even a single day. Within a week, he told me he would stay indefinitely and help me take care of my kids. We looked for jobs. Within a few weeks, we both found full-time jobs with benefits. We enrolled my kids in school, a new kindergartener and a third grader.

Last of all, we got a call from our mother. She said she decided to buy a house near us and rent it to us until she could retire. All we had to do was go shopping and find a house large enough to hold my parents, myself, my kids, and maybe one or more of my siblings.

Eight weeks later, we lived in a new house. It wasn't the apartment next to the huge stack of dumpsters with the "For Rent" sign I had been considering. Hard to believe, we found a house on the country road I'd driven up and down praying for somewhere to live. I'm not kidding. The house was next to a park with a view. From my backyard with a flower garden, I could see a little wooden bridge over a creek. I'm not making this up.

We even had our first ever dog–just a few weeks later. Within three months, my other brother moved from the east coast to go back to school in Kansas City. He moved in since we had so much room. Within eighteen months, my mom and dad moved back to our hometown as well.

Where I had been alone all the time. Suddenly my family was back. My aunt and cousins showed up to watch my kids so I could work. Friends came to help me pack and move. Like a flood, like waves of water, my big prayers were answered in overflowing grace and miraculous love. In a way, I had a new family. In a way I had my old family back. Miracles abounded that were so large, so unimaginable, that each day, despite my grief, waves of healing surrounded me.

So, two months after that first call to *Compassion*, I was able to log in from my computer at our new house. I clicked to pay the very last payment for my sponsored child, Mulu. In all those years, I had only missed one payment. It seemed like so long ago I had been crying on that phone call when I had no idea where my help would come from. That was a very different day from the one where I confidently paid the last school fee, knowing Mulu had graduated. How amazing that I could be a small lifeline of support during her childhood and finish that promise.

As I hit the last button to send, I imagined my sponsored "daughter" was in her town somewhere graduating from her school program and thanking God for the chance at an education. Mulu and I were both praising God, I'm sure. I think maybe we both graduated that day. I thought I knew about prayer, but in the days ahead, I discovered I had only scraped the surface…

❀❀❀

In the seven years since, I've found myself on a long journey. I've had to use everything I ever learned about prayer. My faith has been tested past many places I thought were limits. Where I couldn't find a path to prayer, I invented new prayer methods out of survival, and out of the exhilarating and often frightening faith journey my life has been. I had been someone who prayed continually, but then I became someone who was in a relationship with God continually. I asked God's help to get out of bed in the morning, to decide what to buy at the store, to make it through five minutes, then ten.

I've sought direction for my parenting and peace for my kids through prayer, and everything, absolutely everything else. Since then, things have changed—not just my career, my plans, my life, but me... I've changed. Each step is bathed in prayer. I think that I'm still standing today because somehow, I found a way to absorb the idea of how to "Pray like a Woman." On the way, I'll share with you my journey and the moments, both big and small, that took me on a path to find God loves us and that he cares for us all in every small thing. ✳

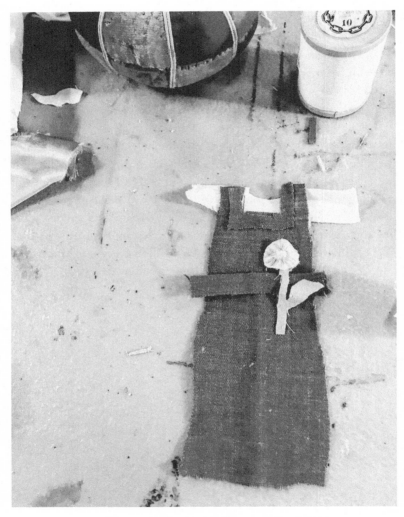

Mother Dress ~Eunice, studio process detail 2019

I

Vision Prayer

PRAY LIKE A WOMAN

Prayer is not selfish ~Eunice's Story

Y ou can learn a lot about a person by getting to know their mother. On a snowstormy night in January, near Minneapolis, Minnesota, my mom and dad prepared for an icy drive from their little yellow house. My mom was nearly thirty-two weeks pregnant and having contractions. They drove through the snow-covered roads to the local hospital.

When the nurse told my mom, "You are going to have this baby tonight!" my parents were surprised. I wasn't supposed to be born for another eight weeks. The doctor informed them of possible risks and complications of a premature birth that included deafness, brain damage, blindness, or death because my tiny lungs wouldn't be ready in time.

My parents worked for a small publishing company and the entire staff were on a riverboat having a work convention.

As a child, I always enjoyed the part of the story where my dad called the party on the boat and let them know to pray for all three of us. Before cell phones, this seemed magical because I wondered how a boat could have a phone. It made me feel special that so many people cared about me.

But my favorite part of the story was what happened next. The doctor gave another dire prediction about my uncertain future right before I was born. But my mother made breath for this answer, "Jesus loves this baby, and she is going to be just fine."

"And you were fine," my mother would always add after she finished retelling the story.

That part was my favorite.

"But there's nothing wrong with my hearing, is there? There's nothing wrong with my lungs, is there?" I'd chant.

"No, there isn't," my mother would answer.

"There's nothing wrong with my eyes. I don't even need glasses!" I would say proudly. I was the only one in the family who didn't need them.

As a young kid, when I felt down about myself and all the things I didn't excel in—sports, social skills, looks, a lot of things, I'd be reminded of that story and feel a bit better. I would silently thank God that my eyes were so good. It made it easier to do all the painting and drawing I loved so much. I always assumed the people on that boat on the night of my birth had prayed for my eyes very specifically. Maybe learning that my life was bathed in prayer at such a young age is what gave me some of the confidence and courage to believe that prayer was something effective but simple. Prayer was just talking to God about ways we needed help, and we could expect an answer that might last a lifetime.

Throughout my school years, my mom always encouraged me to keep pursuing the arts along with my faith. She or my grandma drove me to art classes from preschool through high school. When I had a science or math project, I would invariably panic, but my mom, she'd just smile and say, "Don't worry. We are going to turn this into an art project, and everything will be okay."

I felt those prayers from my parents, grandparents, and friends during an uncertain beginning were still with me, and I used those prayers to help me find my calling in life. To me, they were a lifeline to faith. I believed God protected me and so I believed God was real and that he loved and cared about me. I reasoned that if God cared about a two-pound baby born in a snowstorm, and her parents, he must care about everyone else just as much.

This gave me a certain view of life I wouldn't have otherwise. My mother's story became the first thread in my belief that God hears our prayers.

※※※

There's someone mentioned just once in the New Testament who was a mother and must have deeply influenced her son's life the way my mom influenced mine. Eunice, Timothy's mother is a woman in scripture who is often overlooked. The words about her are few, but they demonstrate something valuable: a specific example of a faithful parent who was willing to speak up about her beliefs.[1] Paul wrote this to Timothy, an important minister and teacher:

"I am reminded of your sincere faith, which first lived in your grandmother Lois and in your mother Eunice and, I am persuaded, now lives in you also," are the words Paul wrote in one of his letters to small Jewish communities that became the early Christian Church in the first century C.E.

Timothy has two letters written to him that we can still read today in scripture. In addition, Luke writes in the book of Acts that Lystra was the town "where a disciple named Timothy lived, whose mother was Jewish and a believer but whose father was a Greek."[2] Timothy came from a mixed family of two races and two religions. His "sincere faith" came from his mother and grandmother, we're told.[3] And part of his story makes me think that Timothy had a whopper of a story about his life that his mother shared with him as well. Paul writes to Timothy about his birth story and his mother's faith. It was such a good one that everyone knew about it. Paul only implies some of the story here: "Timothy, my son, I am giving you this command in keeping with the prophecies once made about you, so that by recalling them you may fight the battle well."[4]

What must that story have been? A story that kept Timothy strong during tough times: times on the road, times in ministry, times teach-

1   2 Timothy 1:5
2   Acts 16:1
3   2 Timothy 1:5
4   1 Timothy 1:18

and even time in prison with his friend Paul for "disturbing the ₋ce" with their shared faith stories.

This unknown story (or prophecy) was either from his mom, Eunice, or she was the one who shared it with her son so much, it changed his life. And it became a story everyone knew. It gave her son a focus and a vocation, his calling to be a teacher. A prophecy is similar to a prayer in that it is a good word spoken about the future over a child. When my mom said, "This child will be fine," she hadn't seen it to be true yet. She was speaking into the future. That's what a prophecy does. It's a prayer in faith. And when she kept retelling the story, it made an impact on my life. I think Eunice was like my mom.

Words that give direction, energy, and insight to the decisions, troubles, and battles of daily life, are powerful. We go back to those words, and so does our family. Some stories, some words are that powerful; we return to them over and over. A prayer or word over a young person's life, if you tell them the story later. It makes all the difference. Eunice's kid became famous for seeking God's direction to be a great teacher. In this case, prayer can't be selfish if it empowers our family to seek out the callings of God's will for their life. If it brings them closer to God, how is that selfish? It's just the opposite: it's generative. It brings new faith, new hope, and new understanding.

❁❁❁

Oftentimes, even with good a word over our lives, and faith stories shared by parents or mentors, hard times come anyway. I imagine Eunice as a lot like my own mother: cheerful, full of singing, and a good story or two. I remember my mom was often so upbeat, so reluctant to let me worry about anything. One summer, I came home from college to find my dad using a white cane with a red tip on the end and a thick pair of sunglasses. He had gone blind, and no one had told me. It was a tough time. I had just come home from school where I was studying visual art. The irony was not lost on me. I literally spent hours and hours a day discussing how things looked, and my dad couldn't see. Later, I found diabetic eye surgery had caused blindness, instead of preventing it.

My mom was the strong one. She decided rather than cower back and be afraid of the future, she would charge ahead. She went away for the summer to work on an intensive low-residency master's degree. No matter the present, she had to think about the future. This took incredible courage and faith on her part.

And for me, at home, I spent the summer taking care of my younger brothers and sister, and my dad. At only nineteen, each day was full of driving around the suburbs of Washington, D.C. (I had a fear of driving) to places like band camp, dance lessons. Those commutes and a million other things were hard for me to do well or patiently. Giving all of myself and my time was so new and so challenging after a year of having been spoiled with the freedom of a college student. I was at my wit's end.

The one thing I remember most clearly: I had to do all the grocery shopping, but without my dad's income, our budget was non-existent. One time, I only had a hundred dollars to buy groceries for the five of us—and I didn't know when more money or groceries would come. I remember counting up each penny on a calculator when I added a second bag of tortilla chips to the cart, figuring they could work for a meal and snacks. Meat and vegetables were the most expensive, so I hadn't bought very much.

One afternoon, I had to make dinner but there wasn't much food left. I opened the pantry, and it was mostly bare. I pulled out one can of cream of chicken soup and some noodles. In the fridge I found a single green pepper. So, I pulled out my mother's cookbook and prayed for a recipe to make a meal out of nothing. Praying was becoming a moment-to-moment activity during that summer, so I prayed God would help me figure out what to cook.

When I came to the recipe for "Three Cheese Chicken Casserole," I felt like I had won the lottery. I carefully followed the recipe and simply omitted the things I didn't have. "It's Three Cheese Chicken Casserole!" I said to the empty kitchen, "only without chicken or cheese." When my dad sat down to take a bite, he never said anything about the missing ingredients.

During that summer, I often cried in the car on the way to work at the local grocery store and–sometimes while at work, which was embarrassing.

One night, in the middle of the summer, after a long harrowing day, I begged God for something to help me get through being the support person for three children under the age of thirteen and one disabled parent. I found a verse in Psalms: "Those who go out weeping, carrying seeds to sow, will return with songs of joy, carrying sheaves with them."[5] The word "tears" struck me because eyes and vision were all I thought about. I kept wondering what was the point of being a visual artist if some people, especially my own father, couldn't see? The one thing I was good at, wasn't helpful to him. Was it helpful to anyone?

The only good day of that whole summer happened late one afternoon. A dark-haired man came through my line to get a few groceries and gave me his tax-free card at the checkout. The card said he was the ambassador from Egypt, which wasn't too surprising since I only lived a few minutes from the capitol. I looked up at him and tried to smile—a rarity at that time. He looked back at me and said, "My, but you have beautiful eyes!" That meant so much to me. It was one of the only positive things I had heard all summer.

I felt hopeless because, everything was telling me to give up my good artist "eyes," quit school, or find a more practical career. "Yes, I have good eyes," I thought, "but what good are they?" Even my positive thoughts weren't getting me through.

Should I stay home and care for my family? Give up college? I didn't know but that verse from Psalms stuck with me. If I kept sowing into my future, even though the tears, I could come back with some benefit for all of my work. I knew "sheaves" were just big piles of wheat tied up, the product of a summer of planting small seeds. If I pressed through now with faith and hope, even in tears, I could have hope that good things would come.

The ambassador from Egypt talking about my eyes reminded me of the stories of my infancy and the miracle of my being able to see exceptionally well, well enough to be an artist. I wished I had someone to talk to about it. My whole world seemed gone. High school friends had moved away. My best friend from college was in Alaska off the grid, so mail and phone weren't an option. I was a mess, and I had no idea what to do.

So, I prayed. "God, will I have to give up college? Everyone needs me here and it's too expensive." E-mail had just become fairly workable that year and my friend Julie from college sent me a few encouraging "letters." She gave me a lot of hope. So I kept praying

"Dear God, is art pointless? Does art just hangs around and say-nothing, do nothing, heal no one, feed no one, teach no one. Is it a joke?"

A song came on the radio right then. "I Know You Know" by Sierra. The words washed over me about how God has a plan for us. The verse Jeremiah 29:11 was an old favorite: that God "had a plan" for me was hard to believe. But I could hold on and wait for direction.

At the end of the summer, my mom came home. She was so grateful that I had taken care of my dad and my three younger siblings all summer. My dad was receiving occupational therapy and doing better with getting around.

"So are you looking forward to going back to college?" she asked me.

I was surprised. "You mean, you think I should? You don't need me here?"

"No," she said. "You should go back to school. We are fine here. I'm just thankful you came home to help us for the summer."

Then, realizing we weren't on the same page, she explained her plans—why she chose this time to work on a degree so she could give our family a better future.

In only a few minutes her hope and strength and faith filled me back up. She was right. I shouldn't give up on my future either. I would trust in the path I'd already prayed about and decided on. I would keep going, follow my mom's example, and keep investing in my future.

That fall, I went back to school. Although I wanted to change my major, I didn't. I trusted my mom's words about me. My eyes were good for a reason. Sometimes while I drew in the art studio or worked in the photography lab searching out small nuances of gray shadow, or lightly grading the scale of a charcoal drawing, those words from my mom would come back. I'd hear her say, the doctor said you would be born blind, and my little preschool voice answering, But I wasn't. I'm not blind. I don't even need glasses!

I was still worried being a visual artist was completely selfish. I didn't even know how to ask God to help me, but he did through those "stories" on my life. My parents' prayer for me from those first day I was born meant "vision" was part of my calling. That's what art was about. Sure, I wanted to quit being an art major, or even quit college when things were hard, but I kept at it. I struggled but, I continued despite my grief at our hardships, and my worry for my family back home.

All those hours working in the grocery store meant I could buy art supplies, so I took Painting 101. At the end of my second year back at school, I finished my first painting course. When I painted it was like my life came into focus. Nothing made me feel so alive. Painting was pure joy. I prayed that God would help me decide if using my eyes to be an artist was a precious waste of time and money or if somehow it was useful in some way I couldn't understand.

❦❦❦

> *In prayer, as in poetry we turn to words, not to use them as signs for things, but to see the things in the light of the words….In poetry, in prayer, the words speak….In our own civilization, in which so much is being done for the cause of the liquidation of language, the realm of prayer is like an arsenal for the spirit, where words are kept clean, holy, full of power to inspire and to keep us spiritually alive. Out of that arsenal we get the strength to save our faith, our appreciation of things eternal, from vanishing away.*

Not long afterward, I found these words in a little blue book on a high shelf in the library while doing research for a paper. It wasn't a book I was looking for. The second-story windows cast light down on all the books in a large gallery of towering shelves, and sometimes the gold letters on a cover would sparkle in a passing sunbeam. Just such a chance caused me to pull the book off the shelf and take a look. In this one passage, I felt solid ground for the first time in a year.

Abraham Joshua Heschel, a well-celebrated Jewish theologian, described my situation with words that were lyrical and direct. They spoke to my hungry soul worried that being an artist, a poet, a person of prayer were useless callings. Even better, he saw them as all the same thing.

Both my grandmother and my dad were now blind and couldn't see my art. That made it feel even more useless. However, I felt Heschel's words must be true. If art was as important as poetry and prayer, then I wouldn't give it up. Visual arts were a hard vocation for me to accept. Everyone I knew valued other priorities. But here in this book, it suddenly seemed so clear to me that working with invisible things like words, symbols, and ideas was not useless. That unseen, spiritual work was just as important as the work I could see, taste, or touch. And that being a painter was not about working with things that people could see, but with invisible ideas available to anyone.

My prayer changed from asking God if I should quit being an artist, to asking for help on how to be both creative and spiritual in a contemporary world. I knew two things from reading the words of Heschel. One, that prayer was important to other people too. Some of them were very well-known and cherished for their work. Two, if someone like him believed prayer was important, equal to the invisible world of writing and the impractical world of art and poetry, but also essential to what people truly needed to live, then I didn't have to abandon my callings for something more utilitarian.

My prayer to feel at peace as an art major was answered for the most part. Nursing, teaching, or social work weren't the only ways to make a difference in the world. I was relieved. Whatever my callings, they were important and useful to God, and now I could take the time to find out.

I wrote Heschel's words in colored pencil on a torn-out sketchbook page and taped it to my locker in the fine arts building. I wanted my final project for the last day of class to show how much I had learned about what vision meant to me. I needed two final pieces. First, I painted a dark railway tunnel opening to the light of the Pennsylvania hills. By the time I began to work on the second, a huge six-foot-tall canvas, I only had one night to finish before it was due.

It was late in the evening before the canvas was ready for paint.

I began a self-portrait. I painted only my head and shoulders. As I painted, the brushes weren't large enough and I struggled in frustration. It was like trying to clean a whole kitchen with a toothbrush.

Around one in the morning, I ran out of paint. I prayed, "Lord, I just want to finish this class well. I want to make something to show how far I've come this year and how hard it was not to give up on this altogether. What am I going to do? The brushes aren't working, the paint is gone, and this is due tomorrow. I'll have nothing to turn in."

What do you have to work with? A new, calming thought made me stop and look in my art box. There I had one tube of black paint and some blue and white left.

I shrugged. It was something to work with. In my hand, I had a rag. It struck me it would work as well for painting as for wiping off the tiny brushes. I felt a sense of peace come over me as I painted with the rag and the black paint, and everything began to flow.

Maybe you couldn't say this was the moment I became an artist, but it was the moment I became a painter. As I was using the oil, some of it began to drip like tears. I remembered the worst moment of my summer when I had been crying tears in broad daylight, not wiping them away, because I knew my dad was too blind to see them. To me that was the lowest point, the most painful. I took the oils and made sure to highlight one single tear coming down the face on the canvas. The self-portrait complete, I cleaned up, went back to the dorm, and got several hours of sleep.

The next day, bright and sunny, finals began. Our painting classroom had a twenty-five-foot ceiling and a cement floor with stools and easels. Enormous box-shaped windows near the ceiling filled the room with light. When I brought the large self-portrait into the room, six feet tall, the rest of the students gasped. It was so large for a freshman painting project, and so very dark. When it came time to talk about my piece, people were silent, simply staring.

"It's beautiful," the professor said.

"It's about my dad," I replied. "He went blind this summer."

It was the first time I had told anyone. All the art students nodded. I felt they understood that I had been going through the impossibility of being an artist creating work that my family wouldn't see. What a relief. Why hadn't I told anyone before?

My painting conveyed the rest of the story for me. A portrait about grief and loss and how to cope with lack of vision—in the painting, a single tear running down my face.

That moment God taught me that my relationship to him and my callings to follow his lead, even in something small like what classes to take, or what career to choose, were more than something I could see. Art was just one way he had given me to tell my story about his faithfulness, to talk about overcoming hardship, about persevering in the dark. The fact that I was even there to tell my story was because God was with me all the way. I knew through answers to prayer he cared about my birth, he cared about my callings, and he cared about even a single art project. God cared about what I cared about, and he made sure I had what I needed, whether it was paint or simply confidence to continue.

I knew I had to keep on studying art. It was another way to remember or mark what was important, to study the words and promises sown into my life. I knew I had to plant into my future whether I was smiling or in tears. Both were okay.

❀❀❀

So how did Eunice's story, an obscure mom mentioned in a letter from one Christian to another in an old Greek text, help my prayer life? It was something I held onto. The idea of a mother who remembered to pray and share hope for the future. Similar to my own mother's story, it meant prayer wasn't so unusual—it happened every day in many families.

Paul wrote, "Timothy, my son, I am giving you this command in keeping with the prophecies once made about you, so that by recalling them you may fight the battle well."[6] Timothy had faith from his mother, Eunice, and his grandmother. A prophecy was some words of hope for the future that kept him on track and kept him believing. Maybe those words were about his calling to be a teacher and a minister. We don't know what they were, but those words took Timothy all over the Middle East, into parts of Asia, and even into prison in

---

6   *1 Timothy 1:18, NIV*

Rome. They took him through months without a home, or a regular place to sleep, bad travel conditions on land and water, losing luggage and being unwelcome; all the while aiding Paul—who most agree had vision problems himself.

Paul again writes to Timothy, "But you, keep your head in all situations, endure hardship, do the work of an evangelist, discharge all the duties of your ministry...[7] "Timothy, guard what has been entrusted to your care. Turn away from godless chatter and the opposing ideas of what is falsely called knowledge."[8]

This tells me there are two types of knowledge. One, what God knows about you, what words he places in your life through mentors and mothers in your faith. Two, what people say about you with good intentions that may not fit your real story.

Maybe you're like me or like Eunice and you're in a hard situation where you are not sure if the good words given to you about your journey are true. Maybe you are pulled between two cultures, or two ways of thinking. Maybe you are afraid to pray for what you need and want because it might be selfish or too small of a thing to pray about. Maybe you are grieving the loss of something in your life or the particular road you must travel. You don't have any new information to go on, but you feel like the path you are on is hard and fruitless and maybe pointless. Maybe you are afraid to pray for your future or your kids' future because you just can't imagine a good one.

This is the time to pray. Prayer does not take away the tears: It uses them to grow a harvest of promises. Prayer is not selfish, it gives vision; it reminds us of God's promises for our future. Here is a prayer I think is something like what Eunice might have prayed. A vision prayer is seeing your future and holding on to hope, knowing God cares about you:

Dear Father of all children of every kind,

You're the one who causes everything to grow. Save me from sorrow. I'm in a hard place where nothing is as easy as I expected. People look down on me and I don't have any kindness left, not even for

---

7   *2 Timothy 4:5, NIV*
8   *(1 Timothy 6:20, NIV)*

myself. Some people doubt me and my good intentions; they don't care for who I am, or the choices I've made with my family. They don't understand my calling or the place you've brought me from. They don't see the good future I know you promised to me and to my family. Help me remember your word. Remind me what is true. Silence the negative voices and give me your words of wisdom. Even though I don't know why I'm on this path, give me the next step and the next step after that. I am crying now.[9] I'm in a lot of pain. Give me the faith I need to trust your word: that nothing I have done is wasted.[10] That all your promises will come back full. That you are with me in this place. Your words over my life and my loved ones are true. Someday soon, I will dance and sing. My arms will be full, not empty. You will take this tiny bit of faith I have and make it grow. You are with me, and I praise you for giving me the faith to invest in the future and for giving me the strength to continue on this journey. ❀

---

9   "You have seen how many places I have gone. Put my tears in Your bottle." (Psalm 56:8 NLV)

10 " So then, Christian brothers, because of all this, be strong. Do not allow anyone to change your mind. Always do your work well for the Lord. You know that whatever you do for Him will not be wasted. " (1 Corinthians 15:58, NLV)

Miracle Dress ~ Tabitha, Quilted Satins on Wallpaper, 8 x 10 in. 2021

II
Patchwork Prayer

Prayer is not magic ~ Tabitha's Story

Many times, a friend has asked me to pray for them. To pray for them to have a healthy baby, to find a life partner, to come back to health from cancer or depression. Maybe people ask you to pray too. I always say yes and go about asking God. It only takes a few moments for me to ask him to meet their needs.

"I feel guilty when I pray for myself," said my friend Fiona. "So many people have it worse."

I stared at her speechless. We were at my kitchen table over a glass of iced tea. It was summer and we had just had a trying Saturday morning. Still in her house slippers, Fiona had come over to help me with a car that wouldn't start.

What an idea she held! Guilty for prayer? I couldn't figure out what to say. Was prayer something that could be used up, something that could run out? Somehow, she had the idea that prayer was like magic and there might not be enough to go around. I thought about it for a few days then I sat down to write her a note:

Dear Fi,
Thanks for going out with me for pizza the other night. I really

needed to be out with a friend. Sometimes I worry I won't make it as a single parent that works so much. That my life will become something I imagine as the worst possible: living on packages of Tuna Helper, never taking the curlers out of my hair or bothering to get dressed. (This must be something I saw on TV once and it stuck with me.) Fears are crazy things. (My image of the absolute end of the road involves Tuna Helper.... Hmmm, what does that say about me?)

I have an idea to help you think about prayer. Remember when my car wouldn't work, and you used soap to grease one of the belts and get it running again? That's what God does. He shows up with an unexpected solution from something we didn't know was possible. He shows us what we have something available to us in abundance that we didn't know was just what we needed.

Remember right after that? We went to the gas station to fill up the car. We were there and probably not looking our best. There was that lady in a size five blue dress with tiny white polka dots. She was filling up her sleek expensive car with gas on the other side of the tank. I remember you had house shoes and I had flip flops while she wore high heels. But oddly, she looked over at us two single moms in our old clothes and said aloud, "I'd trade places with you in a heartbeat."

What did that mean? It's haunted me. What kind of situation would make someone want to give up being beautiful, having a nice car—and probably an important full-time job, to be like us? We were broke with an old car trying to fill up a canister to take gas for my stalled-out junker. But now that I think about it, maybe what she meant was she'd give up everything to have a friend.

I think prayer is like that. We always have a friend who knows more than us. Who helps us, like you rescuing me when my car wouldn't start. It's not selfish to ask a friend for help. Since God is bigger than the universe, he can't run out of time or energy to help us! God is our friend and has unlimited resources!

Fiona and I were together that day at the gas station, but the lady in the polka dotted dress was by herself. I wondered if the woman could tell that we were friends helping each other out. That we could call on someone for help. Could the woman tell Fi and I were women of faith, and we knew we could ask God for help when we needed it? What else is a single mom to do? Whatever it was, the woman noticed something hopeful in us we didn't see in ourselves.

I continued to think about Fi's question. Could I even begin to explain why prayer doesn't run out? What hope did the woman at the gas station see in us?

To explain how I came to my understanding about prayer as conversation between two friends, I must go back to a time in my life when I felt the most burnt out, the most spiritually dead. Just like the lady in the polka dot dress, I probably would have given anything to switch places with someone, to get rid of my exhaustion, my apathy, and my fear.

❈❈❈

I was twenty-two and a newlywed working part-time at a small country church in a beautiful valley in central Pennsylvania. My first place after college was a basement apartment on the church grounds. I liked to say we lived in the "parking lot" of the church—but really it was the bottom half of a little parsonage next door to a small brick building with a steeple, surrounded by corn fields. My spouse hoped to be a minister, so he had a part-time internship. We also did odd jobs, cleaned the church, taught Sunday school, assisted with the youth group, and once or twice led worship when we were needed. We helped start a prayer ministry, an arts ministry, and brought back the donuts-and-juice-after-church thing. For awhile we did praise band, which I loved the most. To say we were busy would be putting it mildly. But during times between my odd jobs at the church, teaching art, and working at a clothing store, I was desperate to hear from God. I felt dry and exhausted.

One thing we were doing was praying. We tried to incorporate a rigorous prayer time: praying for all the kids in the youth group, the women's Bible study, our small group, the community, our families, and friends. There was a calendar, and a chart with lists of names. It was just another part of our exhausting schedule. When did prayer feel like too much work? I wondered. In my tiredness, prayer seemed like a causality loop. If I prayed for a safe trip while driving my car—why should I have to pray for a safe trip again on the second day of my journey? If I prayed for someone who was sick, or for a friend who needed a new job, then why should I have to pray more than once?

Somehow, a woman I had never met found out I loved prayer. She said she would meet with me. It's funny isn't it—that prayer is rarely discussed in church and there aren't prayer classes in seminaries. So those of us that love to pray, when we find each other, often meet to exchange ideas.

It was a weekday afternoon. I walked across the church parking and the sun was setting early during the cold winter days. In the nursery, we left the bright lights off and let the little bit of daylight pour into one of the windows through the cinderblock wall. The woman wore her hair long and gray, not colored and curled as most women her age at the church did.

When I said I didn't remember meeting her before, she explained, she wasn't always in services, but when she heard I wanted to learn about prayer, she had to speak with me. She rocked quietly in a rocking chair waiting to share with me some of her story. On her lap, she held a large and very full binder.

"This is my prayer journal," she said.

Inside were many, many pages of all the people she had prayed over for many decades: notes, handwritten Bible verses, and many dated entries of answers to prayer. We talked for a long time about her prayer life including about some prayer requests that had yet to be answered, family she loved who didn't believe in God. She reminded me prayer was about faith, "continuing to pray" until the answer came even if it took a lifetime. Then she left. I'm sorry to say I don't remember her name.

I went home that day and made my own binder. It was fun finding so many random notes and things around my desk and life that fit into the journal so well. I pasted in greeting cards and old school pictures and little notes. I wrote my prayer requests next to each name. What a great way to keep track of answered prayers.

When I was done building the binder, I had to admit, it was helpful. Also heavy; this too was exhausting in a way. I liked it for organization, but not for every day. The prayer journal didn't answer my questions about how to keep prayer from being boring or why it felt repetitive. Why must prayer be said every day? Why did prayer, or our perception of it, seem so short-lived? Wasn't it strong enough to last a long time?

Soon after I learned about prayer journaling, I met two women who moved their families back to the area after a year studying revival and intercessory prayer at a ministry in Florida. I was excited to find out what they had learned. Soon we were teaching the teen girls' class together and praying together once a week. They introduced me to the idea of something called a daily prayer covering, a way to pray for protection against all the ways life gets off the rails.

Before I knew it, I had an enormous binder with charts, maps, lists, graphs, and this complicated daily prayer that was two pages long. Kind of like a modern version of St. Patrick's Breastplate[1], the daily prayer covering was a long list of daily protections over health, relationships, faith, even finances. Trying out the daily prayer covering, I had to admit it worked great. It was like a shield against all harm, to protect or "cover" against any catastrophe anyone might experience.

Still, something bothered me about it. One, it was painful to pray such a repetitive prayer every day. The first week or two went fine, but it began to get old. Two, it also had that feeling of being more like magic or a protective charm rather than a prayer. However, I couldn't deny my own experience: The days I prayed the prayer covering were much better than days I didn't. But this didn't make sense. Why would a prayer be so wimpy? It couldn't even make it overnight! Why did it have to be prayed again? God is all-powerful, so why would prayer be so limited?

The whole mess kept rolling around in my head for months as I prayed and tried to overcome the many challenges of my new post college life full of adulting. I had problems with my health, finding a decent job, friendships, forgiveness, and finding direction for the future.

Meanwhile the church calendar didn't stop. There were special services for Lent and Easter, revival meetings, youth retreats, VBS planning committee, and Sunday school. Don't forget worship practice, Bible study, small groups, funerals, and more. Those private weekly

prayer times for all the people in the church began to wane. Exhausted, I kept looking for a way to build my spiritual life back up.

"I'm so tired," I kept saying. I studied books on prayer. I listened to
sermon tapes. (Cassette tapes used before digital music and podcasts
were old even then). Everything I tried to understand about faith and
prayer seemed blocked by my questions about prayer being so limited
and time consuming.

However, during that time, I saw many prayers answered. People
who were fighting made up. People who were sick got better. People
who needed jobs found them. Students who were looking for direction for their lives announced they had decided on majors, colleges,
or careers. The church we worked at had been looking for a pastor,
and pretty soon they found a family to come and minister to them.
To me, it seemed the prayers and the answers were related in a specific
pattern. We asked, God listened. God acted.

I still wondered however, what if prayer was so powerful that it
could do anything—could I accidentally cause harm? What if I prayed
the wrong thing or prayed against someone? I overheard some prayers
that gave me pause for concern. For example, praying for a young
person to not to get the job they wanted because they weren't mature
enough yet. Could praying like this cause harm to a young person's
future or set them on a path they weren't meant to start down? If it
could go wrong, how was prayer different in this case than a magic
spell?

Meanwhile, while prayer seemed too strong and dangerous it also
seemed too weak: If daily prayer was something people needed to do
as part of their faith, why was it so tedious? If God perfectly remembered from day to day what we needed, wasn't daily prayer then a
waste of time?

Finally, I broke down and tried something new. My life seemed so
hard with so few answers. I stopped all the prayer journaling and the
prayer covering and decided to ask God about it. Surely prayer could
be the answer? I prayed about prayer. I asked God, "How do I pray?
Where is the prayer I used to have so easily? How can prayer help me
build a life of faith and service to others? I'm tired. I feel spiritually
dead. I need to come back to life. Will you help me find an answer?"

Almost immediately, I came across one thing that changed my thinking. It is the story about a woman in scripture who reminded me of myself: a woman who had a huge ministry but died right in the middle of it all. Yes, you may laugh, but it's true! The story of Tabitha[11] from the book of Acts became my flagship for how to think about prayer, especially when it comes to prayer for those we feel called to serve.

🌸🌸🌸

Although Tabitha is a woman in the background of grander stories, her quiet work acted as a testimony that changed my life and gave me hope again. Like me, Tabitha loved to use her creative gifts, and she loved to help people. Her story is told in the book of Acts, said to be written by Luke, one of Jesus' disciples.

I'd call her work an art-based ministry. She designed and sewed clothes and dresses for widows and orphans. Remember, back before social services and women's legal rights, widows had no property, no income, and no government benefits. The laws of the day meant if women didn't have a son to care for them, widows were reduced to begging. Tabitha saw this need. She wanted to help these women and children who had nothing to wear, so she began sewing clothing for them. Clothing wasn't generic at the time either. Women in each tribe and town wore different designs.

We don't know how she got the money for materials. Maybe she did a bake sale or collected donations. I imagine, back then, fundraising was probably a lot like it is today. I've always seen Tabitha as a middle-aged woman with curly hair who has been through enough trouble that she understands the reality of a hard life. Her rose-colored glasses are off. She notices what other people do not. She sees a need and she fills it. When I looked up her name in Hebrew and Greek (I know I promised I wouldn't, but I think this is the only time) her name means beautiful or gazelle. Whether she was beautiful or not on the outside, this woman with a sympathetic heart, she made

---

11 *Acts 9:36-43, NIV-Acts of the Apostles was written, many say by Luke, the educated doctor, friend, and disciple of Jesus. Written sometime in the first century of the Gregorian Calendar, or 3700s in Hebrew Calendar, -618 A.H. in the Muslim Calendar, 2770s in the Chinese Calendar.*

tiful things for those who had lost everything, restoring their sense of belonging and dignity.

But let's get behind the action and look at this story. Peter plays a key role in it. (He is the disciple of Jesus who disowned him three times before the rooster crowed, then went on to establish the early Christian church). Known for asking tons of questions, some might have said he wouldn't amount to much. When Peter has a complete turnaround, he lives out the nickname Jesus gives him: the Rock, superstar minister, rock-strong-in-the-faith miracle worker. Peter is on the move in this narrative, doing things that Jesus had done too, like healing the sick and preaching.

Tabitha's story begins when Peter is told an important woman has died. Funny how backward this story is, isn't it? Tabitha starts out already dead when Peter arrives. He sees all the widowed women gathered around crying. They are holding up dresses that Tabitha made for them, showing him their beauty, color, and craftsmanship. Tabitha was not only meeting a need, but she was also a friend. And for that loss, the loss of a mentor, a provider, an artist, her community is in terrible grief.

Peter kneels by Tabitha's deathbed. He prays. Then he says, "Tabitha, get up." I don't know why, but these are my favorite words in the Bible. They are really high up there for me. Maybe because these are some of the words that really came back to me many times in my life when I needed them most.

Tabitha "opens her eyes" and looks at Peter. I can see her in my imagination. Tabitha is all about vision. Her art ministry died. Her creativity died. She died. But when she comes back to life, she *sees Peter.*

※※※

Tabitha's story really hit me when I needed it most. It's her prayer that started me on this journey to really think about how women pray—to think of prayer as creatively designing a daily wardrobe, and to see prayer not as a boring repetitive job, but to think of prayer as mending. You'll notice that the artwork in this book is all images inspired from Tabitha's story.

Now the story doesn't say this, but I imagine Tabitha came back to life and went back about her business; that she went back to weaving and sewing and making clothes for the poor, the sick and the abandoned. Those that no one else would help. I also like to imagine that her ministry would inspire later churches to appoint elders to help the poor and widows in their neighborhood.[12]

I took Tabitha's turnaround to heart, and I prayed for God to bring me back to life and whatever remnant of whatever ministry he wanted me to do. Almost immediately, things changed. My friend gave me a car for a dollar, so I had transportation to get a new job. It was an old red Cadillac whose engine would randomly shut off at stop lights and sharp turns. (It seemed to run much better if I played the cassette tape that came in the tape deck, a praise edition by Kirk Franklin.) I called the car "the praise mobile."

Next, I saw an ad in the paper. I couldn't afford to get the paper, but somehow, I came across one. The ad was for a job working at a greenhouse nearby. Plants sounded healing after a long, dark winter. I drove the praise mobile to the greenhouse office and interviewed with the owner of a fairly large operation. The office held a dozen people.

"We don't have any jobs for graphic design," the owner told me, "But you could work in the greenhouse with the other temporary and migrant workers." Maybe an office job would open up later, he suggested.

I took the job. I knew it might be hard work, but I looked forward to connecting with one of my other favorite things, nature! I love green things!

One of the first days, a small dark-haired woman with a loud voice gathered a handful of us ladies into one of the cool greenhouses. She spoke loudly and overly clear as most of us were from South America, and even Laos, I was the outsider. She pointed to a low "bench" the length of two or three dining room tables. Filled with beautiful red and pink geraniums, it was a sight of beauty.

"Take the heads off," she said.

---

12 *"...their widows were being overlooked in the daily distribution of food. So the Twelve gathered all the disciples together and said, 'It would not be right for us to neglect the ministry of the word of God in order to wait on tables. Brothers and sisters, choose seven men from among you who are known to be full of the Spirit and wisdom.' We will turn this responsibility over to them." (Acts 6: 1b-3, NIV)*

"Take the heads off?" I asked.

"Take your thumb—like this." She demonstrated, placing her thumb at the neck of the flower. "And pop the heads off." The blossom flipped off and fell on the ground. "All of them," she added, pointing to the next set of low tables, and on down the rows of over a hundred such benches jammed to the edges with trays of dozens of blossoms.

My face must have fallen.

"They can't grow any larger if they have blooms," she explained, sensing my sorrow. "It drains their energy. They are too small, so they need to get bigger first."

Stunned, I couldn't believe I was being asked to kill a flower in full bloom. How could I waste so much beauty? The other women with me, unphased, immediately began taking all the flowers off the plants and dropped them into empty buckets. I had to warm up to it. The first few decapitations, it was like being asked to drown a kitten. Soon, the full table before us soon lost its color and became rows of small green plants. Hesitant at first, deadheading became easier and kind of fun. The little plants obviously needed room to breathe and seemed to perk up a little taller while we worked.

As I pulled off the buds and flowers, I felt God nudging me to notice something.

Does this remind you of your prayer life? The question came to my mind with more emphasis than my normal inner thoughts, so I took a deeper look at the baby geraniums in front of me. I had to admit, without their huge flowers, the fragile plants revealed stems so tiny, it was obvious they could barely hold the weight of the buds, let alone full blooms. The leaves were the size of small coins where I knew the adult size leaves should be three inches wide. Yet no matter how underdeveloped, each plant still produced full size buds that endangered its survival. The plant did what it was designed to do, almost like a computer program. However, those buds would only keep the plant from its full potential to grow, hiding its leaves from the sun, shielding the container from water, and exhausting its energy by building huge flowers before the stems were ready for their weight or the leaves were big enough to pull in enough sunlight for food and energy.

So strange, I marveled, that this type of flower needed someone to care for it. In fact, it needed daily care to survive. These plants needed a gardener, and I realized, that was me. The word gardener reminded me I'd always heard that God is like a gardener.[13]

"I'm like one of these plants, aren't I, God?" I prayed silently. "I'm small and I have too many buds. I'm doing too much too soon and have quickly exhausted all my energy."

God clearly pressed upon my heart the visual of how much these plants needed a caretaker. They would die if someone did not remove all those early buds. Suddenly, I knew what to do with my prayer and church ministry burnout. I needed a daily way to watch out for too much of a good thing. These plants were just like me. I was killing myself with overproduction. If only there was a way to have a daily fix, a daily gardening session where God could be my gardener and help me figure out what I could handle.

It was hard not to laugh at my situation. I was at the end of my energy. But clear as day, my questions, my problems and the answers were all the same thing. It was only my perspective that needed to change. Here I was struggling with the idea that daily prayer was exhausting me when what I needed was a daily way to connect with God or I'd wither like one of these plants.

Where I had I heard the word "daily" in scripture? You may be a step ahead of me. Yes, it was the Lord's Prayer.[2] The idea of daily bread[14] or a daily relationship with God[15] was such a universal standard idea, I'd overlooked it. I hadn't thought about the word daily as being such an essential part of scripture, or my faith. It dawned on me that I needed a way to be restored and cared for every day. Like the flower, I couldn't do it by my own power. I too had an inner design that got me into trouble. Even when I wasn't ready for it, my natural inclination would be to try to do too much, and trust on my own strength and power.

I needed a gardener as well. I was built to need a day-to-day spiri-

---

13 *"I am the true vine, and my Father is the gardener." (John 15:1, TLV)*

14 *"'Father, hallowed be your name, your kingdom come. Give us each day our daily bread. Forgive us our sins, for we also forgive everyone who sins against us. And lead us not into temptation.'" (Luke 11:2-4, NIV)*

15 *"Keep this Book of the Law always on your lips; meditate on it day and night, so that you may be careful to do everything written in it. Then you will be prosperous and successful." (Joshua 1:8, NIV)*

tual sustenance, the same way I needed daily food and water. It made so much sense. I was a daily kind of creature, in a daily kind of world. This was the natural order of what God intended our relationship to be. Wasn't the beginning of scripture all about the idea of a creation divided up into days?[16]

So, prayer wasn't like magic after all. Magic (my main source of knowledge here was cartoons and folk tales) was something that kept going until it was stopped. Like the story of poor Mickey Mouse who played the magician's apprentice in Disney's *Fantasia*. Mickey sets up a spell to help do his daily cleaning chores. Only he can't get the magic to stop, and the cleaning spell creates too much water and soap, causing a catastrophic flood.

At first, magic, the opposite of daily prayer, would seem to be more powerful. Isn't a magically performed job better? However, magic is a dumb thing: a spell, an equation that can only fall apart in the long run. Prayer isn't like that. Why? Magic is about control, but prayer is about relationship.

Magic is about wanting to have power over someone or something. That is not a relationship, it is only about dominance. A relationship is about nurturing trust. *In a relationship, we trust someone to use their power for good.*[17] We tend a close relationship every day with time, energy, and care just like we would tend a garden with daily tasks–depending on the daily weather season.

Why would God make prayer daily? I guess it's because prayer isn't about taking power or control over our lives. It's about connecting with a real and present Creator God. Someone who cares for even the smallest, most fragile life. Someone who knows what we need and when we need it. I guess this makes God more like a gardener than an equation–a real person, a friend.

A garden magicked to grow would soon strangle itself, knock down buildings, wither away from blight. Daily prayer isn't like that. God, in infinite amazingness, reaches out to each of us. Yes, that reach is big, all powerful, but also incredibly gentle, loving, and terribly just. How could we even approach him without being crushed, over-

---

16 *Genesis 1:1-31, NIV*
17 *"...but God disciplines us for our good, in order that we may share in his holiness." (Hebrews 12:10, NIV)*

whelmed?

No worries. God has a plan for how we can approach him. Is it the same way a tiny flower can meet a waterfall, one drop at a time.

I decided then and there, in that greenhouse, if prayer is about a daily relationship, then my relationship with God would be daily.

It worked.

Over twenty years later, I can say, yes, it is hard. I fail a lot. I'm the flag bearer for people that do too much. Let me say this: daily prayer became my saving grace. The patchwork prayer of daily faith was the way I came back to life. Daily relationship is not a list or a chart or a binder, it is the way I meet a God who wants to help me prevent burnout and stay spiritually alive. Each small spoonful of daily grace brings me closer to knowing the Creator and how to connect with him.

What does it look like? Oh, it's not as fanciful as you think. You know how people who are very close speak to one another: informally, and not always politely. My daily prayer happens even if it means I tune in to tell God I really don't like daily prayer, or that I'm having a terrible day, that I'm worried or tired. It's just being the real me—it's a *here I am.*[18] Instead of treating prayer like a magic charm, hoping I can buy power with perfection, promises, or bargains, I trust God to care for me. The best thing about a relationship with God is that it can't be earned.[19] A relationship with God is a gift. And that relationship is mostly done through prayer. That means prayer is really our response to a loving God.

Daily prayer that focused on my relationship with God, rather than a repetitive recipe or an exhausting list, meant life was different. I found myself with new energy. Slowly, I became alive again. I saw powerful answers to prayer and the most important ones were in my own heart. I felt new.[20] Once I felt strong enough again, I added praying for others back into my prayer life. Instead of praying for

---

18 *"Then the Lord called Samuel. Samuel answered, 'Here I am.'" (1 Samuel 3:4, NIV)*
19 *"So now we have a high priest who perfectly fits our needs: completely holy, uncompromised by sin, with authority extending as high as God's presence in heaven itself. Unlike the other high priests, he doesn't have to offer sacrifices for his own sins every day before he can get around to us and our sins. He's done it, once and for all: offered up himself as the sacrifice." (Hebrews 7:26-28, MSG*
20 *"Behold, I will do a new thing; now it shall spring forth; shall ye not know it? I will even make a way in the wilderness, and rivers in the desert." (Isaiah 43:19, KJV)*

everyone, I tried to focus on just a few people who came to my mind during prayer.

When I prayed for someone over time, my relationship with them changed. More often than not, they didn't change—it was my attitude and heart that did. Prayer to me became the opposite of control. Prayer really wasn't about changing people or situations around me; it was about changing myself.[21]

Seeing prayers answered can be intimidating. But over time, instead of worrying that I might pray the wrong thing, I prayed God's will instead. That sounds self-defeating or circular, right? Well, it's not if you remember, prayer is really about relationship. What is it like to ask for God's will when praying? Does it sound ridiculously short and opaque? Sort of a "Ditto, back at you God." Well, that would be boring. I think it's more than that. I think daily prayer is best explained with the "Our Father" or "The Lord's Prayer."

One of the easiest prayers to remember, and the most *daily* prayer Jesus wrote,[22] and taught. It focuses on everyday needs. It's the perfect frame to make sure I keep my prayers from an attitude of control. How do I ask for God's will? Like a parent checking my homework, I give each prayer back to God. I ask him to find the mistakes, make the corrections, cover over the harmful things. Then I ask God to only let his will through.

If you're like me, you may have heard many sermons on this prayer, or even hundreds of them. But here is how I say the "The Lord's Prayer" when I say it quietly to myself. Below, I added some extra thoughts in italics to show you how I try to make myself slow down and be present in the daily-ness of this prayer.

Having it memorized from when I was a little girl helps, but it also makes me say it too quickly. So here is my "slow" version:

Our Father in heaven,

(You are my father who is out of this world. You are our father, so I'm not alone, I'm in your family. I'm protected like a small child. I belong. You fiercely love me.)

---

21 *"And it will come about that everyone who calls on the name of the Lord will be saved..." (Joel 2:32, NASB)*
22 *Luke 11:1-3, NKJV*

hallowed be thy name.

(You are set apart and so is your name. You are big and holy, strong and powerful).

Thy kingdom come.

(Let your worldview, your presence come here over me and this place like a house, a tent, a telephone booth, a funnel, or whatever shape I can think of. I'm safe in a strong walled space where you are generous, and you are in charge, and you are the protector. I'm in a community of people; there's a whole kingdom of people and resources and readiness for whatever needs I have today. I'm not alone.)

Let your will be done

(And let your perfect plans be done—here in the place just like they need to be, and as you'd like them to be done.)

on Earth as it is in heaven.

(Let this place be more heaven-like: no tears, no sorrow, perfect peace, every need met, perfect health, perfect joy, your perfect presence.)

Give us this day our daily bread.

(Okay, Father God, you asked for daily and here it is. Here is what I could get by with in just the next 24 hours if I don't worry about tomorrow...I'll list out here...my absolute minimum. Here is what I need today and here is what I hope for today emotionally, physically, and spiritually. Oh, and can it also be fairly painless? Oh, and God, what would you like today to be like? I hope it's going to be on your strength because I'm pretty empty. Maybe I'll just give the whole day to you. I was never gonna make much of it anyway. Take it. Let's go together.)

And forgive us

(And forgive us when we miss your will...add personal items

here.)

as we forgive others.

(And let us forgive others...add people here. God, you be in charge. I'm tired of trying to figure them out. They are yours. I give them back to you and leave them in your hands. Here is someone who needs your special help today.)

And lead us out of temptation

(God, please don't let me leave you, don't let me leave your will. Keep me close...add items here.)

But deliver us from evil

(Protect my family, health, finances, ministries, relationships.... add items here).

For thine is the kingdom, and the power,[23]

(This is your place, so I'm not gonna worry. And this is your power, it's out of my control)

and the glory, forever. Amen.

(God, let everyone know how great you are. Show them all your amazingness, so that they can tell others about it! Let everyone see it more and more. Let me see it. Let me praise you and not be shy about it. Don't let me get in your way. It's your day, not mine. Amen.)

So that's my daily prayer. Sure, I miss some of these steps and even whole days. My attitude is not this perfect all the time. I'm human. Sure, I am not always generous, or kind, or forgiving. I don't always see what I need to change about me. I don't always remember not to worry about more than one day at a time. But this helps me...a lot, especially on hard days.

Catholic tradition says that several of these in a row can be med- itative and healing. If you are in terrible trouble, ten of these in a row does help, even twenty. Some would say go further and pray the

---

23 *Matthew 6: 9-13, KJV/NOG*

whole rosary once or many times. Personally, I have to say this prayer maybe four or five times to even slow down enough to think about what any of the phrases mean. Prayer knots and beads have been used since recorded history, to help us focus on prayer.

It's hard to focus on a daily prayer. It is a muscle that grows over time. Length is not depth. Praying longer or over and over may not be helpful or even what you are called to do. One thing that "pray like a woman" means to me is that sometimes prayers are short, informal, or done at the same time as something else. Finding a God who loves the daily me, is the best thing that ever happened to me.

෯෯෯

Maybe you feel like I did. Maybe you feel dead right now. You are burned out. You've lost your creativity, your energy, your hope, or maybe even your faith. Maybe you relate to Tabitha: you feel it's too late for you. Your creativity has died or your great project, your dream, your vocation or calling. Maybe you are like the lady in the polka dot dress. You may feel there is no hope for you, and no one is there to help you. You'd give anything to trade places with almost anyone. Maybe you are like Fiona and I, and you think there couldn't be enough prayer to go around for all your needs. You are like the plants in the greenhouse; overproducing to the point that you're dying. Maybe you really are physically sick and feel your life draining away. Maybe a doctor said you aren't going to make it. Prayer is the way we become spiritually alive.

Don't believe those myths that prayer is weird and pointless, takes too much time, is repetitive, or smacks of something silly or danger-ous. Don't be afraid to pray. If you push past that and try it, you can use the prayer of Tabitha, like I did, to find a way to ask God to bring you back to life.

Imagine a new kind of prayer life with me. It's daily, a patchwork of our joys, messes, concerns, and needs. It's not a magic spell for pro-tection. It's a relationship with a God bigger than we can imagine. Vi-sualize taking pieces of cloth from all of Tabitha's dresses and turning them into a beautiful quilt. Each piece is a story of daily relationship.

That is how I want you to think of this daily prayer. Not as a repetitive painful thing, but as building a colorful quilt that grows each day. I think that if Tabitha could have put words to her prayer, it might have sounded something like this:

Creator God who brings life,

    Save me from death: the death of my spirit, my creativity, my imagination, my faith. Give me a way to come alive again. Give me beauty where there were only ashes. Strength where I had only fear. Instead of this despair, give me peace to wear–a garment made out of Praise.[24] **Help me piece together a daily faith; a way to depend on you instead of myself. A way to let go of control and hold onto patience about your plan and your timing for me. I want to grow alive again, not be weighed down by too much. Let me give control to you and trust you. Let me be in a relationship with the Creator God each and every day. Thank you, God for rescuing me from a kind of death. Thank you for being my friend.** ❊

---

24 *"And provide for those who grieve in Zion— to bestow on them a crown of beauty instead of ashes, the oil of joy instead of mourning, and a garment of praise instead of a spirit of despair. They will be called oaks of righteousness, a planting of the Lord for the display of his splendor." (Isaiah 61:3, NIV)*

Indepen-Dance Dress ~Joanna, Quilted Calico on
Cotton Paper, Gouache, Pencil 8 x 10 in. 2018

III

New Shoes Prayer

PRAY LIKE A WOMAN

Prayer is not a lost cause ~ Joanna's Story

When I was eighteen, I wanted the same things as many people. I wanted purpose, community, and to do something helpful. In a way, I wanted my work to flow out of that rich internal life of prayer that I was beginning to sense was so important to my life.

When I went to a college fair with my parents, I felt like career shopping was similar to shoe shopping, only you'd have to wear your decision for a much longer time. At the fair, a small, trim woman introduced herself and showed me her brochures. "What major are you considering?"

"Art," I whispered. (I didn't say much back then, and honestly, I had been considering several things, but that word popped out.)

"Okay. Well, we are a Christian college, and our motto is that Christ comes first," she replied. "So, if you went to our school, you'd learn how to be an artist, only how to serve God with your art," she answered in one breath.

My little eighteen-year-old ears couldn't believe what they heard. Feeling so guilty for choosing art, I assumed art was selfish and impractical, but here was someone promising me I'd find a way to make being an artist count for something spiritual as well. I went home and the more I thought about it, it seemed the perfect fit for me, just two hours from my parents' house.

Maybe that seems like an impromptu easy choice, but I've probably never been so afraid in my life. A year later, I received my acceptance letter in the mail. I remember the deadline loomed for me to reply if I would attend. The complication: I had also received a full scholarship to a state school into their art program. What was I to do? How could I make the right choice when it would affect every minute of my life for four years and probably the rest of it as well? There just didn't seem to be one way to decide! When I did the math, one college cost less up front but more after four years. It felt like a lot of pressure.

Somehow, I hoped there would be some answer floating in the sky somewhere but thinking and math took me in circles. Finally, on the last day to decide, I flopped down in agony on my bed and probably cried into my pillow. I told myself that I shouldn't be a baby. Suddenly I remembered there was a way to be certain: just ask God about it.

"God, I only have a few hours left to send in my letter," I prayed. "I can't decide this on my own. I'm terrified I'll make the wrong choice. I'm going to read some verses. Please let me know which decision is the best choice you have for the future you have for me."

I opened the Bible and began reading Proverbs. In chapter three I found something:

"Choose my instruction instead of silver, knowledge rather than choice gold, for wisdom is more precious than rubies, and nothing you desire can compare with her."[1]

Now you can get into a lot of trouble playing the open-to-a-verse-game with the Bible. However, after praying about it carefully and regularly reading and studying Proverbs anyway, I felt like it would be all right for this case—especially since I felt this verse was pointing right at my problem.

I had been considering which college was closer or cheaper or more prestigious. However, I hadn't considered what I would actually learn. That's it! I had an idea about how to decide. I looked up the state

---

1   *(Proverbs 8:10-11, NIV)*

school course listings: the classes for my major had no variety. They were all art courses, and not much of interest even there. I wouldn't have to take math or science–only the art courses in my specialty, not a wide range of art at all. The full scholarship was so tempting—amazingly tempting. Plus, wouldn't it look better to have a degree from a big university, in an important art program? But it looked like I'd be learning a lot less.

The other school was not impressive to anyone. I worried that a degree from a little Christian college would be like putting a nerd sticker right on my diploma or even a don't-hire-me sticker. I looked up the list of classes for my degree and there were so many things! So many interesting courses on every subject.

"Wisdom" said the verse. And that word snagged at my heart and showed my off-kilter focus. If I knew one thing about God, it was that physical money and possessions weren't really his thing so numbers wouldn't help me decide. They were temporary, and God wasn't. Wisdom, however, was supposed to be longer lasting and better than rubies. Wisdom meant being close to God, following him not in a fearful way, but in a "I'm following you over everyone else" kind of way.

Which do you think is more important? Wisdom or money? My heart felt this question pretty heavily. Wisdom or money? Which will you choose?

It became clear right then and there, if I believed prayer was not about power, it was about surrender. Then I should think about what wisdom and education meant. If I took this verse and applied it to my decision, it meant choosing a school that wouldn't get me noticed, wouldn't make me sound great or look great, but would give me tools to do some unknown future I felt called to. And hadn't the woman promised me I'd learn how to serve God as an artist? That was the wisdom I was looking for. How to be a creative person and a person of faith at the same time.

Well, I'm an artist and a writer now, and this book is on prayer, so you can guess what I picked. Yes. I picked "wisdom," and I picked the smaller school. The course offerings were like a menu at a restaurant. Instead of one main course of art, I had an endless change at learning so many amazing topics. I marked the box labeled "accept," folded up the crisp manila paper, sealed it, and put it in the mail. At about three days' mail service, the letter would get the small liberal arts college on or before the day of the deadline. (This was back in the day—email wasn't used until the following year.)

In the fall, once I arrived on campus, I chose my college classes the way most people chose ice cream toppings at the *Dairy Queen*. Besides my art classes, I took writing and poetry, I took religion and worldview classes. An immersion travel course took me to Israel where I stayed outside Jerusalem for two weeks and also did a homestay with a Muslim family, visited many churches and mosques and several kibbutzim.

During that time studying in college, I took extra Bible courses and audited some. I joined a lot of groups. I couldn't get enough. I took anthropology about First Nations culture, lots of art history, and on and on. I loved learning. I enjoyed school so much.

Best of all, I made some of the closest friends of my life. Those classes made me feel I gained some wisdom, but I think I gained just as much from good friends. My roommate Sally and I got along really well, which made me try more things than I would have on my own, like choir and drama. Terribly shy and indecisive person that I was, how I ended up with a roommate I had been friends with for six years was an odd story! Sally and I met before college. We met at the awkward age of twelve in a tap-dancing class in a tiny town in Kansas. Tap dancing should have been hilariously fun, but at our age, it was mostly embarrassing.

Somehow, we bonded during our last rehearsal. While sitting around for hours waiting to go on, feeling glamorous and old in our stage make-up and hairspray, we talked about our lives as 6th graders and really connected. As she left that evening, she said, "I'm moving to Germany."

"Let's be pen pals!" I cried out. (It took a few more years until my parents let me have a phone, and no internet or social media yet!)

We wrote typical letters that kids write, and they had tapered off. One day while visiting the college, I was standing inside a dorm looking out over the sidewalk and I saw a girl from quite a distance walking away from me.

"That's Sally!" I told my mother.

"How can you even see her?" she asked. But something about her looked familiar, and her jacket read "Frankfurt" in all caps. How many girls our age looked just like my pen pal from Germany? She was too far away to see me and of course I didn't have her number, but a snail-mail letter confirmed that yes, she had been there. Oddly enough, we both decided to go to the same little college in Pennsylvania, a thousand miles from where we first met in Kansas. For a shy person, this was like winning the lottery. With a friend, I could be brave enough to face anything.

Over those four years, I went back to that verse about wisdom so many times to help clarify decisions. I really wanted my life to be "on track" to have "direction." Maybe even I leaned toward "worry-free." All that to say, my motives to pray and seek God's will for my life weren't always selfless or even spiritual. But God takes us as we are.[2]

I had to make so many decisions during college. Each time I was afraid, I'd pray, "Am I choosing wisdom here?" That helped me. I wanted to make decisions focusing on God as a friend interested in every part of my life, and that he had a plan for me.

What I didn't expect is how meditating on that one verse could change me completely. I moved on to trying more and more new things. I asked new questions because I was focused on gaining wisdom and experience. Can I sit in on this class, not for credit, but just because I want to learn? Yes. Can I be on your drama team and go all over the East Coast with you, take your trip to Philadelphia, your trip to Canada? Yes. Sing Handel's *Messiah*, or lead a club? Yes. Hang art in a new place? Yes. Teach a Bible study? Yes. Take a modern dance class? Yes. (That was a fun one.)

I had so many opportunities to grow out of my shell. Yes, was the answer. What I thought was a simple verse and a one-day decision, grew in my heart over time to a sort of new bravery that the shy eighteen-year-old me could have never imagined.

I didn't know how much I'd enjoy college. My fear, my inability

---

2 *"Come to Me, all of you who are weary and burdened, and I will give you rest."* (Matthew 11:28, KJV)

to ask questions aloud, and my trouble making decisions began to dissipate. I found my place, began to discover who I was, and what kinds of gifts I had to offer.

Then just as suddenly those four years were over, and I felt bereft. I grieved my entire senior year that I would have to leave, and in some ways, I have grieved every day since. I loved classes, I loved my professors, I loved learning. It was my kind of place. I didn't know what to do next with my future. There was nothing to hold up to that verse in Proverbs and ask if it was wise. There was just emptiness. The unknown. I could only focus on what I would lose once I graduated. All the friends, all the books at the library! All the beautiful walking paths. I didn't know what to fill it with. I think my attitude was a bit like the woman I want to tell you about, Joanna.[3]

❖❖❖

Joanna was the wife of a wealthy man named Chuza. Her story is in the book of Luke. (Yes, written by that same Luke who wrote Acts.) Scholars say Chuza was the servant, or maybe tutor, for the household of Herod, the ruler of that region.[4] Joanna had been miraculously healed of a disease or condition by Jesus. So had Susanna, and many other women who chose to support Jesus and his disciples "out of their own means."[5]

When I think of Joanna, I see a lady who's a bit too old to live the hippy lifestyle that Jesus embodied. However, she's doing just that. Jesus heals and delivers her from something. Was it depression, migraines, epilepsy, deafness? Whatever it was doesn't matter. She is eternally grateful. While her husband is working day and night with his government job, she has time and money enough to support this great new cause she's found. A new kind of spirituality where women can take part. Where they aren't third class citizens in their own families anymore. Where they can get to know a Father/Mother type of God[6] in a personal way that changes their everyday life. Joanna is

---

3　 Joanna. www.Biblegateway.com/joanna (Luke 8:1-3; 23:55; 24:10, NIV)
4　 Luke 8:1-3, NIV
5　 "Joanna, the wife of Chuza, the manager of Herod's household; Susanna; and many others. These women were helping to support them out of their own means." (Luke 8:3, NIV)
6　 "Like a [mother] bird protecting its young, God will cover you with His feathers, will protect you under His great wings; His faithfulness will form a shield around you, a rock-solid wall to protect you." (Psalm 91:4, VOICE)

in bliss.

I imagine her paying for food in busy markets, cooking over the campfires, tending to street kids they meet along the way. Maybe she's buying out the biggest leather goods store in the Decapolis because everyone has worn out their sandals at once or getting a great deal on wool blankets when the winter nights set in and the desert air begins to chill them to the bone. I imagine her darning and patching holes while sitting on the beach listening to Jesus teach about happiness a beatitude journey faith can bring; about how to be mended and remade.[3]

Remember, there were more than twelve disciples at first—many people tagged along at different times. Jesus even said it was okay for little kids to hang out with them.[7] I imagine the women were glad to support this rare kind of understanding toward children. There were a lot of mouths to feed. The men were tired from teaching and preaching and they received no income to travel and do this work. Joanna took her time and income to build this dream she wanted to be a part of, because she believed in the message.

Joanna's story stops at the end of the book of Luke with a scene from a garden of Gethsemane. Here is Luke's account of Joanna going to the garden after Jesus was killed:

> *"But on the first day of the week, at early dawn, they came to the tomb, taking the spices that they had prepared. They found the stone rolled away from the tomb, but when they went in, they did not find the body. While they were perplexed about this, suddenly two men in dazzling clothes stood beside them. The women were terrified and bowed their faces to the ground, but the men said to them, 'Why do you look for the living among the dead? He is not here but has risen. Remember how he told you, while he was still in Galilee, that the Son of Man must be handed over to sinners, and be crucified, and on the third day rise again.' Then they remembered his words, and returning from the tomb, they*

---

7   *"People were also bringing babies to Jesus for him to place his hands on them. When the disciples saw this, they rebuked them. But Jesus called the children to him and said, 'Let the little children come to me, and do not hinder them, for the kingdom of God belongs to such as these. Truly I tell you, anyone who will not receive the kingdom of God like a little child will never enter it.'" (Luke 18:15-17, NIV)*

told all this to the eleven and to all the rest. When they came back from the tomb, they told all these things to the Eleven and to all the others. It was Mary Magdalene, Joanna, Mary the mother of James, and the others with them who told this to the apostles. But they did not believe the women, because their words seemed to them like nonsense. Peter, however, got up and ran to the tomb. Bending over, he saw the strips of linen lying by themselves, and he went away, wondering to himself what had happened."[8]

When Jesus dies, it looks like Joanna's dream dies too. No more sunsets, no more backpacking through the region, no more sleeping under millions of stars. No meeting new people every single day. Not being the founder of a movement anymore. No longer the mother/cheerleader to dozens of people all having the same purpose together. Joanna is crushed.

※※※

I think Joanna's prayer is twofold. At first, she was grateful for a healing miracle in her life that caused her to follow Jesus' rag tag ministry. But when the time came to actually pack a bag, leave her household for an indefinite amount of time, give up her income, and give over control of where she went, most everything about her circumstances—I'd call that a prayer of surrender. Joanna discovers that in surrendering to God and leaving on this backpacking journey across the five cities, that she hasn't lost anything—she has gained everything.

After so many rich experiences during the course of some of those three years, that experience ends. Jesus dies a horrible death on a Roman cross and is buried in a borrowed tomb. Joanna goes to mourn with her friends, and to add to the horror of his death, and the spectacle of a public execution they witnessed, they find Jesus' body is missing. Two angelic, glowing people tell them they are looking in the wrong place.

"Why are you looking for the living among the dead?"[9] they ask

---

8   *Luke 24:1-12, NRSV*
9   *Luke 24:5, NIV*

the women.

Joanna's story looks like it ends here at a closed door, an empty graveyard, and a dead end. There she is in a tomb. It's dark. It might have smelled a bit earthy—there in the tomb is another opening to a smaller cave or tunnel which held all the bones from that family. The walls are carved rock. The door is a rock. There's a bed made of rock and it's empty. This is her, between a rock and a hard place. Jesus isn't there anymore. So, what good did all that surrender do for her? Her heart is broken.

But then something incredibly subtle happens. When Joanna turns around and looks back into the garden, she sees the bushes, the paths, the white stones, and the blazing blue sky. In that moment, she hears the words again echo in her mind:

"Why are you looking for the living among the dead? He is not here; he has risen."

That's when she realizes that when she steps out of that tomb into the sunlight, she doesn't have to stop. She can keep following Jesus in whatever way she is called to do next. He's not gone, he's out in the world with her, he's in her heart, she's still on a journey with Jesus, he's still calling her to adventures in his name.

Joanna's prayer was not about being ungrateful for her life, or her miracle. It wasn't about being greedy to ask for more when she already had so much. Maybe you feel like I did when my college journey was over, or maybe you relate to Joanna. Maybe you have had a miracle in your life. You are grateful. You have so much to give, but you don't know what to do next or where to start. You are afraid to ask God for more when you've been blessed so much already. And you are even possibly a bit afraid of what God might ask you to do next if you sat down to really think about it. Maybe you are grieving the end to something good. You've been on a wonderful journey of faith, of service, of community and now it's over. Maybe you feel it would be greedy to ask for anything more when you've received so much. I think in that space, maybe Joanna's prayer will help you like it helped me. This is how I think it would sound:

Dear God of impossible things,

I surrender. You've given me everything. The best I could have dreamed. You took care of me, lifted me, taught me everything. But now I feel far from you. I am lost. I'm grateful for the past, but I need you now more than ever. I want to be part of your will today. I want to be part of your plan, your ideas, your vision. Save me from my fear that you won't be with me in the next step, that you won't be near. Draw close to me.[10] Give me a way to be a part of the journey you call a "kingdom." Let me be a part of what you're doing next. Make my calling clearer.[11] Give me a way to listen to you now that things are changed. Help me meet you, listen to you in a new way. I surrender to whatever part you have for me. I'll give up whatever I need to give up. Let me be someone who listens to your call again. Give me the strength[12] to answer, "Yes," to your next good thing.[13] ✵

---

10 "Draw near to God and he will draw near to you." (James 4:8a, NKJV)

11 "...but to those whom God has called, both Jews and Gentiles, Christ the power of God and the wisdom of God. For the foolishness of God is wiser than human wisdom, and the weakness of God is stronger than human strength."(1 Corinthians 1:24-25, NLT).

12 "Each time he said, "My grace is all you need. My power works best in weakness." So now I am glad to boast about my weaknesses, so that the power of Christ can work through me." (2 Corinthians 12:9, NLT)

13 "With this in mind, we constantly pray for you, that our God may make you worthy of his calling, and that by his power he may bring to fruition your every desire for goodness and your every deed prompted by faith." (2 Thessalonians 1:11, NIV)

Hopeful Dress ~Miriam, Vintage Embroidery, Mom's Wedding Dress Satin,
Bride's Maids' Dress Fabric on Cold Press Paper, 9 x 7 in. 2021

IV

Basket Prayer

PRAY LIKE

A WOMAN

Prayer is not hopeless ~Miriam's story

Tracing back a path to the very beginning, I discovered specifically, one particular woman's story as my earliest foundation for how I think about prayer. This story gripped my imagination with an image of how God works miracles even for little girls.

Ever hear about the story of the burning bush and two sandals in a sea of sand? It is a story of wonder, and direction—a story about Moses, the man who took off his shoes when he approached a living bush that was on fire but would not burn.[14]

My first memory of Moses' sister, Miriam[15] is my mother reading me this story in a tiny book for toddlers. It wasn't until I sat down to write this book on prayer that I realized how much time I'd spent imagining Miriam. I guess you could call it mediating. Maybe it's because my parents brought a baby brother home and put him in a wicker basket cradle. At the same time, my little preschool Bible had a picture of Miriam standing next to her brother in a woven basket. Regardless of how it happened, this is one image I've held close every day of my life.

14 Exodus 3, NIV
15 Exodus 1:22, 2:1-8, NIV

My interest in prayer began with this story. As a child, I didn't have any lofty spiritual goals. I wanted to be a singer or a ballerina; to have friends and a dog. But most of all, more than anything in the world, I wanted a baby brother.

When my cousin Rebecca told me I should pray for one, I must have decided to try it. Not knowing my mother had a recent miscarriage, my little four-year-old self began praying every day. I sang songs about my brother. I made little drawings of that baby wrapped in tissue-paper blankets. I figured God was so big, and I was so little, I should probably try a variety of ways of asking. Plus, singing and art are things kids do.

Did it work? I have two younger brothers and a younger sister. God is a big giver. I think my lifelong interest in prayer must have begun from the simple need to have a friend who didn't have to go home at the end of the day. Today, my sibs are my best friends, but just as in any relationship, it isn't always easy. Similarly, my path to be a person of prayer to seek out God every day and to learn to pray "without ceasing" is more like that ongoing family relationship.

❈ ❈ ❈

In her story shared in Exodus, we meet Miriam as a young girl. She's also a slave–a situation with no hope. Many of us can relate to that. There is a big slavery (a.k.a trafficking) problem in the world right now and there is a good chance that you or someone you know has been in a type of slavery, or still is one. Maybe you are in a debt situation where you are a slave to the work you must do. Maybe you have a boss that treats you like a slave, or a spouse or parent that abusive. Maybe you're oppressed, or trafficked, or in a prison you can't break out of. It's not too far of a jump to relate to Miriam's hopeless situation.

As a girl, Miriam can't imagine a change. She can't even formulate a question. But to me, that is where prayer begins. It helps us find a question. Prayer allows us to see outside of the walls, cages, and bindings, both real and spiritual, that block good things God can bring.

Miriam is in the country of Egypt, and her family is under the same order as everyone in their tribe. It's a decree that any male child born to their race must be put to death. The Pharaoh is concerned with overpopulation as well as control and power. There is nothing for Miriam to hope for. There is no one she can give her new baby brother to that will be able to protect him. She has no power. She has no influence. Her only possible future is as a woman slave instead of a child slave. Fear must be the only emotion in this impossible situation because at any moment, a loud cry from Moses could signal a guard to find and kill the baby.

However, Miriam's mother does something. She takes action with something so far outside the box, I can't even comprehend it. She builds a small boat, a cradle that would float, out of papyrus reeds– something between bamboo and hemp. It could be used not only for weaving baskets, but paper, houses, boats, and musical instruments. As a river reed, it seemed weak and fragile[16] like Miriam and her mother, but in the right hands, it could be made into something that could transport and protect beyond measure.

It's the basket that has always had my focus in this story. Let me explain. Miriam's mother goes down to the water and places her baby in the basket and lets it drift. To me, the basket is the first miracle. It's a powerful force of faith, hope, and creativity. It's complete surrender over to God's intervening plan.

But little Miriam does something unexpected.[17] She stays and watches this basket; she can't pull herself away. We aren't told how she feels or what she thinks. It's not her idea to build the basket. I imagine she fought tirelessly to keep her brother. Her mother gives no instructions of any kind. Is the baby brother in danger of being drowned, lost, eaten by a crocodile? Yes. Could he die of sunstroke or starvation? Yes. Is there any possibility besides death for Miriam's brother? It's slim at best. Here's the thing. I think Miriam watches that basket because she is waiting for a miracle. To me, the waiting and watching is the first second act of prayer. I don't think Miriam imagines good from this disaster. She simply watches and waits for God to act— probably endangering her own life, and that of the infant. If she is spotted in connection to the baby, then it could be killed.

16 *"A bruised reed he will not break, and a smoldering wick he will not snuff out. In faithfulness he will bring forth justice…" (Isaiah 42:3, NIV)*
17 *"His sister stood at a distance to see what would happen to him." (Exodus 2:4, NIV)*

The basket has sparked her curiosity and her sense of imagination. She has her first question. "What will happen to my brother?" Though Miriam's prayer may have grown even larger. She must have chafed at the injustice. As she wants her brother to be saved, she also wants to have hope for herself: to survive the grief and loss of being in slavery. And, as a young woman thinking about her future, I have to imagine this injustice made her long for something more for her family.

What I love about Miriam is that she stays in the water. We don't know how long, maybe several hours. She must follow the boat up the Nile as they get closer to the palace. She must swim, and stay hidden, dodge, try to blend in, swim upstream. She must be silent. And she must have some hope to do this. With each treading of water, her hope is larger than her fear.

If you don't know the story, the baby in his impossible basket of reeds is found by a daughter of the Pharaoh. Yes, the same king who wanted each Hebrew infant to be killed at birth. The princess is the smart one. She knows instantly where this baby is escaping from, and she pledges to raise it as her own.[18] Maybe she wants to get back at her father for his evil law. Maybe she is just moved by this one instance.

But who should stand up and ask her first question aloud? Miriam. "Shall I go and get one of the Hebrew women to nurse the baby for you?"[19]

Here is where we see how prayer changes someone. She is incredibly brave and maybe ingenious. In her place, I could have never imagined this question. I don't think Miriam could have predicted this outcome from the morning's desperate beginning. To speak to a princess?

Waiting in prayer changes Miriam. She learns from her time in the water, hoping and imagining. Her prayer grows larger than one brother, one basket, and covers her family and her people. Meditating on her mother's creative solution helped Miriam pray creatively and when she opens her mouth, a creative question is directed to someone unexpectedly generous. I think this is my favorite story that shows

---

18   *"She opened it and saw the baby. He was crying, and she felt sorry for him. 'This is one of the Hebrew babies,' she said." (Exodus 2:6, NIV)*
19   *Exodus 2:7b (NIV)*

how prayer works.

To me, that makes the basket a good symbol for prayer and a good symbol for intercessory prayer for others: it's a creative weaving, a cradle of hope. Intercession often involves praying for a long period of time for someone or a group of people–not in a repetitive way but a creative one. Praying for someone else means surrounding them in expectancy and hope and weaving those together with promises from scripture, looking for cracks to fill with more prayer and waiting for a solution. Intercession, or praying for someone else, is the kind of prayer that won't give up no matter how dark the circumstances. Intercession is a waiting type of prayer. This basket prayer means giving everything over to God again and again for however long it takes, until, like a dam breaking, the answer pours over the top and carries you to a new understanding of how to speak up on someone's behalf.

Miriam's mother took an astoundingly brilliant risk that only makes sense in the case of extreme hope in her God—hope in the face of imminent death. She risked everything by casting away her child to save him, losing the chance to know what happened to her son.

This must have taught Miriam a lesson that day, one I can't forget: to think outside of the possible, outside of the inevitable, is what sprouts from a creative imagination inspired by a conversation with a creative and loving God. To me, that's one of the best moments in discovering prayer. Miriam's basket became my symbol for prayerful expectancy: the place to put questions and waiting.

Although they grew up in different households, different worlds, I believe Miriam never truly let that basket leave her mind. I wouldn't be surprised if she kept filling it with prayers for her brother, no matter where he was. She had seen the first miracle when God saved her brother's life in such a creative and unexpected way, and by such an unlikely person—Miriam must have had a new way of thinking about God. She filled her basket with higher hopes, bigger faith, and more creative questions.

Later, when her brother, Moses, commits a murder and runs away from Egypt,[20] she hears about what he has done. It's almost impossible that Miriam doesn't continue to pray for her brother at this point.

---

20 *Exodus 2:12, NIV*

He is gone, he is lost, outside of the law. Surely, she must have prayed, and put each one of her prayers over to God. Over the course of a lifetime, I think Miriam's basket of prayers on the subject of her brother, her family, and her nation, is large and heavy to carry, but she continues to let it sit in God's hands.

So back to the day Moses takes off his shoes in the desert far from Egypt in what would now be Medina Saudi Arabia. That was the day Moses knows he is on Holy ground—the day God commands him to become a leader. When Moses comes back home to Egypt with a story to tell about his burning bush experience, I'm certain that Miriam prays some more.[21] Her brother has gone from slave to prince, outcast wanderer, to reluctant co-leader of a social justice movement with his brother, Aaron.

When Moses finally gets permission for his people to leave Egypt, as free people, not slaves—Miriam knows something profound has happened. Again, like when he was a baby in a basket, she follows Moses. She goes with him.[22] And let that image sink in. Both times, she is leaving her fate and the fate of her people in the hands of a God she has come to know as her rescuer.

Clearly here in this old, treasured story, something changed the course of history. It is one of the most important stories that formed the way people relate and understand God as one who cares for us personally. Many say it's the time after this where the Moses and his people eventually had time to write down the scriptures. You could say this story wouldn't have happened without Miriam and her mother faithfully taking great risk. Miriam's family, no matter how much they believed in God at first, no matter the level of daily devotion to their faith—it increased over time.

Moses came home with direct access to God. He and their brother Aaron convinced Pharaoh that it was time to let the Israelites go (with the help of ten plagues). And when they march out of Egypt, they are carrying clothes and fine jewels. They are going to a place away from slavery and oppression.

So, when the life-changing freedom happens, an escape to a new

---

21 *Exodus 3:1-4:14, NIV*
22 *Exodus 12:32, NIV*

vision, Miriam finds new strength. This time, Miriam does not stand in the water all day wondering if she could even hope for a miracle. This time she confidently walks out on dry land. The water is pushed away on both sides by God's hand as they walk across.

Even when Pharaoh changes his mind and chases them down, more miracles happen. Pharaoh washes away into the Red Sea along with his men and horses. Miriam might see it as God pouring out that basket of blessing and protection, pouring out answers from their prayers for deliverance.

Unbelievable? Yes. But now Miriam has seen a lot of miracles. Her family is reunited. Her people have a hope of a future. Miriam adds a chorus to Moses' song. She grabs a tambourine and leads all the women in a song and dance.[23] She becomes a prophet, a writer of music, a leader. She has a voice.

In the end, an outsider might see her celebration song and say it looks easy and spontaneous. But this song of praise comes from years of filling that basket with prayers of expectancy, of watching, of waiting. This song comes out of her whole life of prayer.

❦❦❦

When someone asks me to pray for them, it's the direct, complete and full answers; the quick answers that are the most surprising. My cousin received a house for free after so many years of moving from place to place. My friend published thirty books in a year after trying for ten years to get published. My neighbor found a family, after so much heartbreak.

"You are such a good pray-er," they always say to me.

For one, it's not me. It's God who answers prayer. I know that I tend to say the same thing about other people when I ask them to pray for me. I must remember, it's God. However, I do notice, that whenever I asked my friend Becky to pray for my brother, good things happen fast. So, why do some prayers get heard so quickly? I

---

23 "Then Miriam the prophet, Aaron's sister, took a timbrel in her hand, and all the women followed her, with timbrels and dancing. Miriam sang to them: "Sing to the Lord, for he is highly exalted. Both horse and driver he has hurled into the sea." (Exodus 15:20, NIV)

think it's because each person pours out of their own basket of experience. They pour out of those prayers that weren't answered quickly for them: the consistent prayers, the long prayers, the hard prayers, the unanswered prayers. Each prayer adds up and it never leaves.

Prayers last forever, they aren't empty words that dissipate into the air. A prayer doesn't fade over time like an old letter or outdated technology. Don't get me wrong, they aren't like money you save in a bank and then cash in because you've done your time. No, it's much different than that. Prayer is our expectancy; our faith and hope in God. Prayer is our relationship with him that grows over time into our own song. Over our lives, it simply continues to fill and grow. And we can pour out some of that for others.

My journey being an older sister, is what made me realize how much Miriam taught me. My first experience with prayer—asking for a baby brother—is why I always feel connected to her, but it was the hope of Miriam I focused on when my family ran into trials of all kinds.

When I was around nineteen, my brother ran away from home. As I prayed that we would find him, I pictured Miriam standing in that cool water completely powerless but waiting for God. I prayed fervently while I drove to the school, talked to policemen, bus drivers, church friends, detectives and officials. I prayed when I drove our family van out to a park where we had a lead. And I prayed as we scooped him up and took him home safely.

Miriam's prayer is my meditation for the long game, the life-prayer. I let that imaginary basket hold my focus when over a decade later my brother had several breakdowns, becoming so ill at times he forgot who he was. Later, he became a missing person, we prayed while searching the internet, prayed through days of family flying all over the country to find him. I was at home with my own little kids, so I sat down in the yard and gathered some long reeds from the day lilies and began to weave them into a small round frame. I used that time to pray. I knew time was running out and my hands needed something to do.

"Dear God, please let my brother be well enough to remember how to call home," I prayed.

A few hours later, he did call home. We found him wandering in a faraway state on the coast with just a backpack. He'd forgotten to get on his flight home. He'd forgotten to eat, or how to get help, but he'd remembered to call home. That's how my mother found him and brought him back to me in Kansas City. We had a chance to be a part of each other's lives again.

When we had to go to the hospital and visit him, I was nervous. So, I decided to focus on that image of Miriam, one of love and hope. That's what gave me strength to march through the locked doors and the metal detectors. Other people saw me walking across tile floors, in the mental health wing, but to me, I was wading through water like Miriam. And each day, each hour, through the trials my family faced, Miriam's type of prayer was one I could count on. That basket for my brother always had room for more prayer.

Many times, I begged God for complete healing, but that never came. Often it was just enough to get us through each trial. However, there were many moments of healing, of hope, of stabilizing, of regrouping. Each day there was enough healing for all of us to keep going, keep loving, and keep our faith and hope for a good future.

Throughout much of the ups and downs of the spiritual and mental health and safety of my own family, I've held onto hope. There are times when I've prayed, "God, it's been over ten years now, twenty years now, twenty-five years now…Surely this basket is full. Surely, you can have mercy and healing now at this time and on this day." I call those my "Shirley" prayers.

I can only say that each time, whether my prayer is answered in full or in part, I see God work great miracles that are sustaining. I've seen moments of partial healing for my brother: miracles of time together where we painted a mural, or we both read at a poetry reading. One time, I fixed a wind chime he made of shells and hung it on the porch. He smiled when I told him about it. There were the years he was able to complete seven semesters of college, times he sat through family meetings and gave big brotherly advice, times where he didn't remember us, and times when he called to ask how we were doing. Each of these while battling illness. Each of those joys was a miracle, and full healing is still my prayer.

So how can this be an example of God pouring out? This journey has taken me to a place I never expected, to a faith and compassion that I didn't think possible.

Now I know that with enough steadfast prayer, over time, with faith and creative insight, God will pour out an answer to your prayer. Whatever God chooses to pour out in answer, or when he answers, is not up to us. I don't know about you, but when he does, I want that prayer basket to be overfull and brimming with my creativity, my stubbornness, my expectancy. Aren't those, too, a gift from God? And they are a gift to share with those around me.

I can say this. The more you fill that basket of prayer, the closer you are to the day you reach in and you are no longer afraid. Instead, you have a voice, and you have praises you couldn't expect.

Maybe you are like Miriam. You have fearfully large problems that you can't even begin to face. You cannot even imagine the day when you could see a grain of hope. Maybe your family, or your city, or your people are afflicted, poor, sick, oppressed, or in slavery. Maybe you look into your future, and you see nothing but more pain. Miriam's prayer is something that can move mountains. It is a prayer that can change your life, the life of your family, your country, and your world.

It starts with standing still and watching for God to move. It starts with just being strong enough not to run away from the idea of hope. It means waiting on a miracle. Keep putting more into your basket until it builds hope. Then add more. Waiting on God in hope is not to be taken lightly. For once that basket is full, an entire river could run out of it, and still there would be more to come.[24] Prayer is not for the weak; it builds courage.

If Miriam's prayer were written down, it might go something like this:

Father God who saves me,

You made the water, and the land—Save me from losing my family, my culture, my future to oppression, war, disease, and violence.

---

24 "...*down the middle of the great street of the city. On each side of the river stood the tree of life, bearing twelve crops of fruit, yielding its fruit every month. And the leaves of the tree are for the healing of the nations." Revelations 22:2, NIV*

Give me a way to share my legacy. Give me hope for a future.[25] Help me to trust you with my low and unimportant position.[26] You've put me in this time and place to do the work you've called me to do in the place where you want me to be. Let me see something that I need to see. Please teach me how to watch and pray—how to intercede for others. I haven't begun to hope. Show me the way to not be afraid. Give me creative insight. Give me new questions. Give me childlike faith, to hope with expectancy, keeping my eye on you at all times, and let me use that faith according to your will and your way. Fill me up, so that one day soon, I can praise you with a new voice.[27] �֍

25 *"For I know the plans I have for you, declares the Lord, plans for welfare and not for evil, to give you a future and a hope. Then you will call upon me and come and pray to me, and I will hear you. You will seek me and find me, when you seek me with all your heart. I will be found by you, declares the Lord." (Jeremiah 29:11-14a, ESV)*
26 *"But God chose the foolish things of the world to shame the wise; God chose the weak things of the world to shame the strong." (1 Corinthians 1:27, NIV)*
27 *"Oh sing to the Lord a new song; sing to the Lord, all the earth!" (Psalm 96:1, ESV)*

Preaching Dress ~ Hannah, Quilted Satin, Watercolor,
Pencil on Wallpaper, 9 x 7 in. 2022

V

Journey Prayer

PRAY LIKE A WOMAN

Prayer is not sitting still ~Hannah's Story

Not all prayers are about changing the world. Sometimes you have a quiet longing in your heart that gets stronger and won't go away. You pray about it silently, but nothing happens. I don't think that means God is blocked. But sometimes we are. There are times when prayer needs to become audible, to have a voice. What I mean is that prayer can involve more than alone time. Sometimes prayer takes place publicly, or works like an intentional, physical journey. The old word for that is pilgrimage.

Words have power, yes, but prayer can also be action. Prayer is not always silent. Prayer is not always still. Prayer may happen while you are not folding hands. Sometimes prayer is more than words. It is a visible, physical act of faith.

I met Kay while living at a seminary in St. Paul, Minnesota, just a couple of years after graduating from college. We became instant friends and her insight brightened up that cold, dark, and lonely Minnesota winter. Kay had two little girls and one newborn, but she and I took several day trips together and both volunteered at the food pantry.

Married to a Japanese man, Kay had dual citizenship in the U.S and Japan. She had spent most of her adult life there.

"When we wanted to pray together in Japan, we would go outside together on a hill, stand in a circle, and pray aloud all at the same time," Kay explained to me one day.

We were drinking coffee in a fabulous shop with stained glass windows. She talked while juggling a toddler, a baby, and one on the way. Kay was surprised at how Americans prayed. When she came back home to Minnesota, she saw how many times people never opened their mouths to speak a word during prayer. Sometimes they asked for prayer requests in a group then skipped praying together, assuming that if they prayed later on their own, it would be just as good. She asked, "How can I know what they are praying, if they don't say it with words? How can I pray with them if I don't know what is on their heart?"[28]

Kay taught me a lot about prayer in those few times we spent together. She even taught me a prayer eventually cured my debilitating fear of driving.[4] She taught me, having faith that God wants our safety and what's best for us, cures a lot of fears blocking us from reaching out.

I missed her when she moved, but after a few years went by, I had two little kids of my own. Like Kay had been, I was looking for other women to spend time with. I found a mother's group at a little Methodist church where my daughter went to preschool. I took her there on days I would study for my writing degree. I liked the mother's group for getting out of the house. Before I knew it, I was on the team to plan Sunday night services to help young people and busy families come back to church.

I enjoyed the weekly Tuesday mornings with other young mothers. I often spent the entire time waiting to give my prayer request at the end of the hour. Sometimes, we prayed together silently at the end of the group, while one person prayed over the prayer requests aloud. Sometimes, we ran out of time to pray. For me, this was like going to lunch and running out of time to eat.

On those days, I remembered Kay's question. I didn't really know

---

28 *"For where two or three are gathered together in my name, there am I in the midst of them." (Matthew 18:20, KJV)*

what was on the hearts of these women. I felt like we were all missing out on something, but I felt inadequate and hopeless in sharing more about prayer with the women in the group. Not only was there no time for it, but it was like prayer was a foreign land that I could never hope to explain.

The more I thought about it, the more I sought out some idea that would help me identify what our mother's group was missing when we prayed. I couldn't put a name to it. I thought back to one of my first prayer partners, Vicky. She was an amazing friend I met in college. How had she and I prayed together? I remembered the verse that meant the most to Vicky: "Delight yourself also in the Lord, And He shall give you the desires of your heart."[29]

"The desires of our heart were put there by God," Vicky explained to me one day while we were sitting on the grass outside the college dorms. "So, if we have a desire for something good, then he must have a plan to meet that longing somehow."

My desire was to remember how to pray, and maybe share it with others. That's when I began to have more empathy for the other mothers in my group who didn't notice we were skipping over prayer. Prayer was the best part of getting together. However, there had been a point where I didn't know that. Before I met my college friend Vicky, I hadn't realized what it was like to have someone hear your prayers aloud; to not be alone in prayer. I guess she was one of the first people to hear my prayers, to hear my heart. It was life changing.

※※※

It was my sophomore year of college. Late Friday night in the art lab, I was painfully trying to get an early version of Adobe software to work with the printer. Vicky interrupted me. I barely knew her name. but she invited me over to her dorm for coffee.

"I've got to finish my work," I answered. "I don't think so...maybe another time?"

"It's okay to stop for a while. The printer's not even working," she pleaded. "And I made really good coffee."

After I made up some other excuse, she finally ended with "you

---

29 *Psalm 37:4, NKJV*

can take a break…we're all kind of worried about you." Taken aback, I asked who she meant.

The other art majors in the sophomore class, she explained, noticed I had been working too hard. There were fewer than forty-five art majors in each grade level in our small school of 2,000 students. It wasn't that my grades were too high, or that people were jealous of my work, they were generally worried I never had fun.

I admitted to myself I treated my art major as if it were pre-med. Maybe that was a bit overboard. But I had trouble believing everyone thought I worked too hard!? Processing how tired and lonely I felt, they were probably right. I hadn't thought anyone else noticed.

Vicky kept smiling at me like she wouldn't take no for an answer.

"Well, I guess I better come for coffee then." I smiled back.

After that first night chatting, I decided that coffee with Vicky should be as high a priority as schoolwork. I was a really shy college student and speaking up was hard. Taking time off of schoolwork was also hard. Vicky reintroduced me to some old friends and new ones, other art majors and English majors—most of them were in the popular liturgical dance team on campus.

They invited me to a Thursday night praise and worship service. I loved to sing. Praise and worship night was a student-led event and one of the reasons I had chosen to go to college there. It was such a great feeling to know I wasn't the only one my age who really enjoyed singing praise and worship for fun. However, I was always missing it to do schoolwork. If you've ever been around the "praise and worship" crowd, you know they love a good night of singing to guitar the way football fans take to a great playoff game. My new friends convinced me to come more often.

After the second or third visit to Thursday night singing, I asked Vicky about people raising their hands in worship.

"Why do they do it?" I wondered.

"You're a dancer, right?" she asked. "It's like that."

I had taken dance my whole life but not the liturgical dance class on campus I'd been really wanting to join.

"Just act like no one is watching you," she said. "It's just to help you reach out to God in a visible way."

The next time we were at the praise and worship night, the band was playing, the lights were dim. The tiny little church with pink stained glass windows was packed, even on the balcony. We were singing a song I enjoyed, so I decided to try and raise my hands. It was terrifying at first. What if someone might notice me? But then the most wonderful feeling washed over me—like golden light. It was like my worries and fears were evaporating out of my hands and cool strength was flowing back in. Vicky was right. It was the same feeling I had when dancing, only better.

From then on, I simply had my hands raised while singing. I felt a lot of energy pouring into me. I still feel nervous when I raise my hands during singing, every time. It's funny to feel nervous about something you know is helpful and healing. But I try to ignore it.

As anyone who has ever been to a loud music concert knows, excitement is palpable in a room full of jumping, singing people. Praise and worship night was similar, only it wasn't just happiness—it was a fullness and sense that God really cared about me. Really, it reminded me of prayer, only easier. As the choruses repeated, I was reminded of things I wanted to pray about. Really, it was very much like a guided liturgical prayer service, or Taizé, only the worshiper was free to interpret each song on their own. The music was based on scripture that I usually knew really well, and my thoughts and associations helped me center on God.

By the time the spring semester ended, I was a much more relaxed student. Although I was still the perfectionist in my art classes, I noticed that spending more time with friends made life better. And my grades hadn't slipped. If anything, they'd gone up.

The following year, five of us girls got an apartment on campus. We took turns cooking meals and doing dishes four nights of the week. Fridays were dinner parties. We prayed together sometimes, which was new for me. Praying in a group of people who weren't my family, or a church group, was weirdly intimate. Everyone has a different way of praying, and it was amazing to hear the women's voices, their dreams and hopes, and hear them believe such hopeful and encouraging things for me.

The summer before our Senior year came too soon and everyone went home. I stayed on campus and worked at the natural history museum typing and cataloging old cards in the bird egg collections. Each card contained handwritten notes from an ornithologist written with pen and ink. Thankfully, I had been obsessed with cursive and old books growing up, so I could decipher them.

Every card listed observations about a bird's nest and its eggs— well, really one bird couple. The make-up of their nests were listed: Spider webs, string, hair, moss—You get the idea. The next section described the parents of these eggs and how the eggs looked, their size, shape and color, how the birds worked together, and how many eggs were laid. Then came the part I didn't like: The parent birds' reactions when their eggs were taken by the scientist for his collection.

What surprised me about these stories of birds? If their eggs were blown away by a storm, or collected by scientists, the birds acted in a way I would describe as grief. They would stay by the empty nest for a few days hoping for a miracle. Other times, they would call for each other. Sometimes after reading the reactions of the birds' losses, I'd want to cry. But other times, I had to admire them because they were able to press on. The birds built a new nest and laid more eggs. They never gave up. Birds laid many sets of eggs over one warm season. Their lives were more about persistence than loss.

Outside of my summer job, it was lonely without many students on campus. I missed my friends. I was praying for inspiration when I thought of Vicky. Like those birds, Vicky's trademark was not giving up. She was tenacious about faith, and about her relationship with God.

So, one Wednesday, I called and said, "Why don't you come back from your parents' house and get a campus job here?" Vicky wanted to but couldn't afford it. However, I had just enough money to buy her a plane ticket from Florida to Pennsylvania, and I offered it to her. Thankfully, she accepted, and arrived a week later.

On a typical sunny day that summer, after typing about birds all day (Vicky cleaned dorm rooms), we would hang out. What was amazing to me, Vicky knew how to pray like someone much older than her years. We could pray together, watch movies, have coffee, and talk about our faith, our dreams, and our heart's desires. Getting to know each other without classes was a welcome change.

I was in awe of Vicky's devotional book collection (I had hardly any at this point). She had books on prayer, faith, and relationships. Though classes were not in session, Vicky was still constantly studying. She spent hours on daily prayer and Bible study, especially on her days off. She seemed to enjoy this time, like it was fun.

Another thing I noticed hanging out with Vicky was her commitment to go to church and take part in praise and worship, to sit in the front row, and go early! To her, praise and worship time was like candy.

What would it be like to be waiting every moment for a word from God? I wondered. At only twenty-one years old, I had never met anyone who loved to pray as much as Vicky. She reminded me of myself, except I kept that part of my life so hidden.

That summer, Vicky reintroduced me to the idea that you didn't have to wait to study the Bible or sing or pray until you got to church. Vicky listened to praise music in her dorm room. She'd sing whenever she felt like it. At first, the recorded music sounded loud to me. Kind of fuzzy. There were people shouting, and clapping, and the music was raw and unedited. I couldn't understand why she listened to it. It was so noisy and not really musical!

However, I soon realized that it was the atmosphere the music created that was so special. My attitude would change after the praise and worship had been playing awhile. I felt more thankfulness and peace when I listened to the music.[30] Vicky made me a few mix tapes and they became my favorites. Her prayer life was a natural consequence of believing her spiritual life was something she did every day, all day—not just once a week. Prayer happened during music, during fellowship, during reading, during work, during breaks. To Vicky, prayer was all the time.

Vicky's relationship with God was personal. It was like he was another roommate and an independent study course all in one. He was there for Vicky. I felt this way about my own faith, but again, I kept all of my prayers silent, so no one knew about them except me. I

---

30 *"Is anyone among you in trouble? Let them pray. Is anyone happy? Let them sing songs of praise." (James 5:13, NIV)*

listened to music, but I didn't sing along. I prayed, but only silently. Church was always a big chore. I began to wonder what it would be like to let my love for God show a little.

Soon, I joined Vicky down at her Pentecostal church. It took me back to my earliest memories of Sundays when my parents had taken me to a little stone church in Midtown in Kansas City. I'm not sure how unusual it was, but I adored the praise music. Many Sundays there were liturgical dancers wearing white dresses or slacks. They also wore bright pink and teal-colored matching sashes–the little girl in me had enjoyed the costumes more than the dancing. I liked that childlike faith feeling. As a young adult, I had forgotten about all the joy. Why had my faith become nothing more than getting dressed up in uncomfortable clothing and trying not to fall asleep one service a week?

At Vicky's church I felt like a kid again. Vicky reintroduced me to the idea that praying didn't have to be quiet or seriously dull; it included praising and dancing and singing. It included friends and prayer partners. She treated the spiritual life like it was fun. Something I'd lost sight of.

Whether it was singing, dancing, stomping, clapping, shouting, or flag waving, those church services were not boring. The more I attended church with Vicky over the summer, the more I remembered what my faith had been like when I was a kid. I remembered singing made-up praise songs to myself and dancing around in our back garden. I remembered praying for a baby brother and then drawing pictures about it.

I was new to this church, and it was odd at first to see adults behaving like kids, but soon I realized this childish joy, treating God like a parent and a friend—this was how I had always been underneath. As a kid, when I prayed, I combined singing and dancing and art without even thinking about it. Getting to know Vicky as a friend and prayer partner reintroduced the idea of joy in my prayer life. Not being still and quiet like a rock but thinking about prayer as a celebration—with noise![31]

Living with child-like faith meant joy. In some ways that meant

---

31 "But He answered and said to them, 'I tell you that if these should keep silent, the stones would immediately cry out.'" (Luke 19:40 NKJV)

my prayers became smaller, not bigger. What I mean is "little" prayers were brought to God and he answered them. This made prayer feel like a daily adventure, and God seem very present.

Here's what I mean by little: One Sunday afternoon, before we hopped on the bus home, Vicky stopped to share with me a "little" answer to prayer.

"Look what they had at church! Sponges! I got two." Vicky said.

"Why are you so happy about sponges?" I asked.

"I didn't have enough money to buy a sponge to clean my dishes," she said. "So, I prayed about it, and I said, 'God I really need a new sponge, will you please send me one?' Then when I went to church today, there was a bucket of sponges on the counter, brand new in their packages."

"Were they for you to take?" I asked suspiciously.

"A sign said, 'Free. Please take one,'" she answered. "God really loves us. He even cares about our dishes!"

First, I realized that Vicky had been giving out of lack, to make me fresh Puerto Rican coffee many afternoons, and how generous that was when I realized the money and time involved. She had to get her coffee bar set up without a car to get supplies, or much cash for them either. Second, I realized how much God really did care about the small things. It was amazing he could use all of us to help each other. He even cared about our coffee time and Vicky's need for a sponge.

Through Vicky, I became sure that other people experienced that quiet inner voice in prayer, and we were connected by that prayer. The Spirit led us to share at the right time. One person had extra sponges; another person had extra coffee. I was the recipient of both through Vicky's "teatime" hang-out sessions. Then I remembered how I'd bought Vicky's plane ticket and what a wonderful summer it turned out to be because of it. I guess we all had contributed. I saw how all that generosity wove together into a system where one hand didn't know what the other was doing, but we all were led to work together and there was a lot of joy all around. [32]

Like the birds I studied all summer, Vicky's spiritual life was about persistence more than her losses. It was plain to see that what first

---

32 *"Blessed are the poor in spirit, for theirs is the kingdom of heaven." (Matthew 5:3, NIV)*

appeared easy on the outside—a strong prayer life—was a pilgrimage for Vicky that took many years. Going to school so far from her home in Florida was just part of it.

Vicky's joyful prayer life didn't come quickly. It took years of struggle and trial to find a way to be open to meeting God earnestly every day. She had shared about her life when she hadn't been considering what God might want for her, and how the results always left her feeling empty, hurt, and lost. She'd lost a few friends when she decided to seek out a more spiritual life, but she didn't let that stop her. She wasn't the only one to benefit—everyone around her did.

You've likely had a friend who constantly shared their love for something, like a video game, a band, a movie series or a team. Vicky was like that, only she shared her passion for the spiritual journey with me. Her openness made me more aware of my daily life with God.

That summer there were lots of tears, singing, dancing, counseling, mentoring, Bible study, and enormous hours of prayer on both sides. After a time, Vicky told me one of her prayer requests—to find the love of her life. She shared her prayer to meet a man with a long list of qualities that I wasn't sure she could find: a man of faith, service, and tenderness. It sounded like a high order.

I prayed with her anyway, wondering what God could do. A month later, I couldn't have been more surprised that Vicky's answer appeared so unexpectedly. We didn't have a car and there was no bus service to campus; however, Vicky met Jon—one of the few guys who stayed on for the summer. Every day, they had been cleaning the campus together for the many summer conferences. It was such a surprise to me when Jon was just what Vicky had described. He had a servant's heart (which was even the meaning of his name). He was a gentleman, a music major, and had a great sense of humor. Their friendship grew. A year later, I would be the maid of honor at Vicky's wedding.

Vicky's story sounds sweet and easy, but I'm capturing only a tiny bit of it here. I saw in her life a beatitude kind of journey, with God as her guide. Her example changed me and made me more creative about prayer. After weeks of so much talk about our futures, the desires of our hearts, the prayer sessions and Bible studies, we were both more joyful, more refreshed, and ready to tackle that last year of college that held so many doors to our future.

I had hoped for a friend, for fun, for spiritual direction. The desires of my heart for that summer were more than answered.

⊗⊗⊗

Back at my mother's group in Kansas City, my memories of Vicky brought me the answer I'd been looking for. I knew they just needed to see that prayer was fun and easy. I wanted them to know God brought immediate joy, friendship, and help from praying together. I had been wondering how to share a lifetime of prayer with a group of women who didn't know how to pray in person for each other. Yep, you know me now, I was too shy to ask them if I could share about prayer, so I prayed for an opportunity.

One of the mothers, Sarah, was moving to North Carolina and we all met at one of their houses. We had such a nice time. We really started to bond for once—not being in a stale classroom but in someone's home, having fun together. Suddenly, Sarah stood up and announced her babysitter had to leave, so she had to run home. Everyone said they were sorry to see her go, and they would pray for her. We'd most likely never see her again.

I had wanted us all to pray and now we would really miss it. Our last chance to pray together was dissolving before my eyes. I prayed for the courage to speak up. I knew Vicky wouldn't sit quietly in this situation. Instead of feeling powerless, I stood up.

"Wait! Please. Can we pray for you before you go? Can't the babysitter wait a few minutes?"

The ladies nodded and agreed that it was a great idea. I knew I finally had my chance.

To my chagrin, all the women sat down, folded their hands together, fists clenched, and closed their eyes. They had been filled with life and noise and now they turned to little stones, their eyes squinched, their knuckles white from pressing their hands together so tightly. Everyone waited for one person to pray quickly so Sarah could leave. I assumed they were waiting for me.

I almost gave up and told God that I'd never be able to explain what I meant to my friends. But God gave me more bravery to open my mouth again.

"Wait," I said. "We always prayed a certain way at my old church when someone had to leave." Then I described how one person sat in the middle and the others stood around and placed their hands[33] on that individual's back or arm and prayed aloud. My friend Sue knew what I meant and helped out, guiding us all into a more relaxed formation.

No one seemed disagreeable, but they acted like I was sharing a party game they'd never heard of. I had to pose everyone like a game of Twister: I moved everyone around closer to Sarah.

"We are giving a blessing," I explained.

With whatever blank stares or questions that came back, I tried to convey that this was not a quick word over a hot meal. This prayer was something Sarah would take with her, something tangible.

"Like this," I said. I placed their hands on Sarah's back and those that couldn't reach on each other's backs, like a chain.

I don't remember if I explained why the laying on of hands [34] was important, but everyone was beginning to understand. Mothers know that you calm a baby by laying your hand on its back. They got it.

I just couldn't stand to let our friend leave without a prayer that was empowering and a blessing. I told everyone that it was like "popcorn" prayer. After that they knew what I meant. They could pray one-at-a-time, in random order, aloud, and say what was on their hearts—however they felt led—for our friend who was leaving.

It was an unusual experience for this group. They began to pray one at a time. Soon, they began to pray earnestly. They prayed blessings: for Sarah to have help and a good future; safety for her family; employment; new friends; even a ministry. People prayed aloud who didn't normally pray. Their feelings about how much they cared for each bubbled up, this time in words we could all hear. Laughter and tears overflowed, and the prayers went on for a few minutes more than our regular prayer time.

---

33 *"They presented these men to the apostles, who prayed and laid their hands on them."*
(Acts 6:6, NIV)
34 *"For this reason I remind you to fan into flame the gift of God, which is in you through the laying on of my hands." (2 Timothy 1:6, NIV)*

Afterward, Sarah left for the last time. But for the first time, our group was energized. They decided to stay longer and talk more. A tour of the house was given, and more food and drinks were handed out.

It's funny the way God works. When we invite him into a situation, especially prayer, he turns it from something boring where we hold rock still and silent, to something personal, something bonding, something fun—something that brings fresh hope, life, and friendship. I'm glad he helped me stand up that day and show others a taste[35] of it. God's presence energizes us and those moments of creative energy and friendship last forever. I still feel that moment of friendship in my heart today.

Standing up and being loud about prayer reminds me of another woman who did the same, only she wasn't received as well. Hannah's story takes place in the book of Samuel. It's people like her who remind me that sometimes you're going to be laughed at for your faith, or for your unique style of worship, but that doesn't mean you should stop praying.

※※※

Hannah, like my friend Vicky, is loud and bold about her faith.[36] (Hannah is a woman from scripture who actually gets a ton of lines! PTL.) She is married to Elkanah, a sweet and romantic husband. He loves his wife and treats her well. But Hannah has no children, and she is being bullied by another woman about this "shame." Years go by like this. Hannah is distressed, having trouble eating and sleeping. But one day, she "stands up."[37] I don't know why it's phrased this way (I promised not to look up the Hebrew), but I like the idea that she has had enough grief and that she is going to get up and do something about it.

Hannah decides nothing else would do except to walk down to the Tabernacle and pray aloud in person until she has an answer. This was a house of prayer where God's presence dwelled and never left. It

---

35 *"Taste and see that the Lord is good. How happy is the person who takes refuge in him!"* *(Psalm 34:8, CSB)*
36 *1 Samuel 1, NIV*
37 *1 Samuel 1:9, NIV*

seems like the place to pray. She goes down to the temple and then she begins to pray fervently and loudly. She doesn't kneel or sit silently.

Now, if you read this chronicle from the book of Samuel carefully, you'll find out that prayer like this was a rarity in Hannah's time. The priest does not recognize what Hannah is doing. In his complacency, he thinks that if a woman comes to the temple and is muttering aloud, she must be drunk, so he accuses her of this.

Think about it. Praying aloud fervently is so strange to the priest at the house of prayer that he reasons it is more likely to find a woman drunk than praying. Remember this.

When she's accused, Hannah answers, "Oh no, sir—please! I'm a woman brokenhearted. I haven't been drinking. Not a drop of wine or beer. The only thing I've been pouring out is my heart, pouring it out to God. Don't for a minute think I'm a bad woman. It's because I'm so desperately unhappy and in such pain that I've stayed here so long."[38]

❀ ❀ ❀

Maybe you are often in a place were praying aloud is not acceptable. Showing your faith is weird, forbidden, frowned upon, or against the law. Yes, in many churches and synagogues, it would be crazy to run up to the front and pray. The old Shakers and Quakers got their nicknames from loud, fervent prayer. However, I've been in some places of worship where women have to stay on one side of the building or on the balcony. I've been in churches where a small room was delegated to quiet prayer, and some where people shut the door to hide their loud fervent prayer.

In a regular time for worship where people gather, everyone must consider each other and how loud they might be or how long they might pray. What traditions are in that space? Some places of prayer require head coverings or other considerations. Most places are on a tight schedule and only allow you a few seconds or minutes of prayer. So, finding a time and space to pray is important, even essential. Today most of us feel comfortable praying anywhere; however, setting aside a time and space to pray for a specific request can be truly healing.

---

38 *1 Samuel 1, The Message*

Prayer can be set aside on a hilltop, or a campus, or a sacred space. I've prayed at many holy sites, and even had my prayers mailed to some. I've lit candles in caves and monasteries from Savannah, Georgia, to New York to Palestine. But some of the spaces where I felt the closest to God in prayer were just in my own room at home or driving to a site special to my family or my childhood.

Hannah does this. Her prayer is not quiet, and it is not short. First, she stands up, then she travels to a special destination to pray. In my words, I would call this a pilgrimage. She travels for the purpose of finding a way to connect with God about one particular pain visually, physically, mentally and spiritually, one desire of her heart.

Hannah's explanation of her actions, however, is accepted. The priest pulls himself together and finally blesses her. She goes home. Washes her face. Feels better. Eats, sleeps, has hope. You guessed it, pretty soon Hannah is pregnant. She has a son, and she names him Samuel.

Samuel, he's special. He's someone who will change the spiritual landscape of his country forever. He had an amazing "Here I am," type of attitude. Maybe influenced by the stories from his mother. I guess when you are told that your life is important, that you are a gift, and that you are an answer to prayer, it changes how you see things.

Do you know someone who is an answer to prayer in your life? Let them know. Tell them aloud how much they mean to you. Let them know they are part of a miracle and watch how it changes things.

I knew Hannah's prayer most of my life. That meant if I needed something, I should ask for it. And that it might not be easy. I might be teased or criticized for praying. I might be called names. I might be looked at as crazy for being a person of prayer, but I shouldn't give up. My friend Vicky didn't mind how she looked praying, dancing, or singing aloud. She prayed for small things like kitchen supplies, to large things like finding a partner in life. Speaking up about it was key.[39] Sharing the desires of our heart is part of the process. As anyone who does meditation knows, voicing our dreams and our needs and putting them into words brings about a change in us. It makes us

---

39 *"Therefore, I tell you, whatever you ask for in prayer, believe that you have received it, and it will be yours." (Mark 11:24, NIV)*

ready to receive the good things God has for us.

On the other hand, it's more than a simple meditation. This fervent journey kind of prayer, this pilgrimage to voice the desires of our hearts, is more than setting an "intention" or asking for a gift. Praying is a relationship where you share your dreams with a Creator God, then you give those dreams back to him. Hannah does this. She does not hoard her blessings. She ends up dedicating her young son, Samuel, to the Temple. He lived there in a cloister-like setting and grew up learning the scriptures. Hannah would sew him something special to wear each year and bring it to him. She dedicated the desire of her heart back to God in an amazing act of selflessness.[40]

There is something similar we can do. No, not dropping our kids off to live at church. What I mean is, dedicating the answers we receive in prayer back to God. We can thank him for our gifts and remember the journey we took with God to bring about such big answers. Why not dedicate the future of those answers back to God's care rather than starting over with a fresh fear? Set aside a time and a way to commemorate the journey. Hannah wrote a prayer. Many praise songs sung today are based on her prayer. What could you do? Paint a picture, write a poem, a play, or share your story?

Maybe you have prayed for a job, a child, a spouse, a partner, a business, an education—but now that you have it, things are not going as you hoped. Keep giving your blessings and dreams back to God. Ask for his will and his direction. Hannah's prayer is one that works for both grief and joy. It's a prayer of conversation—a prayer of journey. Because of Hannah, I know prayer is a relationship that you walk with God, together. Sometimes, that means walking literally to a site of pilgrimage like Hannah did. It's a prayer where you accept each day knowing it is part of God's plan, both good and bad, sorrow and joy.

You aren't alone. Hannah had both joys and losses. My friends Vicky and Jon had both blessings and hardships. Vicky's modeling of a daily spiritual life has never left me. She shared with me how to journey with God. I often remind myself to live both grief and joy

---

40 *"For this child I prayed; and the Lord hath given me my petition which I asked of him: Therefore also I have lent him to the Lord; as long as he liveth he shall be lent to the Lord. And he worshipped the Lord there." (1 Samuel 1: 27-28, KJV) (1 Samuel 2:1-10,CJB)*

with God, to ask him about the desires of my heart in a more active, loud way.

There is nothing silent or still about Hannah's prayer. She is recorded as saying, "Lord Almighty, if you will only look on your servant's misery and remember me, and not forget your servant but give her a son."

Your prayer can be as simple as Hannah's prayer for a child or my prayer for a friend. If you have your heart's desire that you've never given voice to—Why not try it today?

Stand up like Hannah and speak your desire aloud. You can go on a pilgrimage by walking down the street to your favorite view, or to a friend's house to tell them. You can share your desire with people where you worship, or at some other special or spiritual place. You can tell the cashier at the grocery store. Tell someone,[41] and tell God. He loves us. Maybe your prayer to ask God to release a longstanding desire of your heart, might go something like what I imagine Hannah's prayer to be:

God who is like a best friend to me,
Please take away my shame and my embarrassment. Let me stand up[42] and ask you for that desire you placed in my heart. Give me the strength not to be embarrassed about you or my faith in you. Let me tell people how much I trust you to take care of me and how much you love me. Let me walk and speak in faith with others. Let me show you that I trust you. You placed a longing in my heart, so I give it back to you and ask you to fulfill it how you see fit. Whatever your answer, let me give that gift back to you. Let me be a part of your plan and your dream. Take away what's blocking my voice, so you can release a future you have planned. Give me a new voice.[43] Give me words. Give me a way to stand up, contribute; to walk in a way of love.[5] I want to be a fragrant offering[44] of your love; to be a part of your journey with you.[45] ✳

---

41 *"Again, truly I tell you that if two of you on earth agree about anything they ask for, it will be done for them by my Father in heaven. For where two or three gather in my name, there am I with them." (Matthew 18:19-20, NIV)*
42 *"... 'stand up on your feet and I will speak to you.' As he spoke, the Spirit came into me and raised me to my feet, and I heard him speaking to me." (Ezekiel 2:1, NIV)*
43 *"In my distress I called upon the Lord; to my God I cried for help. From his temple he heard my voice, and my cry to him reached his ears." (Psalm 18:6, NRSV)*
44 *"And walk in love, as Christ loved us and gave himself up for us, a fragrant offering and sacrifice to God." (Ephesians 5:2, RSV)*
45 *"But thanks be to God, who in Christ always leads us in triumphal procession, and through us spreads in every place the fragrance that comes from knowing him." (II Corinthians 2:14, NRSV)*

Arrival Dress ~Lydia , Fabric Collage on Wallpaper, 8 x 10 in. 2019

VI

Soaking Prayer

PRAY LIKE A WOMAN

Prayer is not about words ~Lydia's Story

In 2007, I moved back to my hometown in Kansas City, Missouri. I had been teaching and showing art in Pennsylvania and then St. Paul, Minnesota. However, in my hometown, I knew no one because we had moved away when I was thirteen. Without those connections, no one would let me show in their galleries. I didn't know what to do and I didn't have room for a studio, so I stopped making art and focused on the house, the garden, and my one-year-old daughter.

After a few years, I managed a small art show in a café in a tiny suburb. Ironically, the cafe closed during the month my art hung there because of the recession in 2009. In fact, we were so poor, I painted the art on wood paneling I had found in someone's trash. My desire to be an artist was a silent prayer. I couldn't put it into words. I just had a feeling that surely God must have a plan for my creative calling even when everything seemed against it.

I picked an obscure Bible verse to help me focus on my dream to find other creatives:

"On the Sabbath we went outside the city gate to the river, where we expected to find a place of prayer." [1]

1   Acts 16:13, NIV

This is part of a passage from the story of Lydia, a businesswoman and artist who worked with purple cloth. I guess my prayer was to find a community where I belonged. I didn't know if I wanted a prayer community, an art community, or help in showing and selling my art. I didn't know. Maybe I'd find a sense of community by a literal river, or at least a wellspring of life and creativity?

I kept hearing about this place down on the other side of the river that was called the Crossroads Arts District. I read about it online and in brochures, but it didn't have an address or hours. But with young kids at home, I didn't know anyone to go with me to visit the art galleries, if I could find them. If I could just get down there, I would know what to do next. At that point, I wasn't even sure I would make art again, I just wanted to see some. I had a wordless prayer that God would help me find a way to use my education in the arts, even when it seemed all the doors were closed.

During the recession, our family used local food pantries and boxed food from church ministries so much, I forgot what the inside of a store looked like. I didn't have a car, so much of my time was at home. Despite the food scarcity and other hardships, we had a lot of family traditions and little celebrations that kept me busy. I taught art classes and did a lot of volunteer work.

One day, I was organizing my desk and I found some old notes, a packet of little papers from a tradition I created called our "annual coffee and vision meeting." Once a year, we went to the bookstore, loaded up on coffee, and picked out books that reminded us of dreams for the future. This was followed by a show and tell. Finally, we would write down our "dreams" in a notebook.

I glanced through the seven pages for seven years, noticing a distinct pattern. Every year, I had new dreams for what I could pursue in life. They were grand plans like going to Europe, opening a Bed and Breakfast (before Air B&B's), opening a retreat center, working on a cruise ship, etc. You get the idea. Each page had the year marked on top with new ideas.

That's when I noticed something odd. On every single page, the lists were nice and even and organized, but scribbled on the corner or side of each page, like an afterthought, even written upside down, there were the same words.

"Get an MFA in writing?" The notes were clearly written by my own hand.

Most of the ideas didn't have a question mark, they were just a list of ideas. But this one had a question mark every time. It was the only consistent dream–dialogue with myself at the end of every vision meeting.

Why did it keep coming up? I didn't think of myself as a writer. I only had one novel I'd written during National Novel Writing Month when my daughter was a baby. Could that be what God had next for me? After so much faith and tenacity to study art, and my continued daily search for art jobs and gigs, why would God ask me to go back and study writing? I could say that I prayed about it, but not really. It's more like I set it on the prayer burner and left it to simmer in the back of my mind.

I didn't see any clear path for me. I was an artist who wasn't making a lot of art. I was a mom stuck at home during the recession, cooking things from scratch I found at free food pantries. I didn't even have a car. I had a young daughter to care for who wasn't in school yet. I prayed about it, but I had no words for this prayer.

It wasn't too long before the idea of writing began to stir questions and little promptings in my mind.

"God, I've never been good at writing," I prayed, arguing away the idea. I saw a red pencil in a tin cup on my desk I had kept since I was thirteen. It read, "Mrs. S. Loves Me." Why had that meant so much to me? My strongest memory from my eighth-grade year was Mrs. S. telling me I'd make a great writer someday.

I continued to pray about it, but I decided getting a writing degree was impractical. Why didn't I wait and write in my retirement like everyone else? (This was funny as I was continually underemployed since I couldn't afford childcare).

This new wordless feeling that I should pursue writing was just too weird for me. My prayer was a constant argument that writing was a silly dream. God wouldn't ask me to pursue it now, would he? I'd do it later, I argued. I reminded God that he had ideas that were too big for me, too crazy to attempt. Finally, I found some words for this prayer.

"Lord, I can't be a writer. I've never won a writing contest or done hardly any writing at all. Art contests, yes. Writing contests, no."

That settled it. No writing for me. (This is often how my prayer time goes. If you are an arguer, no worries. Prayer is conversation, there is no reason not to argue some of the time. It's a great way to think through things.)[2]

One day, not long after, I moved some old journals and saw my eighth-grade diary. Why not look in it to see if there was anything about that memory of being told I could be a writer? I couldn't resist a peek. When I pulled it off the shelf, turning through the yellowed pages, I found a day I had completely blocked out. In it, I described an uncharacteristic gift from my dad: A small balloon, and a bouquet of red carnations. I eagerly read more to find out why.

As I read the entry, I couldn't believe my eyes. In my own handwriting, I described the school award—a bouquet of lollipops. I'd won the award by submitting something to a writing contest. I read it three times to be sure. I didn't remember the contest or the candy, but I remembered the flowers from my dad celebrating my award.

Yep. That proved it. I was an award-winning writer! You'd think I was happy for such a sweet memory. No, that meant this wordless prayer argument about becoming a writer was a battle I was not winning.

What is the one thing you could probably teach or study without stress, without prep, without hesitation, and do just fine? Another nagging question popped into my mind.

Not art, I decided but writing. It was my easiest subject.

I knew the answer had been in front of me a dozen ways for a long time. I'd been having recurring nightmares about graduating high school. In every version of the dream, I would end up in a math or science final exam unprepared. Fearful I would fail and have to stay in high school forever, I'd wake up in panic.

Now that I was considering going back to school for graduate studies in writing, the nightmares stopped. The last dream on the topic started like the others but ended very differently. In my dream:

I was again running around panicking, trying to find my high school

---

2   *"'Pardon me, my lord,' Gideon replied." (Judges 6:14, NIV)*

classroom and my final exam. But this time something new happened. My friend Shelby showed up and took me to my locker. She helped me open it, and even showed me a little light inside. On the bottom of the locker was a row of textbooks that looked really interesting, but I didn't have time to look at them. Finally, Shelby walked me to the class. There I discovered a substitute teacher who had been one of my Bible professors in college, and he announced we'd have an English final instead. I sighed in relief. I knew I would pass an English final without even studying, and graduate with honors. I wouldn't be cursed to stay in high school forever.

I never had that dream again.

The answer was clear. In my nightmare I hadn't been attending class. I hadn't been "attending" or listening to the idea that I wanted to be a writer.

"Fine," I finally admitted in prayer, begrudgingly. "I'll apply to the MFA." I'd lost the silent battle of wills, but maybe I would still wait a while longer. Why go to the trouble of filling out the application when I was so busy? A few more years putting it off wouldn't hurt.

What about readers who need your stories now? A thought argued. I had to admit, this was something I'd never think of myself. This was a conviction from that silent fatherly voice that made my heart thrum with its deep vibration

Not only had I had lost the argument, I was feeling the prompting to hurry. When a silent prayer becomes focused on helping others and goes against my selfish nature to just take care of myself—it was getting serious. To me, this meant that the argument wasn't in my own mind. It was a nudge that I should listen to.

Hah. Still, I did nothing. Yes, that's right. I had a lot of excuses. However, my best friend had ordered the paper application to be sent to me in the mail (online applications weren't a thing yet). When a second application came in the mail, I realized I had a smart friend.

Ignoring a looming deadline wasn't me, so I polished up the first twenty pages of the novel I had written, then mailed in the application for a degree in writing for children and young adults in St. Paul, Minnesota—back to the town I was born in. The degree program was mostly hybrid with only twenty-two days at the University a year.

Surprisingly, to me, I got in. I was going to be a writing student.

For three years, I took classes for my "two-year" degree. I studied poetry, fiction, short stories, and picture books. Sitting in the library with a baby on my lap and my daughter playing nearby, I had to admit that maybe this prompting had been right. My school health insurance had covered the surprise addition to our family, a baby boy. And the homework to read 150 children's and YA books was something that easily integrated into my everyday mom-life. God did seem to have a plan.

I never could have predicted how well and easy that degree would integrate into my world. More importantly, I loved the amazing people I met. One thing that struck me about writers for children and young people—they were a lot like me. They were thoughtful and cared about the future. They were funny and wacky and wrote poems and stories. I'd found a group of people who really cared about the arts more than competition; about each other more than a personal audience. That's what I wished the visual art world would be like.

⌘⌘⌘

Over the course of four years, that wordless prayer to be a part of a community of creatives continued. I'd floundered, failed, argued, made progress. The end of my degree felt like another dead end. Two worlds, both art and writing, called me in different directions while employment never came easy. Of course, when school neared an end, I still wondered about being a visual artist.

"What about my Lydia prayer?" I prayed to God. "Will I ever feel like I belong to a group of creative people? Why can't I be a part of a community more than a few days a year?"

I'll be the first to admit, my prayer life sometimes sounds like I'm a whiner. I kept reminding God that I wanted to find a community with people who loved being creative.

That's when something happened. I still taught a few art classes here and there, and I was on a few mailing lists. Something unusual came to my inbox. The mayor of Kansas City was calling on all artists. He asked that we could come share our vision for the city. During one twenty-four-hour period there would be a dozen or more meetings all over town. All I had to do was come to one. The letter said it was a tradition that had not happened for seventy-five years. What a strange answer to my prayer. I didn't even stop to think about it. I had to be there!

I dropped everything, found a sitter, and drove through some confusing hilly neighborhood south of our home until I found a little out-of-the-way community center. Inside was an ice rink. There, while people were skating, I sat in a tiny, blistering-hot room with about fifteen other artists. It was the last meeting of the day.

As we talked to some of the mayor's staff about what we thought Kansas City should be for artists, I found myself speaking up. I hadn't made much art in five years, but I had an opinion about how much I loved my hometown and how it had inspired me to be an artist.

It felt amazing to know that in community centers all over the city, artists were meeting and talking about our heart for our city. The mayor's meeting inspired me. I wasn't alone as a creative person. Finally, I realized if I wanted to find room for myself in the arts community, I needed to make art. In order to make art, I needed to make room for art in my own life.

Praying again about this felt like I was in the folktale of the fisherman who kept coming back for more and more wishes—the guy who was never content. I now knew I could find other artists. But there was nowhere for me to make art. I had to find space.

"Dear God, I need a space to make art but there is no room and no income to do this!" The answer shouldn't have surprised me, but it did.

Don't you have enough room already? What if you think about it creatively—like an artist?

Sometimes in prayer, you do feel like there is conversation happening back and forth. I couldn't even begin to understand this question. So, I took a tour around my own house.

"Lord, help me to find a creative solution," I prayed

The basement was full of my spouse's office. The kitchen was small, as was the attached dining room and living room—where the kids played mostly. My little girl's room was full of bunk beds and toys and the nursery was a quiet dark little space with a crib and a dresser. The master bedroom was full of bright light and had a corner for my desk.

When my spouse came home from work, I asked him if we could move into the tiny nursery painted with a baby mural so that the master bedroom could become an art studio. I was so thankful for that yes.

So, I moved my kids into one bedroom and told them to share bunk beds. I started painting again. Sure, I was rusty after almost five years, but I knew God must have a reason for giving me a life where two worlds collided, both art and writing.

In the studio, I worked on my books, a novel, a picture book illustration portfolio, ideas, and happy things. Counting the months on one hand since graduation with an MFA, I was running out of time to find a job or get published. Things were desperate financially. The only jobs I could find paid less than the daycare I would need to take them. Finally, I pleaded with God.

"We are desperate. I truly need a job, and I can't wait any longer." At that time, artist jobs were often listed on *Craigslist*, an early site for want ads. I found a job and interviewed by phone. It was teaching "paint and sip" classes. I had just happened to see a documentary on *PBS* about the phenomenon, so I knew about the brand-new craze, inspired by two women who survived Hurricane Katrina and wanted to do something that would cheer people up.

Ironic that, just as I finished my writing degree, I was being paid to teach painting and invent new designs for groups to paint together. I enjoyed it and learned about working in acrylic, something I hadn't learned in school.

That was the moment I just knew life was going to even out. My youngest was about to enter Kindergarten. I had helped my husband get through a second degree, and he was about to graduate and maybe find work that paid enough for gas and food! We had survived the recession. My degree was finished, and I was writing a great book. I even had an agent. Life was just about to be good—maybe even as good as I had always dreamed.

Then everything stopped.

First, a painful, unexpected divorce. My littlest brother graduated college and he came to help me. Then my other brother become ill and needed care. Soon after that, my father died.

All in the course of six months, my family experienced many losses. My mother bought a house in town. We all moved in together. It
was a tight fit, but we all had room.

Sure, my life had fallen apart. I lost everything I ever wanted. I lost
my marriage, my ministry, my church, most of my friends, and my
house—my sense of identity. But I had one thing left: my job.

I felt proud to be a "regular adult" with a decent full-time job at an
office. I had only been working there a couple of months and I'd been
hired the day the "paint and sip " company let me go. I was going to
have a career and it was going to be fine.

In that, I felt like God worked a miracle for me. Instead of running
around at home barefoot and caring for two kids, I felt like I was really somebody. I got all dressed up for work, dropping off my little kin-
dergartner at early daycare and taking lunch breaks with adults! I felt
so cool. I had a pedometer that would get to 10,000 steps every day.
Finally, I wasn't a student, I wasn't a stay-at-home mom, I wasn't an
artist: I was normal. I loved it. I could pay my bills for the first time.
It was incredible and I was finally food-secure for the first time I could
ever remember. Despite my pain and loss, how great to be normal.

It didn't last. For one, professional jobs don't give sick days to new
single moms dealing with funerals, divorces, and a host of family
problems. My standing at work looked precarious for other reasons I
couldn't identify. Maybe I was used to being self-employed and sharing my ideas a little too freely without enough deference. Turns out,
my boss tormented the last three people before me—each of them left
after only a few months by quietly disappearing during their lunch
breaks—without giving notice. I couldn't believe the story about my
job, and I didn't care. I was amazing. I loved having a job. I needed a
job, and nothing could make me leave it.

Soon I began to notice the tension in the office. After three months,
it looked like I was next on the list of people the boss would inspire to
quit. However, I wasn't a quitter, so no one knew whose resolve would
last longer. Okay, everyone probably knew except me.

Work continued getting even more stressful. My absence for my
dad's surgery and then unexpected funeral had raised an administra-
tive red flag that had to do with complicated math I had misunder-

stood about sick leave. Well, there wasn't any. That's what I'd misunderstood.

Things were so bad at work, I began hiding in my car over lunch,
sitting in the parking lot in my old beat-up Hyundai, the only thing
I got in the divorce besides the kids, our stuff, and our mattresses.
During one of those lunches, a song called "Oceans" came on the
radio. It was about trusting God and walking[3] out on faith.

"You're going to ask me to quit my job, aren't you?" I asked God.

*Think of all the open doors waiting for you if you go about doing the
work you feel called to do instead of sitting behind this one door—this
one dead end.*

"But I'll have nothing," I said. "Don't take this too. It's my last
shred of respect!"

But you'll have everything you need.

Now this was unusual. I strongly felt that I needed to do something that didn't make sense to me. It felt frightening and impossible
and upside down. This was not the way things should work. But it
also felt familiar.[4] I recognized that I had been continually prompted
to be ready to do something for a long time. So, almost against my
own will, I went into HR to say goodbye. I didn't want to sneak away
like my predecessors. I quit my job that day, and it was one of the
hardest things I've ever done—and that's saying something.

When I went home to break the news, it didn't go as expected.
Everyone smiled. My mom said, "Oh thank God, I wanted to ask you
to quit for a while. I need your help so much." Then she broke down
with actual tears of happiness.

Well, that was unexpected. So, for six months I stayed home and
helped my family. It takes a lot of work to handle a family funeral and
close out the paperwork of a lifetime, even with someone as organized
as my dad had been.

In some ways, it was like Christmas break that never ended with
all of us in the house together. After the funeral, we helped my mom

---

3   *"But Jesus immediately said to them: "Take courage! It is I. Don't be afraid." "Lord, if
it's you," Peter replied, "tell me to come to you on the water." "Come," he said. Then Peter
got down out of the boat, walked on the water and came toward Jesus." (Matthew 14:22-23,
NIV)*

4   *"Be generous: Invest in acts of charity. Charity yields high returns." Or "Cast your
bread upon the waters and after many years it will return again." (Ecclesiastes 11:1,
Message, NKJV)*

move into an apartment in Atlanta to finish out another year of work so she could retire. I stayed home to help my brother who was ill. We had lots of good times. We played games, read aloud, and took guitar lessons together. Every little thing was an act of grace, and every little thing was an act of healing. I was there for the kids after school, and I spent extra time working on my novel. We had family movies and family dinners and a lot of great fun.

But I had one more leg on my Jonah-styled journey of my word-less prayer to find creative community. I began subbing full time as an art teacher for my friend Dee who had breast cancer. Somehow this had the opposite effect than I anticipated. It was another chance for me to argue with God and tell him that he was mistaken about my callings.

"God, if you had only let me be an art teacher," I prayed. "If you hadn't asked me to be an artist, but an art teacher, I would be happy. I'd have a regular job. I'd have a regular income. I could still make art. I could make a difference. I'd be a respectable adult with a job and a community. God, you've given me the wrong calling all this time."

You guessed it. After eleven days of feeling brilliant as a substitute art teacher, the work became harder and harder. Many days, I would drive to work crying real tears because I wanted to paint so badly. This was strange, because I hadn't been painting for over a year. But the colors of the sunrise were my favorite colors. Every morning on the way to school, my desire to paint those colors became stronger.

Each day, I tried to help students love and learn about art. Many didn't want to make anything at all. I realized that inspiring young people to learn about art is so much different than making art—a different skill set entirely.

I limped on through, trying to learn as I went. The students made beautiful work. We even had an art show. However, I saw my energy depleted. I had tried to convince myself that God was wrong about my calling to do the things he asked me to do. This school was one of a dozen places I had hoped to "belong" to find community, but God knew this wasn't where I was supposed to be.

The school wanted me to stay, but the more I talked with my friend Dee, the more I realized that an art teacher's heart is different from an artist's heart. She couldn't wait to come back and try a new angle on getting the most resistant students to engage.

"I don't have the same giftings as you," I admitted to Dee. "I don't think it's normal to want to paint so much that you cry on the way to work. I've got to go back to my art."

Just as school was finishing up for the year, I heard about a conference on arts and faith. I decided to show up, but as a "writer." Writers are artists too, I reasoned. (I was waffling.)

Going to a conference sounds simple, but my children were very young. Every tiny step involved prayer: To get somewhere on time, to find money to attend, to have patience, to find a way to look presentable with what clothes I had, to act sane during the one-year anniversary of my divorce and not cry in public, and to not get lost. (At the time, I still had a terrible fear of driving because sometimes my sense of direction would simply turn off.) So many strains on my time and attention as a mother made getting to this event seem impossible—but I was determined.

As I drove to the WWI memorial for the first night of the conference, I had to drive up a steep hill overlooking Kansas City. I took a picture of myself wearing a new color I'd never worn before. It was my first selfie with my first smartphone, a gift from my mother–the GPS meant an end to my days of getting lost driving.

It might have been the first selfie I ever took—and I did it to make a distinct promise to myself. "I want to remember this day. Today is the day things will change. Today is the day I will be an artist, and this time I won't give up." Then I walked up the hill past the enormous monument with angels covering their faces with their wings, and into the tiny steep lecture hall with poppy-red velvet curtains on the black stage.

The first lecture by a famous artist, Makoto Fujimura, was about how art creates a place, a space, a community. I didn't understand what Fujimura meant then exactly, but I loved every minute of it. I wanted a community, and this was what my wordless prayer had been about so long ago when I turned my bedroom into an art studio when I thought about finding community "by a river."

The next day was the second day of the conference, more lectures followed on a local campus—my dad's alma mater. But I still didn't understand where God was leading me. I went through the whole conference as a "creative writer." Then, for the last part of the conference, we took a tour of the Crossroads Arts District, the place for artists I'd heard about for eight years but could never find. It wasn't a specific place—it was an area of town where many galleries were located. It didn't have hours because all the galleries had different hours. However, they were open on first Fridays for a community-wide art walk. How had I misunderstood so badly? And why had I been frightened to drive downtown alone? It was easy once I parked and walked around with the tour group. Why had I spent years wondering instead of just coming down for a visit? It was only about fifteen miles from my house.

The irony is insane. I had been so afraid of doing something as simple as driving down to the river in the middle of my home city and walking along 18th Street. It was so easy. More than galleries, the Crossroads had studios where artists worked and made art. The tour guide said they weren't that expensive; in fact, they cost "a lot less than renting an apartment."

Suddenly like a hot air balloon filling up, a huge wish rose in my heart that I'd never had allowed before. Someday, when I was older, wiser, and my children were grown, I'd come back here and get a studio.

You can guess what happened next. At the conference I sat next to an artist at lunch who talked about losing his studio of twenty years. I told him I was sorry, and I'd pray for him to find a new one. I felt so bad for him. As I left the conference to go home, an important question came to mind.

Why do you feel so compassionate for this stranger, an artist who needs a studio to do his work, but you have no compassion for yourself—an artist who has no studio at all?

Now God helped me finally cross that bridge he wanted me to cross. This idea was a shock, one I had never considered. Would it really be okay to be so wasteful, crazy, adventurous, and extravagant as getting an art studio and making art?

Back home, I told my family, my mother and my aunt about the conference and the tour. "I think I should have an art studio someday. Wouldn't it be nice?" I said.

"Yes. How about next month?" my mom answered.

This was the largest slap to my expectations that I'd ever received. She pointed out it was time for her to retire. Her year was up and she was moving home permanently from Georgia. That meant we were one bedroom short. The master bedroom was mine. In the basement I had a tiny art room about the size of a walk-in closet.

Suddenly I understood. My art room would have to become a bedroom. Either I would have to move all my art supplies to the Crossroads Arts District into a real studio or put them in a closet and forget about it, maybe forever.

I think I might have chosen to put the art in a closet, except for the recent conference and that hard experience teaching art. Both reminded me how badly I wanted, no, needed to create. The other thing that changed my mind: I had finally started painting again for a small display at the local library. For the first time, I began to believe if I continued to paint and make art something beautiful would happen.

So, I called around about a studio. I had just done a six-month class on discipleship with twelve women at a church called *Restore* with an incredible amount of Bible study, homework, and journaling. Before my appointment to tour an art studio space, I was already covered in prayer and doing what God wanted me to do. However, I needed a "word" to make sure I was on the right track.

I opened a big leather Bible sitting near the front door as I was about to leave the house. I opened to Proverbs (again, hard to go wrong.) A few words stuck with me: "Wisdom shouts in the streets. She cries out in the public square. She calls to the crowds along the main street...Come and...I'll share my heart with you."[5]

The funny part is there is the only version of the Bible that uses the words "main street." So I went on the tour, and I prayed "Dear God, if the studio we visit today is on or near Main Street, then I'll know it's the one you want me to take." I knew there is precedence for this

---

5   *"Wisdom shouts in the streets. She cries out in the public square. She calls to the crowds along the main street, to those gathered in front of the city gate: "How long, you simpletons, will you insist on being simpleminded? How long will you mockers relish your mocking? How long will you fools hate knowledge? Come and listen to my counsel. I'll share my heart with you and make you wise." (Proverbs 1:20-23, NLV)*

type of prayer in scripture and it was such an important decision and needed to be made almost instantly, so I felt it was okay to ask for a sign.[6] Sometimes, when I'm feeling there is a big decision to make, I try a narrowing prayer like this, asking God for something specific to help me know it's his will. I don't do this often, but for life changing things it doesn't seem like there is harm in asking, especially if you've been praying all along and keeping close to scripture.

Sure enough, we walked past Grand Street and around the corner of Main and onto Walnut Street to visit an abandoned warehouse where I was offered the space to rent a small 12 x 12-foot studio. I thought maybe I was doing the wrong thing to say yes to the studio, but the man who ran the space texted me back, "Thanks for doing 'something new.'" It made me think of another verse I'd been pondering:

"Behold, I will do a new thing; now it shall spring forth; shall ye not know it? I will even make a way in the wilderness, and rivers in the desert."[7]

I'd been praying that verse for months. That's the way it happened. Me, the doubtful, busy, single mom who wanted to be a writer. I began subbing art in March, went to an arts conference as a writer in April, felt called to be a painter again in June, and by July 1st I had an art studio in the Crossroads open on "first Friday" for people to visit me. Now, maybe you aren't surprised, but I would have been just as surprised to wake up one day as a doctor or a detective as a painter.

You know me. I was still doubtful. However, I decided to try it for three months. I'd go downtown every day and make art. Just the summer. If it didn't work out, I could start on my writing again. I'd forget the pile of job rejections and manuscript rejections and agent and editor rejections and start applying again. I had only two things in mind. One, I needed to "share my heart" with people in busy places and I needed to "make a way" for "new things" to happen, especially healing and restoration and community.

I thought about these verses a lot as my car broke down on the way to sign the lease. As my money ran to zero. As my brothers moved

---

6 *Genesis 24:14, NIV*
7 *"Behold, I will do a new thing; now it shall spring forth; shall ye not know it? I will even make a way in the wilderness, and rivers in the desert." (Isaiah 43:19, KJV)*

the furniture in. As my tiny kids used my grandma's kitchen stepladder to paint the studio walls with paint, we were given for free by a friend who had no idea what we were doing.

As I found boxes of old office supplies and tools and home repair materials in storage left by my dad, I thought of my wordless prayer for a "community by the river." I thought of a "new thing" as I ordered blank white canvases in the mail. And I thought of it again as I sat in the stifling heat in an old warehouse—my studio walls painted bright orange and blue, and I waited with my empty canvases for something to come to me.

I was finally down by the river at the place I needed to be—ready for someone to ask me to make art for them, or anything really. I had no idea. It was just me and 144 square feet of my studio and an entire empty warehouse.

At first, the silence was deafening. I kept praying wordless prayers. I imagined a river running through this deserted part of town. I just kept saying, "Make Way," but for what?

Little did I know the whirlwind of activity that would descend on that place. In just a few months it soon filled with artists and studios, people, friends. My art closet at home in the basement never had shows or visitors or meetings, murals, or galleries, but those were the things that came from the studio down by the river.

I was on the start of a journey that began as a wordless prayer. I had to listen day by day, hour by hour, to God, and do art at the same time. I just had to be willing to be a part of the community that would follow.

☼ ☼ ☼

So, this eight-year prayer story of my wordless prayer for community, I would call it a waiting prayer or a dwelling prayer. It's watching and waiting for God to move by being present, ready to take action when the moment strikes.

One person in scripture who reminds me of this prayer is Lydia.[8] She's only mentioned in Acts 16 of the New Testament. As a woman, her story is overshadowed by three famous men, Paul, Silas, and Tim-

---

8   *Acts 16, NIV*

othy, who go traveling looking for places to speak about Jesus. They are preaching that this new "way" will change the world one person at a time. They are having dreams and visions, teaching, making a big deal about circumcision and other male-oriented considerations— like who is in charge. Lydia's story doesn't stand out because it's interrupted by the story where they cast out an evil spirit of a girl, stir up a riot, almost get killed, go to prison, make a political scene, experience an earthquake, and are miraculously freed from prison.

So yeah, the writer of this book inserts a tough guy's action movie in the middle of Lydia's story. Meanwhile, I notice Lydia in the background, quietly going about her work. She's my hero. Lydia is sharing her faith with her community, beginning the first church in her city of Philippi. We don't know much about Lydia from this historical account. We know she was a dyer of purple cloth from the Greek town of Thyatira, a city known for gold and for having several places of worship, some just for women. I always imagined she was tall and thin and very smart. I imagine she's come into some money and is making simple designs to take the high-class market by storm. Purple was a luxury item.

Lydia is a business owner. But this story takes place on the Sabbath. She is down by the river on the weekly Jewish day of rest with other women. They could be dyeing fabric or doing laundry but since it's Sabbath I always thought they were just taking a break to pray together. Paul is there looking for a place to pray. I always imagined the women having a prayer meeting, and that he found them praying and worshiping. Lydia describes herself as being a believer. However, she is moved by the message of hope that Paul shares with the crowd there.

She wants something more. Her wordless prayer is for something new, maybe a stronger faith than she has already. So, after hearing the testimony of these visitors, she is baptized. This would mean most definitely getting dunked under the water, saying a prayer—maybe giving a testimony. Then she invites Paul and his friends to her house for dinner. That's most of the story.

First, I relate to Lydia because to me she is an artist. Dyeing fabric is something we artists call textile design. She's a designer. And she loves color, rich color. Color is my passion. Lydia's story tells me it's okay to love beauty and design. It's okay to have both art and faith in my life at the same time. It's okay to have a career and still want to do some sort of service or ministry. It's okay to be a woman in the background. It's okay to be a woman in this faith.

There is diversity in every story, and if we peek behind the explosive narrative, Lydia is a lot like you or me. She is waiting wordlessly for a life-changing moment. She has some good work going on, her dye business, her friends, but she wants something else. She has a calling to do more, but she doesn't know what. We don't know what losses she's experienced. We don't know what wordless prayer Lydia has in her heart. But Paul's message about Jesus' beatitude way of life moves her. Lydia helps me understand that when I pray like a woman, I don't need to have the right spiritual language to pray. Simply knowing I have something I need. Simply feeling it in my gut. Simply keeping my eyes open when I'm about my regular daily work, or when I am with friends, or when I am praying—keeping my eyes open for that opportunity God is calling me to or to be, is enough.

That is Lydia's prayer. A prayer of waiting or dwelling in the moment.[9] Lydia helps start the first church in her city. When Paul gets in trouble, she feeds him, helps him and his crew, and sends them on their way. Her presence in the story implies she refocuses her family and her community's faith on this new message of grace, on community and hospitality. She's found what she is looking for: a way to use her spiritual gifts and her creative gifts at the same time.

Lydia is my go-to woman for a wordless waiting prayer. Maybe you are like Lydia. You have a lot of things in your life, but you are missing something. That's okay. Prayer doesn't need words. You don't have to do anything special. You can simply keep your eyes and ears open and trust that all the work you've done is not in vain,[10] it's going somewhere. God's going to do something new[11] in you. You want to be with other people who are making a difference? You don't have to worry about having the right words. Sometimes, prayer is just watch-

9   "Rejoice always, pray without ceasing, in everything give thanks; for this is the will of God in Christ Jesus for you." (1 Thessalonians 5:16-18, NKJV)

10   "Therefore, my dear brothers and sisters, stand firm. Let nothing move you. Always give yourselves fully to the work of the Lord, because you know that your labor in the Lord is not in vain." (1 Corinthians 15:58, NIV)

11   "See, I am doing a new thing! Now it springs up; do you not perceive it? I am making a way in the wilderness and streams in the wasteland." (Isaiah 43:19, NIV)

ing and waiting with your eyes open, knowing God is holding you in his hands.

Prayer creates a new place in our hearts for compassion, an openness to others outside of ourselves. That desire isn't from us, it's from God.[12] Lydia soaked her fabric in purple dye, and she soaked her life in prayer. With patience and prayer, she had her eyes open for opportunities, and that made all the difference. Creating a community of prayer meant a new kind of life, a new kind of faith, and made her more aware of God's will. Even if it didn't have words, I think it went something like this:

Lord God who makes a way,

Save me from my regular life, from my regular complacency, my regular faith. Give me a new thing. Make way for your river in my life. Make streams in the desert where there is emptiness or loss. Help me find a way to speak to you. Help me find you. Help me listen to you. Help me find the new thing, the calling you have just for me. Put me in the right place at the right time—that place where I can bless others. I belong to you; keep me on your path. Give me faith to be a leader in each small way you have for me. Give me faith when I need to quit, when I need to embrace, when I need to step up, when I need to say yes to you.[6] �

---

12 *"No one can come to me unless the Father who sent me draws them." (John 6:44, NIV)*

Battle Dress ~Rahab, Oil on Pieced Canvas, 57 x 36 in. 2018

VII
Flag Prayer

PRAY LIKE A WOMAN

Prayer is not about perfection ~Rahab's Story

My friend Fiona and I met at a birthday party. She was my cousin's roommate. Over the years I got to know her, and she amazed me so much. She has a huge heart, a huge personality, and everything about her is big: her voice, her strength, her way of speaking. She is a mighty woman.

Her stories about her life were outrageous. She'd been through everything you could think of. She could party harder than anyone, dance longer, sing louder. Fi lived life to the fullest. As she got older, however, she suffered from bipolar disorder. She had to quit her job and go on disability payments.

Now, I could see how amazing Fi was, but she didn't always see it. Her neighbors loved her; animals loved her. Everyone knew Fi: kids, kids without parents, lonely neighbors, shy people, happy people—they all came to her when they needed a friend. I wanted to hang out with her because of her endless energy for life. At that point, I was new to single parenting, and I felt like I'd lost more than my energy. Fi didn't care. She and my cousin let me come over and sit on their couch, play with their many dogs and cats and watch movies. Fi entertained me with her stories that were better than anything I could ever find at the library or write myself.

Fi had the best stories I'd ever heard in my life. And she was often the courageous one in those stories. After many months, we began talking more about our faith and about prayer. Fi said that she had some prayer requests about her family. She didn't think God would listen to her prayers, but he might listen to mine.

I tried to explain that Fi was uniquely amazing, and she deserved a happy and full life. Why not pray for anything she needed?

"You were there for my cousin when she needed a family. You've been her roommate and like a daughter to her. You are an answer to my prayers for my family because you came when we needed you, so why wouldn't God answer your prayers? It's all interconnected." I kept trying to tell Fi the picture I saw of her: as someone epic, someone who had a great story ahead of her, and a great story behind her.

"You don't know what I'm like sometimes. Sometimes I'm horrible to people," she argued.

The more we talked, the more her doubts about prayer surfaced.

"You don't know me. You don't know what I've done. You don't know what I'm like." Somehow, when it came to prayer, she didn't feel like she was good enough to ask God for what she really needed and wanted for herself.

"Wow. Do you think God cares about any of that?" I said. "He loves you. He loves everyone. You can ask for whatever you need or want."[1]

That's when it hit me. I'd been praying for so long, I had no idea that most people didn't know they didn't have to be perfect to pray, or to be prayed for. You can have as much abuse or illness or regrets packed into your life as will fit, and it's still okay to pray.

Prayer is not for the perfect person. Prayer is for us.[2] Scripture lets us know that we can find safety with God whether we are perfect or not. If you're looking for that ideal spotless moment when you are perfect enough to connect with a perfect God—that moment doesn't exist. Maybe that's why we are naturally suspicious of anything that

---

1   "As for God, his way is perfect: The Lord's word is flawless; he shields all who take refuge in him." (Psalm 18:30, NIV)
2   "But he said to me, "My grace is sufficient for you, for my power is made perfect in weakness." (2 Corinthians 12:9, NIV)

says we can. But remember, God isn't just perfect, God is love.[3] We can find a safe place in prayer. Like a baby bird in a nest, we won't be crushed but protected and cared for.[4]

So, God gives us the gift of certain moments where we can be near him, reach him. How many? As many as we want. Anytime, anywhere, silent, or out loud, with words or without words, we can pray and reach out to God despite our imperfections. It's a unique perspective of the Jewish and Christian faith traditions that we don't have to earn, bargain, or barter for God's attention. It's offered freely; some call it grace.[5] Perfection is not a state we can achieve with practice or earn in any way. But every time we pray, we reach God's ears.[6]

Fi's attitude of worrying about being perfect enough to pray about her needs reminded me how unfair it is that so much gets in our way in connecting with God. Fi was such a spiritual person. I could see so many generous qualities about her. Those are gifts from God, but she didn't feel like she was on God's team.

Then I reminded myself that I had felt like that once. Probably for the better part of three or four years, I wrestled with the idea that I didn't feel like I could connect with God. The daily struggle had made me want to give up on my faith. Expecting Fi to just feel accepted by God in a few moments wasn't fair of me.

If only I could remember. What helped me know that I could come to God with anything in prayer, no matter what? What made me decide I was on God's team?

❀ ❀ ❀

During my senior year of college and the year after, I served as a volunteer youth leader for junior and senior high school students at a small country church. After getting to know the students for about

---

3 "Whoever does not love does not know God, because God is love." (1 John 4:8, NIV)
4 "How priceless is your unfailing love, O God! People take refuge in the shadow of your wings." (Psalm 36:7, NIV), "God is love." (1 John 4:8, NIV)
5 "My grace is sufficient for you, for my power is made perfect in weakness. Therefore, I will boast all the more gladly about my weaknesses, so that Christ's power may rest on me. That is why, for Christ's sake, I delight in weaknesses, in insults, in hardships, in persecutions, in difficulties. For when I am weak, then I am strong." (2 Cor 12:8-10, NIV)
6 "Since ancient times no one has heard, no ear has perceived, no eye has seen any God besides you, who acts on behalf of those who wait for him." (Isaiah 64:4, NIV)

a year, and going to their Wednesday night services and events, I was asked to go on the youth retreat. As the only woman leader, I worried I wasn't spiritually ready. The teen girls, however, didn't come to me with any spiritual or personal questions. Instead of learning, praying, meditating, and fellowship, the girls were fighting, gossiping, and sneaking out of their dorms. It was chaos. I asked the youth minister for help. I wanted him to remind and encourage the young women on the basics on how to approach a spiritual retreat. My request for backup was rejected. "Girls will be girls," was the answer.

I didn't take it well. Sometimes it seemed the underlying message was that only one gender mattered in church ministry. Soon, that message began to affect my prayer life. I didn't realize how low I felt until I went on a women's church retreat, as a participant, a few months later. The country retreat house sat alone in a valley near a small stream with high sulfur content. (It was pretty but didn't smell great.) No one seemed to mind this feature except me. The well water for the house had a high sulfur content too, so we were told not to drink it. I was so thirsty. Worse yet, I took a shower and came out covered with itchy red spots. I was allergic to sulfur.

That evening, we began Bible study with some singing. My spirit felt like my body: thirsty, itchy, and out of sorts. Then we split up into smaller groups of two or three to fill in a blank worksheet. One question asked, "How do you get closer to God?" I'm pretty sure we were supposed to write in the blank, "Prayer and Bible study." I have a pet peeve of worksheets that keep people from creative conversation, so I was already losing patience.

I tried to hold back my disappointment in the weekend. Here I was, finally getting a chance to hang out with women of faith. I was dying for some real conversation. With no men around, maybe we'd get a chance to speak up and share some of our own perspectives. It seemed like that wasn't going to happen. Suddenly, I blurted out the most argumentative answer that came to me. I shared that after nine years of intense study and reading through the Bible, I was sick of reading it. There had to be other ways to build up faith. I wanted us to explore something besides the easy answer, but the women were taken aback.

After talking some more, I discovered the other women in my group hadn't read most of the Bible because it was opaque or ancient. It seemed unrelatable. Their issues were bigger than my bad day. Everyone in my group felt at a loss to answer the question. Where could we go to build up our faith? We didn't know.

Dejected that the women's retreat hadn't been helpful, I went back home and agonized over my inability to connect with God. I prayed about it.

Finally, I wondered if it was a gender issue. The men preached on Sundays and Wednesdays, and told only stories about men, written by men, with words directed at men. Could that be why we weren't connecting with God?

Back home, I analyzed why Bible reading was also not working for me. What really hit my heart the hardest? When we would finally meet a woman in scripture, their stories were terrifying. I'm sure the speakers in church felt they were sharing stories of forgiveness, or at least stories with context from Biblical times. To my ears, they sounded like stories of abduction (Bathsheba, Esther) and worse, assault and or rape (insert almost every Bible story about women here). It was hard to gain spiritual insight for my daily life as a woman from stories about women who lived in oppressive situations told by men from privileged situations. The historical context of my own faith tradition felt anti-female.

To sum it up, worship time, church, Bible reading, prayer, leadership, and even spiritual retreats were not working. I couldn't find a way to connect with God. Was there a way to break past all the issues to insight? My worst fear was that I was expecting too much—that there wasn't anything to glean from the scriptures I had held close for so long.

I told God in no uncertain terms that I felt blocked in connecting to him. Maybe "he" seemed a bit too masculine. No matter the gender-neutral word for God in the original Hebrew language, God had been called "he" for thousands of years. I knew that was a human thing, not a God thing. After praying about it, I decided it would be crazy to give up my faith over this problem of disconnection and disappointment or over a single misused pronoun. Some women managed to keep the faith without abandoning their sense of identity. I would find them.

I went in search for some fresh perspectives—a search that's still going on today. I read anything I could find with a feminine perspective: old books on women saints, and Mother Teresa's book, *In My Own Words*.

My prayer about feeling left out went on for two more years. At first, it got worse. We moved to Minnesota to a campus at a seminary. I really wanted to study and get a degree in theology, but it was super expensive. There were no "two for the price of one" deals for married couples. I knew I'd be expected to serve as a minster's wife, most likely unpaid, so this seemed unfair to me. After visiting a church where both ministers were ordained and married to each other, I checked another seminary. It was from a more informal denomination, but it was just as expensive and offered the exact same classes.

When I looked at the course offerings, none of them were on prayer or community building–the things I wanted to learn about. That was disheartening. I decided I'd help my spouse get his degree and I'd just do independent study in the library. Surely, that was free.

My first trip to the seminary library, I excitedly walked up to the front desk and asked for a library card. They told me I couldn't check out any books because I wasn't a student.

"But I live here," I explained. "My spouse is a student." Holding my emotion in check, I sought a compromise. I explained that most college libraries let the community check out books. Didn't they have a community library card? I was told yes, but I'd have to go over the university library, not the seminary library, to get one.

"That will be fifty dollars," the librarian said once I finally reached the college side of the campus. Still working for minimum wage, that was a day's wages and broke the bank, but I paid for the card.

I soon discovered that very few books at the seminary were on prayer, so I began to use the interlibrary loan option. It cost the University a dollar and twenty-five cents to order a book from another seminary library within the Midwest. These were Baptist, Lutheran, Catholic, Episcopal, Presbyterian, Pentecostal, and Methodist Seminaries, and I was excited for the diversity. I figured if I checked out thirty or forty books, I just might make my fifty dollars back.

Okay, I'm laughing at myself now, but at the time I really felt like I was a second-class citizen. Unintentionally, the university made me feel that even information was guarded for only men, or the few women who somehow found enough money to attend. I'm not sure if I found even thirty books on the topic of prayer. I didn't keep count. I audited a few classes, read all my spouse's textbooks, and mainly studied at home by taking notes. I made art about what I learned instead of writing papers.

The seminary wives group invited me to join them. We had some fun doing crafts and talking about cooking and knitting, but again, I wanted to talk about prayer and faith, and it didn't come up as much as I hoped.

Finally, in January 2002, I went on a four-day retreat. I'd lost my job and was at the end of my rope. I needed rest and direction. A small farm run by three retired nuns rented me a one-room log cabin named after St. Clare. Clare of Assisi from the thirteenth century was considered by historians to be the first woman to write a rule for her religious community at a time when they were always written by men.[7]

Those four days, I tended the small wood stove that heated the cabin. I read books, took long walks, worked in my sketchbook, and was fed three hot vegetarian meals a day by the loving caretakers. All day, every day, I talked to God about what was on my mind. I just wanted to know that he loved me and that we were on the same team.

One of the buildings had a public hot tub. Above the water was a meditation to pray while soaking. Sitting there, I felt like I was in a tub of tears. I attempted to recite the prayer aloud about soaking in God's presence but all I could say was that I had been "thirsting" for God for four years and it wasn't getting that much better. Afterwards, I got out and dried off. There on the table, with pamphlets and brochures, someone had left a book of stories about women in the Bible. I sighed at the list of names.

"God, is this all you have for us?" I prayed angrily. "A few people

7 Sotelo, Nicole. "Can Women Write the Rules? St. Claire of Assisi Did." https://www.ncronline.org/blogs/young-voices/can-women-write-rules-st-clare-assisi-did

whose names are synonymous with abuses and oppressions. If this is the casting call, this is the team. How are women expected to find ways to connect with God through scripture? Maybe we don't have much to go on."

Through my tears and prayers, God helped me see things in a different light. After that retreat, I again found meditating on scripture to be energizing and uplifting. I made art every day working on a show about healing in scripture. It wasn't that I accepted the mistreatment of women. Instead, I began to respect my own voice more. Maybe St. Claire' story inspired me because I rewrote my own inner rules. I made space for my own voice. Sure, there were gaps, searching times, but God didn't let me down. I kept talking to him about my angst, my need to be heard and understood in a fair and just way, not through bias or misogyny. I felt God listen. The scriptures didn't change. The world didn't change, but I changed.

I got to know the women students at the seminary. I audited more classes, read more books. I lead a summer prayer group for students going on missions. I had a solo art show about healing and prayer. But I think the biggest factor that made me feel like I was part of God's family again happened at my neighbor's church in Minneapolis. The church was called *Elim*, and their logo was a well.[8] You know the kind that holds drinking water from an underground spring. If anyone was thirsty, it was me.

There I met Pastor Penny. She was the first woman pastor I had ever met. Each Sunday, she spoke about faith from a different perspective than I was used to hearing. She wore a long black dress on Sundays with a high collar. It had fine embroidered details that were hard to see as they were all hidden by the dark color of the fabric. To me they were "secretly" beautiful, showing how the feminine could be a part of spiritual leadership if you looked closely enough.

Pastor Penny gave sermons, but she was always careful to be creative with sharing her faith. One time, she had made sure a needle and thread were given to every person who came to church one morning so we could see how small the eye of a needle would be as we talked

---

8 *Exodus 15:27, NIV*

about Jesus' words on the subject.[9]

After a few weeks at Elim, I sighed with relief. Better than the water meditation at the retreat center, sitting in that beautiful round sanctuary shaped like a well, I felt like I had found what I needed. I finally stopped feeling spiritually thirsty. My faith journey, dry and narrow, suddenly felt more open minded. I would look for ways to honor my faith tradition. I felt heard, invited, accepted.

My heart opened up to finding a woman's perspective in my own faith tradition. To me, that meant a perspective of creativity, not being blocked by the idea of perfection, or a toxic masculine culture. I needed a faith in God that wasn't an emphasis on old lexicons alone: I wanted wisdom to celebrate women's intuition; I wanted to help others but not control them; I wanted to speak up with my own viewpoint, yet also hear and share testimony about what God does in lives today, not just 3,000 years ago.

Most surprisingly of all, I went back to those scripture stories that had hurt me the most, and I found healing in them. It was at this time I really came to love Rahab's story. Yes, Rahab, of all people.[10] Embedded in her story was a prayer of faith from the feminine perspective. Sure, it was ancient, but it was one that felt fresh because of its fearlessness. I saw her story with new eyes: Prayer was not about fitting perfectly into the stereotype of my time and culture but claiming faith in the way that was personal to me. Rahab taught me it was okay to want more, to demand more, and to expect more than the small space I had been told to live my faith in. She helped me understand that prayer isn't about boxes or walls any kind.

❖❖❖

Rahab.[11] She is always mentioned by the writers of the book of Joshua as someone of faith. She is a woman of quick action, wit, intuition. (And I know I said I wouldn't, but…) I looked up her name in the original Hebrew, because Rahab is a cool name. It's a masculine term. It means big, expansive, strong and powerful as a dragon. It means—"oncoming storm." How would you like to be named Ra-

9 Matthew 19:24, NIV
10 Joshua 1-6, NIV
11 Joshua 2:1-3, 6:16-25, NRSV

hab? It's a name that would have fit my friend Fi, a powerful person full of energy.

Maybe, like Fi, you are worried a life of faith is too narrow, that it might not fit your big personality, your natural temper, or your life experiences. A big God loves people of every stripe.

Because of her name, I imagine Rahab as a strong woman: loud with an epic personality. I bet she tells stories that would scare you to pieces, or make you laugh so hard you peed your pants. She is labeled a "prostitute" by the male authors of her story. We don't know if she chose this profession, or if it was the same job as we understand the term today. However, I think this point is often emphasized the wrong way, as if she was a "sinner." Despite some historian's debate, I don't see proof that there were many professions for women back in the sixth century B.C.E. I see only a few labels for women: wife, mother, virgin, prostitute, widow.

Some scholars argue that the words for prostitute and innkeeper are very close. A few are coming around to admit that the Western Church both Catholic and Protestant have overemphasized the "prostitute" adjective for women in scripture and that this interpretation should be reexamined. I think they all overlook that women did not have a choice about which role they were given.

All that to say, Rahab's life isn't easy. She could have been abducted into a job as a temple prostitute. Or she could have been a widower or a businesswoman who had several small businesses looked upon with suspicion or envy by her neighbors. Whatever this woman has been through, she has trouble. Even with her oncoming-storm personality, she fears what any single woman with few resources might. Rahab, like my friend Fi, doesn't want to be alone. She wants to feel safe, and she wants to be provided for. She is looking to God for answers.

Whatever is happening in her city of Jericho, Rahab is not a fan of the current government, the Canaanites, also called the Phoenicians.[12] On the positive side, they had taken great strides in travel and mathematics, and they were called the "purple people" because of their obsession with purple dye. Some women even owned land in their culture. This town in particular worshiped the fertility gods.

---

12 *https://www.ancient.eu/canaan/*

That sounds great at first, doesn't it? Living in a town that worships the goddess of love and the god of thunder—how cool is that?

Looking closer, however, it doesn't seem beautiful at all. Most evidence points out that these people also believed in sacrificing children—killing a child as part of a spiritual ceremony for favor with the local deities for good weather and plentiful crops.

That may seem archaic and evil. No one would ever consider such a pagan idea now, right? But stop and think about it a different way. Do you know anyone who sacrifices family or relationships in order to try and feel safe and in control about their future? Know anyone so obsessed with their bank balance, or their perfect life path that they might endanger others? How about any companies that put their financial security over the health and safety of others, maybe even child workers or mothers?

It happens today too. There isn't any human on earth who hasn't spent a moment where they put money, power, or control first. But in this culture, unfortunately, wanting a perfect, plentiful life—a big pantry—meant a culture that involved a ritual we would call murder.

You know, it strikes me I've never heard anyone mention that Rahab or other women she knew might have lost children to this practice. To me, that's the most important part of the context. When Rahab later names her family, she doesn't list a husband or any children. And if she worked at a temple with ritual prostitution and ritual child sacrifice, we can put two and two together, and make a guess as to where the "unwanted" children might end up in this culture. When I look at that picture, as a whole, I see a woman who has little power or control over her life, who may have seen more loss than we care to imagine.

The writer of the book of Joshua describes Jericho as a fortified place to be spied out and conquered by the newly freed Israelites who had left slavery. They wanted a permanent land to live in. It seems like the culture of child sacrifice needed to end for a new culture to begin.

Jericho must have been a beautiful city. Some of the excavated mud brick from that day still exists. I spent a whole day in Jericho once, and I enjoyed the green vistas and the palm trees. I could see for miles. The far-off water in the distance and the flat beautiful plain.

When I was there in the late nineties, I spent the day in a glass shop. Artisans made beautiful blue and green glass into bells, plates, goblets, and vases. To me, it wasn't too much different than the tiny town where my grandmother grew up—just a place in the middle of the plains. I think back in Rahab's time when Jericho was a fortified city, it might have seemed wonderful to an outsider too, a place about the worship of the sun, and love. But underneath, something was going on that made Rahab desperate to find a way out.

So much so, when two Hebrew spies come to figure out a way to take over the city, she gives them free room and board. And in a small town with no secrets, it isn't very long before soldiers are at her door demanding the spies be released to them.

"Yes, the men came to me, but I did not know where they were from. And it happened as the gate was being shut, when it was dark, that the men went out. Where the men went, I do not know; pursue them quickly, for you may overtake them."[13]

Rahab is quick on her feet. This readiness is what I admire about her. She's smart and she gets rid of the inquisition. Then before the spies, Joshua and Caleb, leave, she explains why she helps them. She tells them how she heard of the God of the Israelites, about Pharaoh being tossed into the sea. She learned of this God of miracles and knew spies were coming to stake out an upcoming battle.

To me, Rahab is looking for a faith that is about real love rather than power. With a woman's intuition, she knows the days of her city are numbered. She knows they are in danger and that her city's culture of death is about to be wiped out. The amount of things Rehab knows ahead is uncanny. Like a chess champion, she's even ready to bargain with the spies. She tells them in exchange for her help, they must "... spare my father, my mother, my brothers, my sisters, and all that they have, and deliver our lives from death."[14]

Rahab's readiness can only be the result of a woman of prayer. She is meditating, expecting God to break through with safe passage.

Rahab's courage when it comes to defying an unhealthy culture is important. It's not just one case of harboring an enemy spy and

---

13 *Joshua 2:4, NRSV*
14 *Joshua 2:13, NRSV*

letting them escape. She uses her gifts and what she has available. First, she hides the spies under stacks or sheaves of flax,[15] the plant that makes fine thread, linen, and rope. The spies must notice this because they tell her to hang a red cord out her window (red, not the purple that is the city's color). They tell her when the army comes to attack, no one in her household will be harmed because the red cord will signify their change of allegiance.[16]

Whenever I picture Rahab, I see her standing by her window lowering down this enormous red rope and hanging it there. Maybe she also made braided rope regularly for extra income. We know she let down the spies by a rope strong enough to hold the weight of a full-grown man, and as long as a city wall (because her house was in the wall of the city).

Have you ever felt you were holding on by a thread? That you were at the end of your rope? Imagine how Rahab must have felt knowing the entire city would be knocked down by a God ready to end its climate of death. The only thing between her and annihilation is this red colored cord. I imagine she must have braided and dyed it herself. She literally changes her colors. She chooses another team. You know how one sports fan in the wrong color stands out in the crowd? That's how Rahab stood out with a red cord instead of a purple one. Rehab literally changes teams, her flag, her everything.[17]

What kind of prayer can we attribute to Rahab? I see Rahab's prayer as more than a defensive prayer for protection; it is a prayer of certainty, a prayer of battle. Her prayer is a prayer of faith; a prayer of loyalty to God, claiming him as her rescuer, her banner.[18] When I was growing up, it's what my mother would have called a "hedge of protection" prayer. But again, it's not just a prayer of protection,[19] It's one of allegiance.

---

15 Joshua 2:6, NRSV
16 Joshua 2:17-19, NRSV
17 "Moses built an altar and called it The Lord is my Banner." (Exodus 17:15, NIV) "Now, therefore, fear the LORD and serve Him in sincerity and truth; cast aside the gods your fathers served beyond the Euphrates and in Egypt, and serve the LORD. But if it is unpleasing in your sight to serve the LORD, choose for yourselves this day whom you will serve, whether the gods your fathers served beyond the Euphrates, or the gods of the Amorites in whose land you are living. As for me and my house, we will serve the LORD!" (Joshua 24:14-15)
18 Exodus 17:15, NRSV
19 "And I sought for a man among them, that should make up the hedge, and stand in the gap before me for the land, that I should not destroy it..." (Ezekiel 22:30, KJV)

What's a hedge of protection?[20] A "hedge" is an old term for a natural fence. It was fairly easy to plant a hedge of thorny bushes around a vineyard or garden to keep people or animals out. Think about forsythia or willow and how easy it is to get branches to root into a natural fence. If you aren't a gardener, think about the story of Brer Rabbit who lived in the Briar Patch. The rabbit's home was a natural barrier of thorns that no one could enter. Still don't know that one? How about the story of Sleeping Beauty? To protect her sleeping kingdom, a wall of briars grew up so thick, no one could enter for a hundred years. That is a hedge of protection. A wall of briars appears in our folklore, and in nature, as a common wall to keep something precious safe—like vineyards and farms—a family's yearly supply of wine, food, and oil.

It' the same for payer. See how the invisible wall of prayer, a spiritual hedge of protection, keeps Rahab safe, while the man-made walls don't protect her at all. Rahab didn't think small, and she didn't pray small. When she heard of a God that could do miracles, that's who she thought about; that's who she wanted to follow. Maybe these small-town-gods worshiped in Rahab's city had created a culture of sex trafficking. Possibly their culture normalized the abandonment or killing children for sacrifice. We don't know the whole story, but we know she saw a real problem in her culture. She wanted to serve a God who valued and protected the life of the weak and innocent.

Notice that Rahab doesn't take on her bosses or try to change her reputation. She doesn't call everyone else in her city evil or proclaim herself perfect. Changing that deep-seeded culture isn't her agenda. Rehab doesn't start a war, cultural or otherwise, nor does she become a terrorist. She submits to God for help. She simply turns over her own heart to God and leaves it in his hands.

What I like about Rahab was that she wasn't ashamed. She wasn't cowering or self-defeating. She didn't apologize for her hard life or make any excuses for her situation. She knew that at this point, purity was not going to keep her away from a Holy God. She was going to

---

20 "Hast not thou made a hedge about him, and about his house, and about all that he hath on every side? thou hast blessed the work of his hands, and his substance is increased in the land." (Job 1:10, KJV)

come running for him. She would climb up as high and as hard as it took to reach him. That's the kind of faith and the kind of life she dreamed of. And she was going to take her whole family with her and pull them up too.

Maybe you are like Fi, or Rahab. You've seen something that makes you angry. You've seen injustice done to you, your town, your kids. And you are mad at others, or even yourself, for things you've done. You are seeing red. That's okay. Coming to God with your emotions is okay. If you come to God from a place of imperfection, or sinfulness, it's not a problem to him—and recognizing injustice and being angry about it is not a sin.[21]

Rahab knew what I wish everyone could know. When you see something is not fair, God wants to hear about it. He wants your take on it. And he loves your ideas of what we can do to make the world a better place. He partners with us in our prayers. That's where the walls that hem us in are knocked down, and that's where the walls that protect us are built. Rahab knew prayer is not about being sinless; it's not about being pure of heart.[22] It's about coming forward and raising your hand and saying, "I want in. I want into God's family. And I want that sense of protection. I don't want to be alone anymore."

What's strange is how Rahab's story ends. It's one of the weirdest battles in history. When the spies come back with their army, they don't fight. They march around those super thick walls in complete silence. Silently they march. First day, one lap. Second day, two laps. Third day, three laps. Fourth day, four laps, and so on until seven days and seven laps. Very creepy, I'm sure, to those inside. They follow God's orders, and on the seventh day after the seventh march, they blow trumpets and yell, and the walls simply fall down on their own accord.[23]

Rahab and her father's household and her brothers and sisters are saved, unharmed. Rahab is adopted into the family she hopes to belong to. She has a new life as part of God's family.[24]

---

21 *John 2:15, NIV Just Like Rahab, Jesus makes a rope—but for a different reason—while they lived in different times and places both were angry about a religious culture profiting from injustice and hurting the poor and innocent.*
22 *"Blessed are the pure in heart for they will see God." (Matthew 5:8, NIV)*
23 *Joshua 6:20, NIV*
24 *Matthew 1:4-6, NIV*

❋❋❋

Rahab's prayer is unique in that it is so powerful and so simple. Are you at a point where you are tired of those in charge of your life? Maybe you don't agree with their values, or you don't feel safe. You want to be a part of God's kingdom, and you want to see some of that kingdomness, that goodness, in your horrible situation. You are desperate for change. You want to be on God's team, put him in charge, and let him fight your battles for you, protect you from harm, and give you a family so you aren't alone. If you have a prayer as big as Rahab's, I can't begin to give you words for it. But I can put a few words here in the spirit of what someone like her might say:

God, who is my banner[7] and my rescuer,

Save me from my past. Save me from everything that brought me to this place of desperation. Save me from injustice. Save me from grief. Save me from despair. There is no way out of this one. You will have to break me out. Send a miracle. Rescue me. God over all the Universe, I praise you for having a plan to help me escape from tragedy and despair. I praise you because I know when I accept you, I've already escaped. I'm gonna be healed. I praise you because I'm gonna be whole. I praise you because you've already made a way for me. You've already solved this. You are going to take this mess, this terrible mess of my life. You accept everything that I am, everything that I've done, and you accept me and you love me. You are going to bring something good from my life, my imperfections, my bigness, all of it. I don't know what it is. I don't know how you are going to do it. You are going to restore this.[25] You are going to rebuild me and rebuild this place of desolation.[26] You are going to rebuild my house, my sanity, my body, and my

25 *"Your people will rebuild the ancient ruins and will raise up the age-old foundations; you will be called Repairer of Broken Walls, Restorer of Streets with Dwellings." (Isaiah 58:12, NIV)*

26 *"You yourselves are a case study of what he does. At one time you all had your backs turned to God, thinking rebellious thoughts of him, giving him trouble every chance you got. But now, by giving himself completely at the Cross, actually dying for you, Christ brought you over to God's side and put your lives together, whole and holy in his presence. You don't walk away from a gift like that! You stay grounded and steady in that bond of trust, constantly tuned in to the Message, careful not to be distracted or diverted. There is no other Message—just this one. Every creature under heaven gets this same Message." (Colossians 1:21, MSG)*

spirit. Me and my family, we belong to you now. We are yours. You are going to provide for us and build us up into a new place of safety. You put a hedge of protection around us, and no evil thing can get in. You are my banner of the colors you call me to wave. You are my God. I shout your name. I say Hallelujah because I worship a big God with big possibilities. I worship you. I praise your name, God. And let everybody praise you. When they hear about what you've done for me, everyone is going to praise you. Because you are bringing a miracle. You fight my battles for me. You've already brought a miracle. It's done. It's done. It's done. Praise the Lord. ❀

Liberty Dress ~Esther, Quilted Calico, Pencil on Cotton, 8 x 10 in. 2019

VIII
Prayer Walking

PRAY LIKE A WOMAN

Prayer is not "eyes closed" ~Esther's Story

When I was a junior in college, I would often stay up until two in the morning finishing a portrait for painting class, a group of bowls for a pottery class, or a paper. For me, it was about getting the highest grade. I was a perfectionist. I still am a recovering one. I wanted to surprise my professors with the best possible work.

Those fairly high grades didn't really fill whatever artist-type need I had for praise and admiration. I was sleep-deprived, and my creativity suffered. I found time to pray occasionally, maybe a sentence or two while falling asleep, but my spiritual life was on hold.

One day early in September, I noticed a friend of mine, Chad, had put notices up all over campus that said, "Prayer Walk: Sundays at Midnight." This intrigued me because praying was cool; walking while was praying was even more interesting.

My question: why would anyone have an event on Sunday night? That was homework night. Plus, what would people think about a group of random students walking around with their eyes closed?

Over the first few weeks of the semester, I kept thinking about the prayer walk and noticing the posters. I found myself wondering how the group was doing on Sundays at midnight, especially on cold or rainy nights. After a few weeks, when the weather wasn't too bad, I ventured out, heading to the spot right off campus where the poster said to meet.

The night was dark and foggy. Not unusual, it was often misty at that time of year. As an art student, I was usually out at midnight, or later, walking back to my dorm from the art studio. The streetlamps on this night cast a hazy orange halo. My steps echoed off the walls of the campus apartments contrasting with the eerie silence. I walked past lit windows where students were hanging out or finishing their homework on time like I desperately wished to be.

Finally, the sidewalk ended at the entrance to campus, and I had to walk along the road, which was really an overpass crossing train tracks. At night, it looked like an open mouth. Crossing over, I came to stone archways and columns at the entrance of the school. Wrapped with rustic wisteria vines, they cast eerie shadows anyone could lurk behind. I shivered.

The road was deserted. The sidewalk, empty. Where was everyone? Quaking with fear of imagined ghosts, wild animals, or prowlers, I was ready to run back to my nice warm apartment, but I waited a few more seconds. Finally, I heard two cheerful voices and the sounds of footsteps. Then a few more. A handful of students arrived, and I knew I had been ridiculously fearful.

Chad gave us a few words and a Bible verse to think about, and off we went. Walking in a group made the event fun. One thing I noted: You can't really prayer walk with your eyes shut. I liked that.

We walked along the outskirts of campus past a creek, past the sports complex, around the farthest student dormitory, behind the back of the President's house and Starry Field, then along the creek with its lush weeping willows. Finally, we headed on past Old Main and the schoolhouse. There were many moments of silence where we simply walked. Other moments, someone would say a prayer aloud for the campus or the students. The prayers were about current events, or the time of the year, the semester, the work. They were about the staff, the faculty, the students, and their families.

Soon we were back to where we started, circling the eleven acres or so of the college in just under an hour.

If you've never done a prayer walk, you'd be surprised at the number of things a group of people can think to pray about over the course in the cool, quiet night. It's a lot. We said our goodbyes then went back to our respective parts of campus.

Thinking back, I don't remember the other students' names, and I'm not sure we ever met outside of the prayer walk. There was less judgment; more spontaneity than a prayer session in a church where we would have been sitting still with eyes closed.

When I went back to my apartment that first night, it took only an hour for me to do my homework, and I was in bed by two as usual. Monday was great. I couldn't believe I hadn't lost anything from taking time out to pray. How silly I had been to be afraid. I was sure that next time would be easier!

You might already know this, but it wasn't easier. Every time I tried to attend the prayer walk, I was worried about my homework. If I even made it out of the apartment, I was filled with fear all the way to the meeting place: What if I was funny at praying? What if others could hear me? Second semester, I had a lingering twisted ankle, so I worried, what if I couldn't walk around the entire campus.

You know what? The fears were unfounded. The prayer walk was awesome: fun, safe, energizing. I began to realize fear was a trick.[1] Any other night that wasn't the prayer walk, I'd walk around campus totally unafraid. So, fear was a faker, right? Fear was the enemy.

The reality was there is a lot to be gained when people pray. I thought my understanding about the fake power of fear, and the belief in the importance of prayer, would clear everything up. Still, my jitters never dissipated until we were actually on the prayer walk. The next week, the fears would begin fresh again. In the end, the only thing I could do was expect their return and ignore them.

With just a few more weeks till the end of the semester, Chad told everyone he was going to be gone in the fall to study at the other campus in Philly. He asked for someone else to lead the prayer walk. No one volunteered. I definitely wasn't going to do it because it took so

---

[1] "What else is there to say? Just this: be strong in the Lord, and in the strength of his power. Put on God's complete armour. Then you'll be able to stand firm against the devil's trickery. The warfare we're engaged in, you see, isn't against flesh and blood. It's against the leaders, against the authorities, against the powers that rule the world." (Ephesians 6:10-12, NTE)

much time. Imagine being outside every Sunday at midnight, rain or shine, every week? It was crazy. No one needed this prayer walk that bad, I told myself. When no one spoke up to lead, I thought, well, it was great while it lasted.

Knowing me a little by now, having read this far, you'd be right if you guessed I couldn't let it go. I couldn't let the prayer walk end. What if something important to the campus would be lost? Months went by, and I did nothing. Finally, with only a few days left of the semester, I knew I had to speak. This was before social media, so once the term ended, I wouldn't see or hear from the group again. I found Chad one day on his way to class. (Only if you are a very shy person, will you understand that, for me, asking a question was like climbing Mt. Everest.)

Chad was a very unassuming person. He stood there and waited for me to choke out my words. He was wearing his customary Christian T-shirt, a bandanna around his forehead, a large cross necklace, and his WWJD bracelet. The added friendship bracelets made him look like the perpetual summer camp counselor type we'd all come to admire. When I finally said I'd take over the prayer walk, he told me that he really appreciated it. I pulled out all the stops and decided to say one more thing, "So what...how do you lead a prayer walk?" He was like, "You just pray. And you walk."

Chad walked off into the afternoon of lazy spring finals week while I stood there on the lawn thinking that this Yoda-sounding advice seemed oversimple and definitely not enough.

Suddenly, I realized what I had just done. I was now responsible for something! I was the leader of a group—or was it an event? And that thing had to do with prayer. I had taken on some sort of spiritual responsibility. What had I done? I had no qualifications to lead. I knew nothing. My fear grew and grew.

All summer, I sat in an office doing an internship outside Washington, D.C. I sat in the office every day, wore a dress, took part in donut Fridays, listened to gossip, and endured boredom. For some reason, the office didn't need me. I colored in a coloring book. I stacked mail. I sat. I made copies. I put school out of my mind.

Soon, it was the last week of summer. Time to pack up and go back to college. Reality set in. I wasn't ready for the prayer walk, so I coped by getting into my typical procrastination posture: lying on the bedroom floor, agonizing over my fate with my hands over my face. I hadn't prepared at all! I needed to learn how to pray, and fast!

"Dear God, help me. I need to learn how to pray. I don't have any money or time and I don't know where to go to find what I need," I prayed. Then out of the corner of my eye, I saw something in the hallway outside my bedroom. It was on top of a shelf right next to the ceiling. I wouldn't have seen it unless I was lying on the floor. It was a royal blue binder about eight inches tall. The large white letters on the spine read, "School of Prayer."[2] I'm not making this up. There on my parents' basement shelf in Northern Virginia, the answer stared back at me. I laughed, untangled myself from the floor, and took three steps to the hall where I reached the book by standing on my tiptoes.

Later, my mom told me she had been given a copy of the manual and done the training before I was born. This little notebook didn't look like much, but, to me, it was a bright blue life preserver. Different than how I learned to pray at home, this book emphasized praying by scriptures that built up faith.

Wait. You think I studied and read the whole book before school started, don't you? I tried but no, I didn't. Typical college student, I decided to read it as I went along. I mean, as a full-time student I didn't have time to read a whole book ahead. Right? I'm laughing now.

So, my senior year of college I led the *Prayer Walk*. Every Sunday night, I'd read one chapter from the "School of Prayer." It was so deep and so wide, hard for me to take in, so I read each chapter twice. Then I would create a newsletter (by hand to give myself a break from the computer). I called it "The Prayer Walk Newsletter." I'd draw little cartoons and write what I'd gleaned from a chapter. I'd fold each newsletter, address it, and put it in the campus mailboxes for each person in the prayer walk. That way, on Sunday nights, I had new insights fresh in my mind. On Mondays, the team would get the newsletter in their mailboxes to remind them about the next week. I also gave it out to friends and professors who might think it was fun.

---

2 *Dick Eastman, 1983.*

It always felt a bit embarrassing—kind of like writing this book—but I did it anyway.

Before social media, it took some persistence on my part to get the word out. I taped up fliers and left group voicemails for a certain number of campus phone numbers. Maybe you think this great 1990s-era marketing plan, along with my willingness to get out there, got rid of fears too. Nope: the fear of going on the walk, the fear of leadership, the fear of speaking in front of people, the fear of the dark, the fear of being cold, the fear of doing something silly or impractical, the fear of actual spiritual or social danger from trying to stand up and do something so disruptive to the status quo... the fears were palpable. And the fears kept coming: fear of failure, of ghosts, bullies, fear of no one showing up. (I think there was only one walk I ever took alone, and it wasn't terrible.) Ultimately, I chose to accept the fear. There was nothing left for me to do except give the fears to God. I knew they would dissipate each time I walked through them.[3]

After a few weeks of leading the prayer group, my viewpoint on fear began to change. Fear was not a physical, solid wall stopping me from where I wanted to go. No, fear was a mist, a mirage. Its opposite was prayer. Prayer was the solid real thing I never imagined it could be.

Sure, it still felt ridiculous to lead an invisible club doing an invisible act of service with no measurement of success. Yet, I met so many people on the prayer walk. People could share more easily while walking. I heard people's prayers, their hearts. I met students from all over the world and from all kinds of backgrounds, faiths, and cultures. Most of all, I saw answers to those prayers. I began to imagine that our prayers were inscribed on the stones to the entrance next to the school motto, as well as the prayers of the people before us. Over the months, instead of a sense of fear, I felt a sense of peace and protection. To me, prayer became something tangible, built like a wall,

---

3   *"For God has not given us a spirit of fear, but of power and of love and of a sound mind." (2 Timothy 1:7, NKJV)*

solid as an inscription on a metal plaque.[4] Prayer wouldn't wash off or fade; it was a tangible way of connecting to God and each other. Prayer pushed past fear one step at a time.

The *Prayer Walk* gave me time to connect, my conversation with God continued all week. We talked about who I was, my giftings, my callings, my heart. I could ask God what he thought about those things, where he wanted me to go in life. My artwork became much more creative. I wasn't up all night in the studio, racking my brain for ideas. Surpassingly, my work was received better during in-class critiques. More importantly, I didn't worry as much about what others thought. My artwork wasn't trying to please others; it expressed the journey I was walking by faith.

When decisions came up during that pivotal time, there was less fear and more certainty about where my path lead. I stopped being so awkward and uncomfortable. I had this ongoing "conversation" of prayer with a God who loved me and was rooting for me like a best friend. My decisions were easier. Fears, they were still there of course, but it was harder to pay attention to them when I had this great conversation going about hopes, dreams, and everyday joys with a creator God who loved me as a friend.

Did that mean life was perfect, that I never made poor decisions again? No. I made plenty. But it meant that whatever happened, it had already been given to God in prayer. Whatever I was experiencing, he had my back. I wasn't alone, so I was much less afraid. I was so much more comfortable being the real me because, in prayer, I had found someone who was comfortable with the real me. That conversation molded me, over time, into the person I am today—someone willing to share myself and my thoughts with other people. Something I would have never had the courage to do without prayer to begin with.

I think one reason I had the courage to pray on the prayer walk was because of a story I loved about a woman stood up to fear. For a long time, I thought that the book of Esther was one of the only sto-

---

4   *"Coming to Him as to a living stone, rejected indeed by men, but chosen by God and precious, you also, as living stones, are being built up a spiritual house, a holy priesthood, to offer up spiritual sacrifices acceptable to God through Jesus Christ." (1 Peter: 4-5, NKJV) "You yourselves are our letter, written on our hearts, known and read by everyone. You show that you are a letter from Christ, the result of our ministry, written not with ink but with the Spirit of the living God, not on tablets of stone but on tablets of human hearts." (2 Corinthians 3:2-3, NIV)*

ries about women in the Bible.[5] Esther is an entire book of scripture that takes place while the Israelite people were living in Persia (480 BCE). Now this is an incredible story, and it's the instigating event for the celebration of Purim. Movies and whole novels have been made about Esther. Unlike the few verses or words other women get, Esther gets a book. There are even animated film versions of this story: claymation, and one made with cartoon vegetables, really. So, I won't dig as deeply into this story as I could because it's a volume in itself but let me give you a summary if you haven't read it.

⊗⊗⊗

Esther is a beautiful woman who is caught in a series of political dramas. Her name is also translated as Hadassah or Myrtle— an aromatic shrub that has fragrant white flowers all year. (In some cultures, it's connected with the goddess of love, and some make wine from its berries.) So, Esther starts out a bit like the story of Snow White in that she is a sweet and beautiful orphan who innocently gets caught in political intrigue because of her heritage.

The first political problem is about the position of women in the kingdom where she lives. After a seven-day lavish party, the King commands his wife to come be "looked at" by all his friends because she is beautiful. When the King's wife exerts her authority and won't answer King Xerxes' call, she is punished by being publicly divorced and a new queen must be found.[6] This beauty contest makes the TV show "The Bachelor" look like a walk in the park.

After all the hoopla, the king picks Esther, of all people—a Jewish orphan girl who had been raised by her older cousin, Mordecai. She is sent to live in the king's harem where she is told she has to receive a year of beauty treatments before she meets the king.[7] Every day, Esther is told she must become more perfect, and she must live to serve someone who will divorce her or kill her if she doesn't fulfill his every whim. (People often don't stress this part, but I'm giving you the women's perspective). If a person entered the king's presence without his permission, the king could have them executed.

---

5   *Esther 1-5, NRSV*
6   *Esther 1:19, NIV*
7   *Esther 2:12, NIV*

Now I suppose some of us can relate to the fear of perfection. When I taught my fifth semester of college English, I had a student fall to the ground and cry out in fear because she couldn't decide what to do. If she took time off to do the final exam, she would lose her job. Fear grips us, especially when we are powerless to make our own choices.

Esther's life was full of fear too. Goodness, if she even turned a corner in the palace while lost in thought and ran into the King unexpectedly, she could be killed. Anything she said or did, even her appearance, could be used against her. She was a queen, but she was also a slave.

Esther graduates to queendom and is put with the King's concubines. Her cousin, Mordecai, also begins to work at the palace. Mordecai has his eyes open. He knows what's going on everywhere all the time. He turns in a tip that keeps the king from being assassinated.[8] But this government doesn't even send him a thank you, or really notice. It's simply recorded and forgotten.

Later, Mordecai gets into an all-out social battle with a guy named Haman. Haman is appointed lead noble, and everyone bows to him when he enters the gate—everyone except Mordecai. This makes Haman angry. He persuades the absent-minded King to sign a decree that every Jew in Persia—the entire race of people that Mordecai belongs to—will be killed on a certain day.[9] Haman goes from pride straight to genocide.

Now King Xerxes has his faults. He doesn't know Esther is Jewish. She is about to lose her people, her entire culture, her nation. And Esther's cousin makes it clear that Esther needs to do something about it.

You know how you feel asking your boss for a promotion, or your teacher for a higher grade, or your neighbor to turn down the music? So how would you feel to ask your King (a slave master with a propensity to chop off people's heads) for a meeting to tell him to fix a mistake that he made?

I wouldn't want to do it, no. I wouldn't. It's easy for us readers of

8   *Esther 2:23, NIV*
9   *Esther 3:14, NIV*

Esther's story to think that she should just get on with her task. Why not just tell the King he needs to get it together? Esther, who has never been allowed choices in her life, now has to make one with a life-or-death risk attached to it. Esther is battling fear. Her family is facing certain death, but she's inside the king's palace where it's safe and beautiful, it even smells great. She has attendants to serve her. She has the best place in the women's quarters. She has enough skin care to turn an elephant into a baby seal. She's rich by any woman's standards. But she's about to lose her people to genocide if she can only speak up. I think the fear is what was killing Esther.

Let's count the fears. Worst case: she will be killed for entering the King's presence. Second worst case: she will ask the king about changing his law, confess she was a Jew, and he would dismiss her to her people so she can die with them. Third, maybe she would ask the king for pardon, receive it, but none of her people would. She could end up the ultimate orphan with survivors' guilt. She could live out her days with the man responsible for wiping out her entire family and race.

The fourth and greatest fear arrives in Mordecai's not so gentle letter with his final plea for aid:

> *Do not think that because you are in the king's house you alone*
> *of all the Jews will escape. For if you remain silent at this time,*
> *relief and deliverance for the Jews will arise from another place,*
> *but you and your father's family will perish. And who knows but*
> *that you have come to your royal position for such a time as this?*[10]

Mordecai says that if Esther, in fear, turns her back on her own people–people of her own faith—then it's possible God will save them somehow some other way. But if she turns her back on her people, her immediate family would be cursed and die for going along with such an evil plot. Whew. That is an extreme unexpected guilt trip of Biblical proportions.

None of the outcomes look great. And the likelihood that the King would listen to Esther's question or do something about it was laugh-

---

10 *Esther 4:13-14, NIV*

able, even impossible. What King would ever admit he was wrong to all of his people? It wasn't in Xerxes' character. His first queen was punished simply for not showing up when called. The king wasn't the forgiving type. Heck, he wasn't even patient.

Here is where Esther suddenly has an unusual response:

> *Go, gather all the Jews who are present in Shushan, and fast for me; neither eat nor drink for three days, night or day. My maids and I will fast likewise. And so I will go to the king, which is against the law; and if I perish, I perish!*[11]

Looking through the information I find in scripture about fasting, I'm not sure fasting had ever been used this way before. In other earlier cases, men usually called for fasting and usually to ask forgiveness for a sin. Fasting was used like a kid being grounded: Go to your spot and think about what you've done wrong. Fasting was like a punishment or at least a way to humble oneself.

In Esther's case, she uses fasting in a different way. I guess it's a woman's view of fasting. She uses it as a time to prepare. She uses fasting as part of the conversation, and part of the community building, part of building a relationship to serve a God whom she is afraid has abandoned her.

The story doesn't say she walked around the palace for a prayer walk, but she tells two sets of people to fast, so she is making the rounds. The people with Mordecai at Susa, however many people that might be, and the people with her, servants and friends, are praying while doing other things. I don't imagine they got time off from their work or their scheduled duties to pray. They had to go about their business. This was not the old type of fasting by sitting in ashes, as historical fasting often occurred. These people were walking in prayer. They had their eyes open; keeping every other thought pulled toward their prayer and petition to God. They asked for favor from the King, protection from death, and courage and creativity for Esther to find a solution.

So, Esther's friends and family pray with her and fast with her for

---

11 *Esther 4:16, NRSV*

three days. They aren't being punished. They aren't asking for forgiveness. They are doing something different, praying for insight. They ask for new openings, new creative ideas, bravery; for the situation itself to change, or if not, for their own wisdom and viewpoint to change. They pray for favor: for a new window of favor with the king. Favor to be listened to,[12] favor to be spared. Favor is the key word.

Esther's problem was that she needed a creative solution since the King's law could not really be changed. Once firm, even the king could not cancel a law. He could add another one, however. And what law could he add that would spare the Jews from being killed? Could a creative counter law could be found? If not, open hunting season was about to be declared with Esther's people pictured on the posters. Something must be done. Esther prayed for answers.

I don't know if you've ever fasted before, but it's powerful. I used to tell my friends that fasting is like Super Mario Brothers when one of the brothers touches a star—they become invincible. For a few seconds, nothing can hurt them. Fasting feels like that. Prayers seem to go through more easily. A word, direction, or new ideas seem to come through more easily. I remember one time I fasted with my dad who was going to have surgery. As a mom with two young kids, I suddenly could think more clearly. I got out a quilting project I hadn't been able to work on for years and was able to cut and sew straight lines for the first time in a long time. I finished a few beading projects too. "I can focus," I shouted, "like when I was sixteen!" Fasting cleared the fog from my concentration.

I read recently that walking barefoot on the earth could give a person a great sensation of focus and energy. It seemed silly at first, but when I thought about it, I could remember every time I consciously went around barefoot in nature. Something about those experiences involved increased memory. Fasting is like that. It's like finally taking your shoes off and putting your feet in the grass. Everything becomes clear and life is less muffled. You'll remember what happens when you fast. And what happens while fasting stays in your memory.

Sure, it also may be uncomfortable, but I can't say enough about

---

12 *"Then he said to Him, "If now I have found favor in Your sight, then show me a sign that it is You who talk with me." (Judges 6:17, NRSV)*

the experience. It's challenging, hard but also full of fears and dis-tractions. Yet it's worth every second. I remember using the small sensations of hunger to remind myself to pray. Every thirty minutes, another reminder. It's enough, I think, to pray about how God wants you to spend your fast, more than how you will stick to it. It's impos-sible to pray every minute of an entire day kneeling on the floor. In-stead try a conversational style of fasting like Esther. You could listen to music, go about your day, or spend some time in a book or study that you've felt the need to read. Not too hard right? No. It is hard. But it's worth it.

I asked a prayer partner once, "What do you do as a mom trying to fast? How do you remember?" As a mom, every time I tried to fast, I'd forget, and end up putting something in my mouth, so I felt the whole day was ruined. Feeding kids or grandparents several times a day makes it hard for a caretaker to do fasting. This friend, Sylvia, was from Africa and had a beautiful family and a great job as an engineer. She was a spiritual person who loved God and loved prayer, and I knew she would have the answer. "I do forget," she said. "So, I just spit that bite back out." I laughed. This friend was truly dedicated to prayer. She was not going to lose a day of fasting or an hour of fasting over a forgetful moment. It was something I had never thought of trying, and in a pinch, it would work!

Now, if you have suffered from an eating condition or a health condition, consider giving up something else besides food. You can fast from anything that you do all the time. The whole point of fasting is to make more time for prayer and focus. I've fasted in all kinds of ways: Once I gave up wearing boring colors! I've fasted from dairy, or grains. I've fasted from avoiding faith-based music. (Yes, a double negative. I fasted by listening to music.) I've fasted from caring so much about what friends think of me. I've fasted from television. I could say that doing my college Prayer Walk was a fast for me from putting my homework above all other things. Fasting can be avoiding anything that takes your attention away from listening to God. Try it. You might love it, and here is what God did for Esther when she fasted and prayed...

Esther managed to fast three days. By the third day she is changed.

We can tell because of what happened next. Each step she takes into the king's presence, she relies on God's leading. (So already the prayers are being answered!) Instead of asking the king to spare her people, she asks him to a dinner party, and she throws something else in there. She asks to have Haman come to dinner too.[13] She is slow and careful. She gets the king's attention, then carefully goes forward.

This is something no one could have ever dreamt up in our wildest imagination. Esther doesn't strike me as scheming. She's not a genius in this story, just a simple girl who everyone likes.[14] To me, her reticence to be involved in the whole problem shows that she was not hateful or vengeful. She was not indifferent, rather just fearful for the lives of everyone involved.

That first dinner leads to another, and to a third until you can't help but laugh at the King and Haman thinking that something surely must be up.[15] Prayer and fasting has changed Esther. She is speaking up not once, but four times. Prayer must have given her these creative new ideas.

Finally, on the third night of eating (after three of fasting), the King is begging Esther to tell him what this is all about. He is begging her for a request, even up to half his kingdom. Now that's a switch. Esther's prayer has been answered already. She has been given favor by the person she needs to convince to save them. And Haman all the while has set himself up for an epic plot twist. He's built gallows in his yard in hopes to use on Mordecai. So, when Esther finally confesses what Haman has done, there is proof in his own front yard. He cannot deny that he has tricked the King into a binding law; that he is evil enough to attempt genocide for a personal vendetta. The king learns that person is Esther's cousin, who has saved the King from attempted assassination once already.

When the story comes out, the King finally sees that the proclamation means his own queen could be killed, and all her people will die. This was not a small-town event. His kingdom held one hundred and twenty-seven provinces that scholars agree ranged from present day Ethiopia to India. Xerxes realizes he's wiping out an entire culture

13 *Esther 5:4, NIV*
14 *Esther 2:15, NIV*
15 *Esther 7:3, NIV*

over a false charge. If his smart, beautiful wife is part of these people, they surely deserve their freedom.

The King has both favor and insight too (another answer to prayer). He finds a way to at least stop some of the damage. He re-posts his message that says what day the Jews may be slaughtered, but he creatively adds something. He declares that on that same day, the Jews may "defend" themselves.

So, when the day comes for her people to die unjustly, they are all armed at the ready and with the King's blessing. Sure, it looks crazy, like the King started a gang war in the streets because he can't keep his laws and proclamations straight. But really, the Jewish people battle those few left who still come to fight them. They overcome any dan-ger. They are not wiped out. And they live to fight another day.

Purim is now celebrated with feasting and delicious food and a re-enactment of Esther's story. Purim honors and remembers this great escape through fasting into feasting—celebrating favor that was granted instead of annihilation.

❀❀❀

Fasting and prayer, including prayer walking, has helped me to truly find my creativity and my faith, to conquer fear and gain creative insight. Maybe it's the answer you've been looking for. Do you need direction? Need to see things in a new way? Do you need a window where there has only been a closed door for so long? Fasting and prayer[16] is helpful to anyone stuck between a rock and a hard place. It helps us fight our way out of a prison and into a place of freedom. It helps us see hope, find a personal, tested, faith. It gives us clear focus to a problem we can't solve. It generates creativity in new ways we thought impossible. It builds relationship and conversation and creates time between us and God. I'd say if I could put words to Esther's prayer, it might read like this:

---

16 *"So He said to them, "This kind can come out by nothing but prayer and fasting." (Mark 9:29, NRSV)*

Dear God, who knows all mysteries,[17]

You made me and my people. Save me from my fear. Let me rise above each wave of fear that crests until I can begin to hope in you. Pull me out of this dark prison and into your light. Save me. Save my family, and save my people from destruction, from death, and from unbelief. Give me new ideas and new insight to walk in your will. Give me favor[18] with the situations or people that are trying to harm me. Open my eyes. Give me a creative way, using my gifts to fight this battle as a person who walks on your path.[19] Make this way easier and lighter[20] and full of hope. Put love where there is fear.[21] Give me a sound mind where I have been confused and indecisive. Put your way in me. Where I have been of two minds, cast out fear and give me focus on your one path for this situation. Make me who you want me to be, because who I am now just isn't enough for all you've called me to do. Hold my hand and lift me up and walk with me the rest of the way. Let me be quiet so I can hear what you want me to say. And Lord, let me be loud when I say it. ❀

---

17 "The king said to Daniel, "Surely your God is the God of gods and the Lord of kings and a revealer of mysteries, for you were able to reveal this mystery." (Daniel 2:47)

18 " May the favor of the Lord our God rest on us; establish the work of our hands for us— yes, establish the work of our hands."(Psalm 90:17, NIV)

19 "Your word is a lamp for my feet, a light on my path." (Psalm 119:105, NIV)

20 "For My yoke is easy and My burden is light." (Matthew 11:30, NRSV)

21 "For God has not given us a spirit of fear, but of power and of love and of a sound mind. (2 Timothy 1:7, NRSV)

Choices Dress ~ Abigail, Quilted Fabric,
Gouache, on Wallpaper, 9 x 7 in. 2019

IX

Quick Action Prayer

Prayer is not slow ~Abigail's Story

The first time I purchased a cell phone was 2009–a bit later than many Americans. New technologies made me nervous. In late June, I got a babysitter for our kids who were one year and four-years-old. It was a relief knowing I could be reached in an emergency.

The first call on our new mobile phone I received was one no one ever wants to get. Our house was on fire. We instantly raced home with firetrucks passing us on the road.

For some reason, I didn't worry about our kids' safety. I could see them in my mind; absolutely sure they were safe and sound with the neighbors across the street.

When we pulled up in our car, sure enough, the house was on fire and the firemen were having quite a time putting it out. My gaze went right to my neighbors'. Directly across the street on their front porch, Kristin and Mel (a mother and daughter who I talked to frequently) each held one of my kids in their arms. They were standing right where I had pictured them on their tiny front stoop. My daughter had her shoes on backwards and was in tears, but the baby didn't even know what had happened. The babysitter had gotten the kids to safety and called the firemen. My four-year-old was the hero, she had accidentally started the fire with matches I had left out, but rather than run and hide, she managed to admit it and get help quickly to save herself, her brother, and the house.

At that moment, running home to a burning house, I was spared so much worry, fear, and pain because of a great sense of peace. I knew where my kids would be and that everything would be all right. I hardly had time to pray, it was more of a quick action. It's not the same as knowing the future, although I've heard the term "future memory" applied to this kind of intuition. I'm sure these moments come from God.[1] They happen when we need quick and certain help.

I think the best scripture that describes the phenomenon well is from the first chapter in Proverbs, "The fear of the Lord is the beginning of knowledge." Sometimes I've heard this called the prayer of knowledge. The term "fear" is a puzzling word I deliberated on for almost a year when I first discovered this verse in high school.

I would have abandoned trying to figure out what fearing God meant except my dad gave me a t-shirt that said, "Fear God" with the chapter and verse written below it. I loved the gray green color of the shirt, so I wore it. But everyone at school gave me odd looks. One guy who sat in front of me in calculus turned around and spoke to me for the first time in four years. He said, "What does your shirt mean?" It challenged me to find out. I had no idea.

Finally, after reading Proverbs a few times, it came to me that "fear" is used to mean reverence and awe, even respect. When we are in a relationship with God—we respect God and are guided by him, believing he is all powerful, all knowing, all loving, and all just—that is the beginning of wisdom. That wisdom includes knowledge too—intuition guided by God's Spirit. We know more than we know, quite literally. When we invite God into our lives, our heart, mind, and soul, we have access to the same comforting holy spirit.[2]

Three years later, I again came to rely on this phenomenon of instant prayerful knowledge while I sat reading about a woman in scripture named Abigail.[3] She was someone I only remembered briefly as

---

1   *"The fear of the Lord is the beginning of knowledge" (Proverbs 1:7a, NIV)*
2   *"But the Comforter, which is the Holy Ghost, whom the Father will send in my name, he shall teach you all things, and bring all things to your remembrance, whatsoever I have said unto you." (John 14:26, KJV)*
3   *1 Samuel 25:1-38, NIV*

one of the smartest women in the Bible.

❀❀❀

Abigail finds herself married to a rich man in a community located near the desert. He has a huge property and a lot of resources. He is from the family of Caleb. Now Caleb had been someone legendary for his upstanding wisdom above all others—honest, fair, and strong in his faith. Abigail's husband Nabal is not. He is the opposite of those things. His name—one letter off from meaning noble—actually meant "wit," but came to mean something more like the English word "nitwit," or fool.

Abigail's story takes place in the same time period, after Samuel the prophet, Hannah's son. Samuel is the one who discovered and anointed a young shepherd boy as the future King of Israel. Not yet king, this teenager had become rock star famous for defeating a giant with just a slingshot. Yes, David, in this story, he's currently an outlaw, hiding from the present King who keeps trying to run him through with a spear. It's a lot of drama and intrigue, but Abigail is a calm presence in the storm.

In that time and place, people would take large herds of sheep or goats out into the arid landscape to find green wild plants and shrubs to eat. Sometimes, as green growing things were scarce, they climbed up the mountain ridges, or down deep cliffs. While they roamed, shepherds kept their sheep and goats safe from falling into holes, eating poisonous plants, or getting attacked by wild animals with a trusty shepherd crook and staff. Every night the sheep and goats were divided and put into pens.

Poaching was a common danger as well. So when Nabal's men brought their large herds into the wild area where a certain outlaw was hiding with his mighty men, it would have been easy for sheep to go missing. A few goats for a nice meal for David's mighty men would have been seen as a sort of tax for entering the "neighborhood," wouldn't have been a surprise or too much to pay. Turns out, David's men were the more than fair. They protected those shepherds and the sheep from thieves and were downright neighborly not taking a single one. If you know his story, David had been a shepherd as a child. It's not surprising he would have a heart for the shepherds and their flocks.

Now David planned a journey that took him past Nabal's large estate. No fast food or hotels back then meant a rich house would be expected, even honored, to serve as an inn or pit-stop for travelers. Hospitality was the epitome of that culture and taken very seriously. Maybe this because of the physical lack of alternatives, a traveler's life could be in danger of cold or hunger. Or maybe the emphasis on hospitality was the spiritual tradition of caring for strangers.[4]

David sends along a servant to say they are coming to visit Nabal's household. He's sure that Nabal has heard about their neighborly protection of traveling sheep and shepherds, so he expects a warm welcome. Just in case, he sends along a servant to remind Nabal of the story of their friendship and to ask for the right amount of food to be prepared for the literal army-sized group about to show up at their gate.

Now this message is sent during sheep shearing time. That season meant more money from the sale of wool. The extra workers on hand meant huge meals would be prepared for masses of people. Nabal already has extra food, extra people to cook the food. It is almost a spring festival type of atmosphere. It's a good time for guests. The more the merrier.

However, Nabal sends back a mocking refusal, accusing David of being a runaway "slave." Why doesn't Nabal want to help this great guy? Everyone knows who David is going to be. Only a stupid man would pretend not to know the future King, no, to go so far as insult, the defeater of giants.

Abagail is busy running her household. And she is an active, kind matron. While David is on his way with an army of hungry men, he receives the mocking message. So, he tells his men to get their swords and prepare. It's the wild west; his hungry army will just take the food anyway. It seems the protocol for a King, whether he was in hiding or on his throne, still came with an off-with-their-heads mentality.

Abigail is still in the dark about the whole situation until a servant

---

4   *"Be not forgetful to entertain strangers: for thereby some have entertained angels unawares." (Hebrews 12:2, KJV)*

comes to warn her. The servant says to run for her life and explains it:

> *David sent messengers from the wilderness to give our master his greetings, but he hurled insults at them. Yet these men were very good to us. They did not mistreat us, and the whole time we were out in the fields near them nothing was missing. Night and day they were a wall around us the whole time we were herding our sheep near them. Now think it over and see what you can do, because disaster is hanging over our master and his whole household. He is such a wicked man that no one can talk to him.*[5]

Abigail acts "quickly." She doesn't stop and kneel. She acts. She prepares "two hundred loaves of bread, two skins of wine, five dressed sheep," sixty pounds of roasted grain, "a hundred cakes of raisins and two hundred cakes of pressed figs." She piles the food on donkeys and then walks alongside them until she meets David personally with his men behind him. They meet in a narrow ravine, a wadi.

※※※

Sometimes when we are in a narrow place where a crisis can be averted, we instantly know what we must do. Other times, something we are supposed to say, and in many cases, knowing the right words to pray. One time this happened to me.

As a sophomore in college, I received a bill that said I owed over $1,000. I was in a state of panic. I didn't have any money and I didn't want to ask my parents for money, because they were broke. As I stood in line in the business office, my mind spiraled into worry and worse case scenarios, including having to drop out, I stopped to pray.

"God, help me know what to do and say. What if they kick me out for not being able to pay my bill? Wasn't it your idea for me to go to this college? Maybe you can do a miracle for this payment? I have nothing."

"You just watch me!" were the words that suddenly lit up my mind with hope. I distinctly sensed a change of heart. Suddenly, I wasn't afraid. I knew God could find a way to make his own will come

5   *1 Samuel 25:14-18, NIV*

about. He could help me stay in college or fix this bill, even though I had nothing to contribute.

So instead of crying or worrying or yelling at the poor woman behind the counter, I stepped forward with as much of a smile as I could muster and said something reasonable—something my nineteen-year-old mind couldn't have come up with without God's presence.

"Would you help me? I don't understand my bill."

The woman looked at it. She seemed confused.

"I don't know what this means. Let me look this up." She typed something into her computer with a frown on her face.

I simply watched her and waited for my miracle. I tried to focus on God and not on my worry. I just couldn't think what that miracle he might do. But I waited and watched.

"This is your balance," she finally said.

"I really owe over $1,000?" I asked holding onto hope that it was a mistake.

"No," she explained, wrinkling up her face. "I can see your file. This means you have a credit. You have extra money in your account."

I couldn't believe it.

"I'll take a hundred dollars out then," I said, cool as a cucumber, as though I had expected that was the case.

I walked away in shock. That still small voice had saved me a lot of embarrassment. Instead of crying or pleading or worrying, I had asked a simple question. That was so against my nature. This proved to me that my constant worry and doubts were unfounded when I was simply following the path God asked me to. It was hard for me to trust his plan, but he helped me learn that trust on the way.

Quick action is sometimes insight about what to say. Other times it's insight about what to pray. That prayer may not even need words. It is a response that is done while knowing you are in God's hands, and you trust those hands.

My earliest memory of beginning to pray, or my first prayer, was also a quick decisive action. When I was four years old, I used to sit in the back seat of my dad's station wagon, jamming to his seventies mix tapes. Some were praise bands with unbelievably slow, but joyful, songs. I adored the harmonies!

As my dad told the story, one day instead of shouting out "Song, Dad," then quietly listening and looking out the window, something different happened. One tape by an artist named Evie had a particular song I liked, "Come into my heart, Lord Jesus." It must have really struck me. I remember the words to this day.

It's funny to me I could even understand the song. That I remembered preschool and kindergarten Sunday School lessons about prayer. Somehow, I connected my ideas about prayer and Evie's song. It was a prayer too! We always prayed at home before meals or bedtime, but somehow, I knew that this was a special prayer and I needed to act quickly even while I was still strapped into the car seat at the back of the blue station wagon.

Dad said I was about four years old the day I told him I wanted "Jesus to come into my heart too," so we prayed together.

I guess I would say that a quick action prayer, the knowledge that you must act immediately, comes from having a prayerful inner life that is about praying "continually"[6] or desiring one. According to scripture,[7] God is all knowing and all loving, all goodness. So anytime we reach out to find goodness or love, that's not us,[8] that's God and asking for the chance to be closer to us.[9]

Now prayer is not magic, it's about relationship, so that doesn't mean that a single moment seeking God is a magical solution, a math equation that means life will always be perfect from then on. That's up for the theologians to debate, however, it seems to me, prayer is a journey. Augustine called it a "beatitude" or a journey of attitudes, a path for the heart and soul to take with God.

I know the result from that prayer more than I remember the prayer itself. From an early childhood I had a rich prayer life, someone to talk to and share my journey with; insight, empathy and energy that didn't come from myself. Sure, I was still lonely, awkward, sassy. I still got in trouble; I stuck my tongue out at my mother. In

---

6   *"Rejoice always, pray continually, give thanks in all circumstances; for this is God's will for you in Christ." (1 Thessalonians 5:16-18, NIV)*
7   *"If we had forgotten the name of our God or spread out our hands to a foreign god, would not God have discovered it, since he knows the secrets of the heart?" (Psalm 44:20, NIV)*
8   *"We love because he first loved us." (1John 4:19, NIV)*
9   *"Look! I have been standing at the door, and I am constantly knocking. If anyone hears me calling him and opens the door, I will come in..." (Revelation 3:20, TLB)*

fact, my memory serves that I was an overly whiny, discontent little complainer as a kid, especially on the outside. Thankfully, that prayer began to change me. On the inside, my heart was constantly growing, praying for God to help me be a more understanding, patient daughter and sister, student, and friend. Believe me, in my natural state, I had a long way to go. Thankfully, God started early on me.

By the time I hit my teenage years, however, my childlike faith was waning. Anger and envy were my constant companions. I dealt with some really harsh bullies in fifth through seventh grades, even worse they harped on my personal insecurities. About seven different kids in my small class of twenty-four were bullying me in seventh grade. I struggled. I had even made friends with one of them, managed to at least feel empathy and pray for a second, but as I ended seventh grade, I was losing the battle of the bullies.

My angst turned into anger at my family, especially how much time I spent helping my parents by babysitting and cleaning. We had a big old house and five people which made for a lot of work. I wanted to spend more time with friends. Well, I wanted friends. Sometimes, I wished I could just get away and have some alone time. What if I had been an only child? Would it have been better? By the time I was thirteen, I hated my school, myself, and even my family. I'm not sure anyone knew how much I was falling apart, even me.

That summer, my parents sent me for a week at a church-based summer camp. One night, after a fairly normal youth service with singing and a lesson, they had a call for people to come up for prayer. I felt I should come forward and pray for a new life. Just like that time when I was a little kid. It felt like something I needed to do quickly. A do-over, a reboot, was what I needed. My heart was a mess. The person I had become was someone I didn't recognize or like.

I ran to the front and prayed to rededicate my life to following God's plan and to have Jesus more in my heart, to let him be the leader of my life. It was a simple action. I didn't have any words. I just wanted things to be better. I wanted peace.

Right away, things felt different. After the meeting, I suddenly had a strong impression that I needed to apologize to my brother for the way I had been treating him. I tried to put it off. There was only one payphone at the campground for 200 campers. But I couldn't ignore this feeling. I couldn't walk away from the area by the payphone. Finally, I had to give in and call home. After talking to my parents, I asked them to put my little brother on the line. I don't know if it made much of a difference that night by asking to talk to him, and I was too nervous to explain why, but I know everything changed from that moment on.

Later that summer, my life and relationships began to turn around. I started to reconnect with my faith. I read my Bible and journaled every night—for hours sometimes. I enjoyed my family again. Not too long after that, my dad told me we had the chance to move across the country to the east coast, but only if we wanted to go. With my newfound confidence and peace, I chimed in, "Let's go for it! Yes!"

Looking back, it seems clear to me now how terrible the next year could have been if I hadn't said that prayer for God to remake my heart during summer camp. That quick action turned my focus around. Within a few weeks, my family had left their hundred-year-old house in a tiny town in Kansas and moved to the Washington D.C. area. My friends, my cousins, my grandmothers were gone. I had no one except my brother. (My baby sister was there too but she had just learned to talk and walk). I cried myself to sleep most nights because I missed everyone so much. I replayed those goodbye hugs in my head over and over. How terrible it would have been if I hadn't had my brother for a friend. How terrible it would have been if I didn't have God for a friend.

Our new rental house and the big move came with a lot of surprises. I began to reconnect with my family in a new way. Instead of fighting, my brother and I took long walks exploring a stream hidden behind our rental house. The beautifully clear water twinkled brightly with crawdads and rocks to play with. I bought a little wooden boat with my allowance, and we sailed it down the creak wading up to our knees. Best in my mind was the name of the boat we sailed. We named it with our initials, the PJ Waterlog.

I'm so glad that quick-action prayer meant the next year was a delight instead of a disaster. On the east coast, my Midwest accent and manners, my hair and clothes stood out like a sore thumb. Walking to school the first day of eighth grade, everything was different. Instead of twenty kids in my class, there were hundreds.

"God, help me find someone to connect with," I prayed, "so I won't be so afraid."

With my slip of paper telling me what classes to go to, I found room 101, English. Mrs. Steinhauser wore a red dress with little white flowers. She said, "Welcome," with a beautiful smile. I can't remember what else she said, but I knew everything would be all right. First thing, every day that year, I had someone who smiled at me and acted like I was important.

My locker was near my homeroom, and Mrs. Steinhauser's cheerful creativity held my center in all the newness. She was from the Midwest too, and her smile was infectious. Somehow, she knew I was a Christian, and sometimes we would talk about faith. One day, when I took her a large drawing as a thank you gift, she returned one of my short stories and said, "Polly, have you ever thought about being a writer? You'd be excellent!" Well, you know, I really took that to heart.

That one decisive moment of quick action in summer camp changed my life. Those problems I thought I had, those plans I thought I had—to stay in that small town and spend as much time by myself as possible—were given back to God. I found myself in a big city with a lot of new friends.

It wasn't easy. Faced with so many new pressures and a totally different life and culture, I needed help. Thankfully, prayer was again (and yet somehow a new) source of strength filling me with a new purpose, a sense of connection. God was my source of hope and renewal. I was less afraid.

That same summer held more. My mother had another baby, another brother for us. A few months before, I might have cried at my bad luck, but now I celebrated. I happily made up the nursery for my mom. When she brought baby Mikey home from the hospital, I enjoyed helping take care of him, marking each new growth and discovery in his little baby calendar. I took him for walks and sang him to sleep. The change in me was remarkable. A new heart was really what had happened to me. God's spirit changed me. If you had told me that in six months, I would be living 1,000 miles away from the bullies, and best friends with my little brother, and happy for more diapers to change, I would have fainted.

That year turned out to be a game changer, thanks to that one quick action to rededicate my life to God. God's spirit changed me. There have been many times since then that I asked God for a new heart, a new life, or had the sudden knowledge that a quick action must be accomplished—even if I didn't know why. Listening to our own heart, and to that still, small voice from God's Spirit, truly makes life a journey of discovery instead of despair.

※※※

Abigail was a woman who experienced quick action. When faced with an oncoming threat, she knew that her next step that very minute would direct her future and the future of her family. When she knew a hungry army was to arrive in a few minutes, she could have prepared for war. She could have told her husband he was a fool and thrown things at him. She could have run away or hidden under a pile of wool till it was all over. Instead, she cooked a feast and had it delivered herself with a prepared speech. She saved her family with quick insight.

Imagine Abigail's moment. Everyone is in shock. Abigail has taken charge as the master of the house while her husband is drunk somewhere sleeping off too much wine. The household's panic is subsiding. The visiting men are eating and happy. Abigail then has time to speak up.

She could have told the army that they had been fed, and now they must leave and never come back. They had been paid for their guard services and now they were even. She could have snuck away to yell at her husband and throw things at him. Instead, Abigail gives David a blessing.[10]

"God will certainly make a lasting dynasty for my lord, because you fight the Lord's battles… but the lives of your enemies he will hurl away as from the pocket of a sling."

A blessing, in that day, was more like a gift of words. Today, the equivalent would fall somewhere between a lifetime supply of coffee,

---

10 1 Samuel 25:28, NIV

a treasure map, or a prophecy. A blessing acted like a engraved plaque. It was real. Abigail gives an eloquent one, poetic and full of metaphor, referencing David's one-on-one battle with Goliath—the time he beat the nine-foot hero with a single slingshot when he was just a young shepherd.

❀❀❀

No matter whether our hearts are young and free, distressed, or depressed, God can save a heart any day, or he can remake a heart. Whatever your heart needs, he has it in spades. The last time in my life that I needed the quick action prayer was when I was a young mom suffering from a problem I couldn't name. I had one baby in preschool and one in second grade. I had more time for art and turned one of the bedrooms into an art studio. I had finally found a part-time job that paid above minimum wage, and I'd finished my master's degree. Our house had been rebuilt after the fire; I even had found a church to be part of. I expected a smooth path, but it wasn't. Life was so unbearable that I felt like I was being buried alive. My marriage was falling apart and nothing I did seemed to fix it.

I had found an old devotional book by Charles Spurgeon called *Morning and Evening*. The words were so beautiful, and I enjoyed reading the daily inspiration. However, so much fighting erupted in our house that I would run back to that little, green-covered devotional and read it again and again, fighting despair and hopelessness. I found myself locking myself in the art studio at my desk, reading my devotional three, then four, then five times a day I knew something was wrong. My life had become so unbearable I could barely make it one hour without running into my prayer closet.

One day stands out in my memory because I found myself hiding in the bathroom with my Bible. Another sign that things were not right. I sat down on the cool toilet seat lid. The bathroom was very pretty. I had designed it myself. It had the most beautiful sage-green walls, and oval porcelain knobs for the cupboards like my grandmother had. The shower curtain was this fun antique fleur-de-lis design, and the tiles were a pale olive, more of a white gold. The mirror was a sweet oval shape with a fun frame.

The only thing in the bathroom I hadn't picked out was the toilet because I had stood in the hardware store with my husband in a full-blown fight in front of the contractor. My husband had won. The toilet wasn't as pretty as the rest of the design, but it probably fit the space better I admitted later.

Things had been rough, and they were getting worse. I had tried to be the best wife I could be. Many times, God had helped give me more acceptance, patience, and love, but I was beginning to think it might not be enough.

Sitting in the bathroom with the Bible on my lap, I read Abigail's story and it was like reading it for the first time. I prayed:

"God, I'm hiding in my own bathroom. I'm miserable. I've done the forty-day-save-your-marriage-plan workbook. I've prayed, I've fasted, I've talked, I've gone to counselors, but it's not working."

My prayer from the little sage bathroom was, "Please make it work. Lord, please don't let me be like Abigail where I have to rescue myself and be my own head of the household."

My whole family was suffering, but I didn't want to stand up and do something about it. Breaking a promise was wrong and I could never hurt my kids by giving them a life of family separation. There was nothing that I'd wanted more in my whole life than to be married. I didn't know what to do.

God reminded me of my own dreams. Dreams to be a part of a church where I could invite people to my house for a Bible study. Dreams to have more kids, to travel, to have a dog. Dreams to be close to my parents and cousins, to be an artist, to write books, to live on a farm, to take walks, to have a beautiful garden and a swing to sit in.

None of those things were happening. And I knew none of those were ever going to happen unless I stood up and took charge of the situation.

I begged God to save my marriage and my sanity; to let everything stay the same but work better.

"What about all the adventures we had planned together?" I felt the argument come back to me.

"All I want, more than anything in the world," I told God, "is a fifty-year anniversary plate to hang in my kitchen."

I was losing the battle between my faith and my marriage. I had to finally admit I loved God more than a plate. Finally, I had to admit that my pride was nothing compared to a real future with faith, hope, and love. Plus, how would I hang that golden anniversary plate if I never left the bathroom?

"Fine," I prayed. "If I am like Abigail, if I am in a foolish, dangerous situation, please rescue me, just rescue me right now, quickly, before it's too late. I leave it all up to you."

The next few hours are too painful and too private to share. But about three days later, I woke up alone in an empty house.

God had rescued me against my will.

I went through years of wracking pain from separation and divorce. But I had to choose how I would live in the unexpected life I found myself. I took Abigail's method to heart. Blessing was the only way to stand up and keep finding a way forward.

How prideful and judgmental I'd been of other people in my same situation. I assumed divorces happened because people didn't try hard enough, or didn't pray about it, or didn't consider their path forward. I didn't realize sometimes they didn't choose it. But now I had to get rid of all my stereotypes. My future had to be about life outside the "norm."

Every day since has been affected by that one quick surrendering prayer conversation with God in my fancy fleur-de-lis bathroom—the prayer I learned from Abigail.

It's still a long road. When you experience a quick action prayer that saves your heart or breaks your heart, that saves a household, or upends your life—a quick action prayer doesn't really end. It changes the direction of everything afterward.

I think we can learn a second thing from Abigail's method. One, we should be aware of blessing and its power. Action and blessing. The jab and the upper cut. The quick one-two will put out any opponent. And let me be clear that our opponent is never people, but the evil in the world, the lies, and the strongholds of abusive power. It's not people who are our enemy, it's foolishness, greed, selfishness, pride. Abigail's way is to put our hearts in God's hands and trust his guidance over our plans.[11]

I've learned by experience to be ready. Be ready for quick action, for a still small voice; to hear or see direction when things get rough. And that action is usually followed by blessing. Whether it's a thoughtful lady at the bank counter, help from the friendly fireman ready to give a stuffed teddy bear to a little girl who lost all her toys, or a patient contractor who builds a beautiful healing space, it's time to bless. Bless people wherever you go. Bless when you go in, Bless when you go out.[12] Bless when you meet friends, or enemies. Bless when you don't know what to say, when you don't know what to pray, and when you aren't even sure what just happened. Bless when people leave, bless them when they come in.

The prayer I use the most often when I'm upset and angry is "Dear God, bless them anyway." Blessing is better than cursing, and it can move mountains. Blessing releases you and leaves everything up to God and his plan and his purposes. You may be surrounded by school bullies, or abusive coworkers, or people that are making you feel unsafe. The first step is to get to a safe place. But cursing a bully can't help them or yourself. Blessing is the most freeing thing you can do and the widest platform for God to work on.

You may not be able to bless those that curse you. It's hard. But you can give them over to God. Let him deal with it. And while you give those problems to him, look around and find a way to walk toward his calling for your life. You don't have to say anything, just let him into your heart.

If I were to rewrite Abigail's story into a prayer, this is what it would sound like:

Dear Mother God, who watches over the weak and quiet,

Put your wings over me like a mother bird[13] over her nest. You see me and my humble situation. Thank you for speaking to me. Thank you for your insight. Thank you for your still small voice.

---

11 *"In all your ways submit to him, and he will make your paths straight." (Proverbs 3:6, NIV)*
12 *"You will be blessed when you come in and blessed when you go out." (Deuteronomy 28:6, NIV)*
13 *"He will cover you with His wings. And under His wings you will be safe. He is faithful like a safe-covering and a strong wall." (Psalm 91:4, NIV)*

Thank you for giving me wisdom and quick wit. Thank you for providing everything I need. Give me a generous heart and light feet.[14] Bless those who love me and help me, who are patient with me. Bless those who make my day. Bless those who inspire me. And then dear God, bless those that hurt me. Bless those who curse me, who neglect and manipulate me—who try to have power and control over me. Bless them anyway. And let me be free. Give me a new heart.[15] Remake me. Give me peace.[8] Protect me. Free me from dangers and from attack on my mind, my body, or my spirit. I don't have to pay back evil for evil.[16] You'll take care of me. I give my situation to you. If I've misjudged innocent people, show me the truth. Put grace back into my heart. I wipe my hands of being the judge over others.[17] I'm free, I'm clean and I'm released. I'm your child and you have a plan for me. You will rescue me. If I am in a foolish situation, you'll break me free. If I am under the oppression of an army waiting to tear down my life, you will turn them around. If I am battling on all sides, you will put me in a clear space. If I am simply in need of patience, you will provide it. I give everything to you. Put your words in my mouth.[18] Put your words on my tongue. Don't let me say anything I'm not supposed to.[19] Put your vision in my heart. Guard me. Just let your will be done in my words, my hands, my feet, my spirit—all of me. Make me courageous, as strong as a lion. Make my wisdom as wise as a serpent. And make my love as gentle as a dove.[20] �֎

---

14 "For you have delivered me from death and my feet from stumbling, that I may walk before God in the light of life." (Psalm 56:13, NLV)

15 "I will give you a new heart and put a new spirit in you; I will remove from you your heart of stone and give you a heart of flesh." (Ezekiel 36:26 NIV)

16 "Make sure that nobody pays back wrong for wrong, but always strive to do what is good for each other and for everyone else." (1 Thessalonians 5:15, NIV).

17 "He will judge between many peoples and will settle disputes for strong nations far and wide. They will beat their swords into plowshares and their spears into pruning hooks. Nation will not take up sword against nation, nor will they train for war anymore." (Micah 4:3, NIV).

18 "Keep thy tongue from evil, and thy lips from speaking guile." (Psalm 34:13, KJV)

19 "May these words of my mouth and this meditation of my heart be pleasing in your sight, Lord, my Rock and my Redeemer." (Psalm 19:14, NIV).

20 "Therefore, be as shrewd as snakes and as innocent as doves." (Matthew 10:16, NIV)

River Dress ~Mary, Found Quilted Fabric on Cotton Paper,
9 x 7 in. 2018 installation Beggar's Table Gallery

Seed Prayer

PRAY LIKE A WOMAN

Prayer is not warm thoughts ~Mary's Story

On an early spring day, I drove from my little apartment, about an hour north of Gettysburg, Pennsylvania, to my parents' house in northern Virginia. Highway 15 was one of the nice things about the drive. There was this one view near Emmitsburg which always took my breath away.

Seeing the Mount Saint Mary's University's campus with its little tower on the cathedral and the gentle slope of the rolling green hills was my favorite part of the journey...that, and the little Irish restaurant near Thurmont with the thickest cream soup in the country.

Every time I saw this spot and the exit sign for The Grotto of Lourdes, I wanted to stop there. But each time I'd drive on past. You may have felt this before too: A certain place on the map beckons, but for some reason you don't go.

That day, I was driving home for my sister's graduation from high school. As I approached the familiar hillside, I suddenly realized that I had driven by this site countless times over almost a decade, but I had never visited, not once. I swerved off the highway, calculating mentally that I could take a whole hour walking around on this beautiful day and still not be late. Also, I had something on my mind. I just needed a moment to stop and pray.

When I parked my car and got out, I was standing under an extremely tall statue of Mary, her arms outstretched, and her gaze directed at me. I suddenly felt like I had been late for an appointment.

Some Protestant Christians might not feel comfortable stopping at a Catholic shrine, but as long as we are thoughtful and reverent, why not? As a girl, I attended St. Xavier's Catholic school for fourth and fifth grades. I made some of the closest friendships of a lifetime. (My education echoed reformation church history, in a way, with my sixth and seventh grade years at a Lutheran school where we studied their catechism.)

At St. Xavier, we attended Mass every Thursday. I was allowed to participate in almost everything. My mother was the music teacher for the upper elementary school. As the only Protestant in the school, we somehow had come to the agreement that I would participate in all the church-related school activities except confession and communion. I guess there needed to be a line somewhere. So, in those parts of the Mass, I sat out.

There was one other thing I didn't participate in. In each service, I said all the prayers, sang all the songs, some of which I really loved. I did everything except pray the "Hail, Mary." Someone must have asked me not to say that particular prayer. To many Protestants, the difference between Catholic and Protestant is centered on the understanding of Mary.

Maybe it was odd being immersed in a culture I was only a cousin to[1]—I could only take part up to a point. For example, my fifth-grade teacher gave everyone in the class a plastic rosary. I chose a pink one. I kept it in a box of special treasures instead of learning to use it. As a ten-year-old, the Rosary was a mystery. I worried saying prayers repetitively might be rude. Would God be offended? Surely, he heard us the first time. And what if praying to Mary wasn't right either? I wasn't sure she could hear me. Was it even okay to pray to someone who had passed away so long ago?

I was thankful for my Catholic friends and upbringing. Different

---

1   *Protestant denominations branched off from Roman Catholocism during the Reformation period just as Catholics branched off from Orthodox Christians centuries earlier.*

faiths were exciting, like visiting different countries. I spent my young prayer life thinking about what people before me thought about prayer and faith. I learned some of the Catholic faith straight from the source, and then later about the Reformation and Martin Luther's *ninety-five Theses*[2] in a weekly religion class at the Lutheran school. It was like learning Church history in order by visiting important historical sites, but I didn't travel—I simply walked across the street.

This experience turned out to be a treasure. I didn't know how grateful I'd be for that openness later. I never could have imagined as a child, the circumstances in my adult life that would cause me to feel blocked or stuck in my faith. I couldn't know that times would come when I would be so desperate and hurt that none of my old paths to prayer would work for me.

Despite the beautiful blue skies on my drive that day through the green hills of Maryland, I wasn't okay. The last year had been especially hard. I remember an inconclusive visit to a fertility specialist and then a few months later, an appointment at the adoption agency. Sitting there in a small office on a high-backed striped sofa, we found an adoption would cost at least $10,000.

For us, that was half a year's salary. I worked teaching part-time art classes in a small community center in a refurbished barn. I gave private painting lessons, even found a small gig teaching art in a preschool. As a career girl, I had never found full-time work. As far as ministry went, we were paid "part time" to the point of almost being volunteers. Even with all those jobs, I didn't make that kind of money in a year. (The social worker didn't mention that there were cheaper adoptions through the state, which would have been good news to me. The internet and search engines were still in their infancy, so I took her price tag as a no.)

In despair over not being a mother, I couldn't look at a baby or I would cry. I still didn't have any children, and I'd been married for what felt like a very long five years. All I could think about was being a mother, but I couldn't start a family. I felt left out. One night, I had cried so hard and for so long about not being a mother, I had broken a blood vessel in one of my eyes. I was at the end of a long year of

---

2 *October 31, 1517 Martin Luther's Reformation begins.*

disappointments.

My prayer life was in shambles. All my normal methods of prayer hadn't worked. I wanted to talk to God but felt like he wouldn't understand. Sure, I knew God was neither feminine nor masculine. But I had been trained to hear that "he" pronoun. How could I address my prayers to the masculine ideas of God the father or even God the son when I had all these needs that seemed only to relate to the feminine? How could a masculine God hear my prayers about birth, women's rights, fair treatment, equal pay, and motherhood? The irony became too much.

Driving past the shrine, I remembered Mary's story and suddenly decided my twenty-five years of passing over her prayer were over. It was time.

Nearby was a walking path. I knew a pilgrimage was a journey of prayer and that kind of prayer worked better if you set a specific intention or question. I knew exactly what I was going to pray for. While I walked up the hillside, I'd pray for my family and all their needs and concerns, but on the way down I would pray for a baby of my own.

From my reading and a few sites, I visited abroad, I knew vaguely about spiritual pilgrimages. The artist in me recognized it as a freestyle form of prayer, like baking a loaf of artisan bread. A pilgrimage could be short or long, to a faraway place or just off the highway. I'd heard of pilgrimages taking weeks or months, but this one hour would be mine.

I walked and prayed. This path wound up a very steep but beautiful hill. The air was clear, the green was amazing that time of year, and the walk was really not too long. Wonderful sculptures and beautiful bronze reliefs were carved in each station. Bronze plaques were engraved with verses and prayers to say at each station up the mountain. I said each prayer.

At the top, a little cave or grotto held candles where palmers (people on the pilgrimage trail) could go and light a candle to say a special prayer. The suggested prayer was the *Hail Mary*. After years of "skipping that one," I paused. I remember thinking, God loves me. He created me to be a woman, and he had a mother. I think it's ok to say this prayer. I need to say it. I just need relief. I need to talk to someone from a woman's perspective, and I need to feel there is a feminine aspect to my faith and a feminine empathy over my life. So I prayed the Mary prayer for the first time.

Back down the mountain, I prayed about being a mother. I felt like I was arguing with God the whole way. At the bottom of the other side of the hill, at the end of the path, lay two sculptures in white stone. One was Mary joyfully holding her baby child. The other was of Mary holding Jesus as he lay dying—a Pieta. Jesus was killed on a Roman cross by crucifixion, and Mary was there to see the death of her son.

I was moved by these last two images. I remember feeling that Mary's message to me was that if I was really going to accept motherhood and all that came with it, I must accept the pain and the failures, and the loss mixed in with the good. Her message to me was that motherhood held all joys…and all sorrows.

So, I prayed one final prayer of release. That I would accept whatever God chose for me. I would accept motherhood and all its pains and sorrows, or something else—adoption, or no children at all. I'd accept whatever God wanted. I'd made clear what I hoped for but my prayer of acceptance felt right. I climbed back in my car and drove on, keeping a brochure picture of the grotto so I wouldn't forget that day.

❀❀❀

I didn't convert to Catholicism from that one prayer, although I've known Protestant friends who switched to Catholicism and vice versa. However, diversity in prayer can be a good thing. If prayer is a relationship, it makes sense there would be variety, growth, and exploration. That Hail Mary prayer, one I had been forbidden to pray, was the answer to my broken heart that day. I found peace on that hillside–a way to talk to God where I had previously been blocked. Thankfully, since I began my prayer life at such a young age, I knew God was my friend. And so, when I was hurt or angry, I knew it was better to tell him I was having a problem. He could handle it. Knowing there were so many other faith traditions of prayer meant that I could focus on meditating on God rather than worrying about what type of prayer was "wrong."

Not all of us get to experience so many traditions. But that diversity helped me. I'm not advocating getting rid of all our traditions or trying to merge them into one. However, I think the most hurtful myths keep us bored, uncreative, and stumped with prayer. If a stereotype about prayer keeps us from God maybe it should be re-examined. Mary was known as someone who meditated on God. Yet, growing up, I remember hearing some people preach against meditating. They warned meditating (yoga for example) was emptying your mind. This they surmised was dangerous; "emptying" your mind might leave room for "evil spirits to fly in."

Limiting our understanding of prayer to just one kind never seemed reasonable to me. Don't we profess faith in such a big God who is timeless and all powerful and all creative and all loving? So why would our prayer life look like one loaf of bread instead of a bakery or a whole grocery market? So, I wondered about this no meditation rule through my mid-twenties until the day I took part in a volunteer house building project. Before the second day of nailing repurposed barnwood as the siding on the eco-friendly house, the sore work crew was lead in some yoga stretches together. When everyone bent to do the "downward dog" pose, I was so surprised by the innocent and joyful humility of the name and their gestures, I burst out laughing and had to excuse myself. I couldn't believe this had been what I was told to avoid. It was obviously something so helpful and innocent—a tradition for a millennia of laborers stretching out their morning stiffness.

If our prayer life is stiff, and sore, it needs to be stretched, right? It's funny what we are told not to do spiritually in one circle or another. Yes, I do have lines I'd be hesitant still to cross, and I have wilder stories than this, but the more traditions I experience, the more these myths about prayer seem like micro-aggressions and arguments from outdated campaigns. For example, Protestant friends warned me never to pray to a saint, only to Jesus and no one else. To them, praying to saints smacked of idolatry. At my grandmother's Methodist church, we prayed liturgical prayers; something my nondenominational friends thought was too formal. They said repetitive prayers weren't personal and so weren't real enough.

My upbringing on prayer: my parents' prayers were a mix of their Methodist and Southern Baptist traditions with a bit of Pentecostal prayer oil and faith healing thrown in. My Pentecostal friends emphasized praying in tongues, while other friends said speaking in tongues was the result of demon possession. Some advocated praying for miracles while others thought this was old-fashioned. They said miracles didn't exist anymore–which makes me laugh. And my Catholic friends would be a scandalized if they knew we sometimes prayed over our own communion ceremony at home wihtout a priest, or even used crackers and orange juice if we didn't have the wine and bread.

I see so many beautiful things about the strengths, giftings and diversity of so many traditions. For me, it became clear, it was my relationship with God that was more important than how I chose to pray. When I was told to look down on another person's type of prayer, that pride seemed the opposite of the whole point.

Now that I'm in my midlife, I can say I've been to almost every kind of western Christian prayer service from Jewish to Christian and many more besides. I've been healed from a lifelong illness while people spoke in tongues. I've kneeled silently during prayer from the Catholic Missal and recited lines from *The Book of Common Prayer.* I've been to house churches and campuses and to hospital prayer rooms. I've been to baptisms in swimming pools, streams, and lakeside. I've attended mainline churches that felt Pentecostal[3] and Pentecostal churches that felt mainline.[4] I've prayed in holy sites, retreat centers, and the International House of Prayer. I've seen people pray by painting, waving flags, or lying on the floor, shaking, jumping, singing, or not doing anything at all. I don't think any kind of prayer is "evil" or the result of bad spirits. Each time we reach out to God, no matter our tradition, that's prayer. In each place I've visited a prayer or worship service, or sacred space, I found people seeking God and finding answers.

Yes, random rumors about how to pray and not pray have always been around—both inside and outside Christianity. I'm not denying

---

3　*Pentecostal movements branches out from Protestant denominational churches during the Holiness movement revivals in 1901 and afterwards.*
4　*More formal worship styles of older Protestant denominations, such as the United Methodist Church, Evangelical Lutheran Church in America, Presbyterian Church (USA), Episcopal Church, Christian Church (Disciples of Christ) and United Church of Christ.*

there is evil in the world, or that even human prayer can be full of greed or other problems that humans can't help but be saturated with. However, how can our faith be effective if our only choices are: to hate those that pray differently from us; give up our faith when it stops working for us; or both? I don't accept those as my only options. I'm a layperson and not a theologian, but it's been my experience that there is a way to be more trusting. If you are meditating on God in prayer with an eye toward scripture and tradition, then the only danger I've found is a richer interior life, a closer walk with the creator, and more acceptance of God's grace.

When there is a real need, or someone is sick, dying, lost, or in danger, even my atheist friends will ask for prayer. In our time of need, no one gets an answer to prayer and then calls back to reject those prayers that aren't in their tradition. We don't get a miracle and then say "never mind." We don't check to see whether our answer to prayer came with the use of Rosaries, silent meditation, candles, a pilgrimage to a shrine, or use of a special prayer language. No one asks the people that prayed for them what kind of baptism or music they preferred, or what hot-button issues they have sided with. No, when we ask people to pray, we are just looking for answers. So, if we can accept these diverse prayers in an emergency, shouldn't we consider them acceptable every day?

Since that is the case, it seems to me that, like Augustine and other saints have said, it's about love. What would it look like if our relationship with a loving God, and grace that helps us love others, was more important than our different traditions and arguments?

It's easy to say it. But much harder to act it out. I still find myself nervous in unfamiliar territory. I found myself fearful to stop at the Catholic pilgrimage site. It's always a bit nerve-wracking doing something unfamiliar. But I'm so glad I made time and humility to explore a new kind of prayer. My reward was a better understanding of Mary and a new experience with both pilgrimage prayer and meditation. Getting rid of fear and bias about meditation led me to be open to explore ways of praying I hadn't before. It helped me not to give up on prayer.

⚶⚶⚶

You may already know her well, or maybe you don't. Mary was the mother of Jesus, a young girl in Nazareth engaged and later married to a builder named Joseph. The building materials in Palestine are mostly rock, but Joseph could do carpentry and probably build just about anything out of any materials.

In the Gospel written by Luke, the doctor, he mentions twice that Mary was a thinking kind of girl. She would weigh thoughts for a long time. She meditated. What did she think about? The most famous line by the writer Luke mentions Mary "pondering in her heart[5]" a visit by shepherds who have a wild tale to tell about angels, a star, and a message that her newborn son. They call him "a Savior, who is Christ the Lord," the long-awaited Messiah.

Later, when an eight-year-old Jesus goes on a walking caravan trip to Jerusalem, he sneaks away to debate and discuss the scriptures with learned men in the Temple. He has been missing for three days. Here is where Mary stands out among mothers throughout literary history. Instead of punishing her son, she "treasures"[6] Jesus' ability to debate and answer questions about the law with adults.

Is pondering the same as praying? I think the difference is Mary is meditating on God's words and promises. Pondering or reflecting on words in your heart sure sounds like meditating to me. So, what is the difference between thinking repetitive thoughts versus prayer? To me, the answer from Mary is simple: Thinking is a solo occupation, while prayer is done with God.

Mary is a really unusual girl. When an angel appears and tells her she's going to be pregnant before ever getting married, she's a little inquisitive but she doesn't reject the idea at all. "I am the Lord's servant." she says. "May everything you have said about me come true." She accepts these wild words from a stranger. She decides to be okay with this stupefying miracle, this strange prediction. And knowing some about her time and culture, the consequences that could result for Mary were, at best, a ruined name, reputation, and marriage. Worse case, local law could call for the loss of her life for breaking her engagement.

---

5   *"But Mary kept all these things and pondered them in her heart." (Luke 2:19, KJV)*
6   *"But his mother treasured all these things in her heart." (Luke 2:51b, KJV)*

How is it that Mary is able to accept this news of a virgin birth, the possible consequences, and the sudden upheaval of her life with such a gentle reply? It's almost as if she is saying, Oh, okay then. I'm in. You're from God. I love God. Well, I'm sure it will all work out. What a childlike faith! To me this is only the result of meditative prayer. It is the constant pondering of God and his word. Sometimes, I like to call it a seed prayer because it is a small prayer with just a few words or one image that is held for a very long time. To me, it seems only someone who has been meditating on God's word could have an answer like that ready.

Mary's name meaning evokes the image of burning bitter herbs or the idea of the pearl made inside an oyster. Something good coming from a long uneasy savoring. So Mary's name could almost mean meditating. Prayer and meditation go hand in hand. I consider meditation a way of prayerful thinking.

Don't get me wrong. The first time I ever tried meditation prayer I was in my early twenties. Led by the spiritual transformation group at a Baptist seminary, we sat in a small chapel through a guided meditation called centering prayer. I failed. I couldn't make it for three minutes. I shifted in my chair, I scratched my knee, I rolled my eyes at the ceiling. Before the last exercise, I had nearly bolted from the room in agony.

All I can say is it takes practice. Two decades later, when one of my close family invited me to the local Buddhist Temple, we were asked to meditate for eight minutes. Proud of myself, I made it the whole time! The difference, I chose something to meditate on, resting in God's love. That made all the difference. It didn't matter which faith group I was sitting with; it was the state of my heart and my practice to wait on God. I'd spent so much time pondering God in my heart, meditation became easy.

For me, I don't have to agree with everything someone else believes to pray with them or spend time with them, even in their sanctuary. God is love and he loves all people, so why can't we pray together and love each other? That's my ten-year-old Protestant-girl-in-Catholic-school heart. That's my prayer from learning to pray as an outsider. Thankfully, since I'm not an evangelist, or a theologian, only a layperson, I can say that this works for me.

At times we may disagree with each other violently, and even want to run from the room or disown someone because we disagree so much. That's a sure sign we need to focus more on how God loves all of us. I think before you judge someone, pray with them, then you'll know their heart.

Coming from a background where meditation was feared, and praying through or about Mary's story was banned, I'm glad I kept exploring enough to try out meditation. I had to fight fear and prejudice for a way to connect with God. Now my ability to meditate is a gift. Now I've learned stillness[7] is an asset. To me mediation is the art of allowing a truth, a word, or a sense of rest to purposely permeate my mind, body, and soul. It's a form of prayer I can use at any time or take anywhere. I can meditate while doing something else. It's not about understanding or knowing the right way to empty my mind. Instead, it's accepting one moment—and then another—as God's moment. It makes prayer into sort of a pilgrimage, a journey of reflection and meditation. A "Zen-like transcendence," my friend called it once. I'd call it an awareness, a constant state of prayer. [8]

Mary's story is the one that helped me understand mediation. In a sense, it's like brooding. And what is the other meaning of brooding in English? It's what a hen does when it incubates its eggs. It keeps those eggs warm until they hatch into little chicks.[9] Funny how the word is the same for both. Mary is literally sitting on this promise. She is keeping these words and these promises[10] warm in her heart; waiting for them to blossom at the right time.[11]

The writers of the gospel proclaim that Mary bore God. They say it was not a metaphor. Scripture says her son was really a sinless perfect child straight from heaven. None of us will have that experience of being the mother of the Savior, but we can have the same faith

---

7 *"Meditate within your heart on your bed, and be still." (Psalm 4:4, NKJV)*
8 *"Always be joyful. Never stop praying. Be thankful in all circumstances, for this is God's will for you who belong to Christ Jesus." (1 Thessalonians 5:16-18, NLT)*
9 *"He will cover you with his feathers. He will shelter you with his wings. His faithful promises are your armor and protection." (Psalm 91:4, NLT)*
10 *The difference between warm thoughts and prayers is adding scripture, God's promises to meditate on in faith and relationship with the creator God who is all knowing, all loving, all powerful, and all just.*
11 *"O God, we meditate on your unfailing love as we worship in your Temple." (Psalm 48:9, NLT)*

experience of meditating with trust and openness to God's picture for our life, whatever that may be. We can savor, soak, ponder, permeate in God's word and his promises. This shows me that Christian meditation seems to be a filling, rather than an emptying. Mary exemplified fullness. And this fullness, pondering, waiting, thinking, holding onto God's promise, is a kind of prayer.

On some days when I felt discouraged, when my heart hurt the worst, Mary's prayer was really a consolation. Without Mary, we wouldn't have Jesus. One woman's open and gentle faith allowed for everything which happened after. Mary made room for God. Mary's prayer helped me understand women were important to God, and women had an equal and unique opportunity to hold, envision, and pursue their faith.

Over time, Mary's prayer began to be a meditation that helped me through my feelings of powerlessness.[12] Her innocent way of praying, her slowness to anger, reminded me that I wanted that childlike hope back in my own faith. Yet, she also prayed with an amazingly wild assuredness, a vitality that I wanted.

Looking back to Mary's story. She chose to accept and meditate[13] on God's promises. She chose to take one step at a time on the journey she was given; to keep her heart open and aware of each word and each event that might speak to the message of hope she received. Her focus was on God, his messages, his signs. That is where she kept her focus through the rest of her life.

❧ ❧ ❧

A year later, after my one-hour pilgrimage, I had a beautiful baby girl. I came home from the hospital with her on an extraordinary June day. In my lap, I held a bunch of roses. The weather was impossibly lovely and cool, much like the day I prayed on the mountain. All the day lilies had bloomed overnight, along with Blue Chicory and Queen Anne's Lace, my favorite roadside flowers. Everything seemed a celebration, and every petal felt like a miracle as I carried that baby

---

12 *"Even princes sit and speak against me, but I will meditate on your decrees." (Psalm 119:23, NIV)*
13 *"Study this Book of Instruction continually. Meditate on it day and night." (Joshua 1:8, NLT)*

home and enjoyed every minute with her.[14] My sister came up to spend time with me and you know, the three of us girls enjoyed that time together. We really did.

After that, I was able to let go of a lot of the anger and sorrow of being childless. When I took the baby out I stopped to let people say hello and smile. Children were a gift. I knew more than every that a life of prayer meant forgiveness and grace, it meant persistence, and it meant accepting both sorrow and joy while focusing on God as the author of life. I had to trust God's timing and look for creative ways to overcome issues that blocked me from staying close with God. Sometimes that was forgiveness. Sometimes that was persistence. Sometimes that involved looking at things in a new way. But it always means meditation on God's word and the closeness God promises for those willing to make room for the spiritual life.

☒☒☒

Maybe you are like Mary, and you feel like you have a lifelong meditation that you are savoring. You are looking for a promise to be fulfilled in your life and you want to keep it close to your heart. Maybe you are like I was. It is a child you want to have, or a loved one you want to see grow into a person of faith and wholeness.[15] Maybe you feel empty and barren. You've lost your love for the spiritual journey, you've lost your faith, or you've lost your energy to pray for a good future. Maybe your life is on a track you didn't expect. Mary's prayer is something that could lift you up. In scripture, we can read Mary's prayer or "Mary's Song," the "Magnificat."[9] Why do they call it that? Because she is magnifying God. In her small way, she makes him bigger through her meditation of faith and expectancy.

Prayer does not fix our situation. Prayer doesn't save us. It grows us into a new person who makes room for God's Spirit in our life. Prayer does not make us bigger or more powerful. It makes us smaller, more open, more ready to notice what good God plants into our lives and to let that word grow in us. We become someone who magnifies him.

---

14 *"I will meditate on your majestic, glorious splendor and your wonderful miracles."* (Psalm 145:5, NLT).
15 *"Meditate on these things; give yourself entirely to them, that your progress may be evident to all." (1 Timothy 4:15, NKJV)*

Here is my version of what that prayer is like. I call it a seed[16] prayer:

Dear Father God,

I'm someone who loves you a lot. I want to be part of your family and I want to trust you with these events in my life that don't make sense. Sometimes, I see my life as impossible, frightening, and dangerous. Sometimes, I feel that if I let you in my life, I'd have to face a path I'm not prepared to take. I am completely unable to become all the good things I wish I could be. I can't save the world. I can't even save myself. I'm just small and ordinary. But, God, I trust you. I'm going to trust you right now. Not just today, but for the rest of my life. And the small idea I have right now about you, I'm going to meditate on that every day. I'm going to think on it while I'm at work, while I'm traveling, while I'm at home. Whatever relationships may come and go, whatever governments may change, or hardships I have to face, I'm going to think on the word you placed into my heart.[17] I'm going to savor it.[18] Every moment, my goal is to focus on you and what you might be doing in my life and in the life of the world around me. Let me see you more. Let me know you more. Let me have your spirit inside of me. You've always been here. You've always been the rescuer. You've always known that there is a way to understand your mothering kind of love, an expectant kind of new life. Let me have that understanding. Let me have the kind of love for others like you do for me. Whatever you give me, whatever you take from me, whatever happens, I belong to you. I am yours, and I will love you and serve you forever. ✖

---

16 "The kingdom of heaven is like a mustard seed, which a man took and sowed in his field which indeed is the least of all the seeds; but when it is grown it is greater than the herbs and becomes a tree, so that the birds of the air come and nest in its branches." (Matthew 13:32, NRSV)

17 "I call to remembrance my song in the night; I meditate within my heart, And my spirit makes diligent search." (Psalm 77:6, NRSV)

18 "Finally, brethren, whatever things are true, whatever things are noble, whatever things are just, whatever things are pure, whatever things are lovely, whatever things are of good report, if there is any virtue and if there is anything praiseworthy—meditate on these things." (Philippians 4:8, NIV)

Contented Dress ~ Ruth, Quilted Velvet & Satin, Origami Paper Collage,
Pencil, Ink, Gouache on Wallpaper 8 x 10 in. 2020

Dedication Prayer

PRAY LIKE A WOMAN

Prayer is not seeing the future ~Ruth's Story

During the time my life was the most normal, I lived in a little yellow house. I had two children and a cat. My husband had a full-time job and I taught art classes once in a while. Best of all, I had my own little garden with roses and crepe myrtle bushes, tomatoes, pumpkins, and other vegetables.

One morning, I picked fresh peas and lettuce from the garden, ate them for breakfast, and decided I had a good life no matter what anyone said.

Despite all this, I felt like the backwards girl. Something about me was different from the other moms at the mothers of infants and preschoolers support group. It was more than the fact that I couldn't afford to bring a Starbucks drink during our Tuesday morning sessions. It was more than the fact that, while other moms didn't want their kids to get dirty when they played outside, I told my kids to please play in the mud and have fun. No, it was something else, but I couldn't put my finger on the issue.

We'd lived in the house for about a year when I had an unexpected blessing. But this pregnancy with my third child was different. Something didn't seem right. I felt really tired. I looked worse than normal, and my mind just wasn't as clear as it usually was.

About nineteen weeks in, I realized I hadn't gotten ready for the baby as much as I had for the others. Fearing it was unlucky, I immediately went out and got a beautiful rocking chair from a yard sale, and one baby outfit. Considering my budget this was extravagant.

The next week, I remember walking up the small hill with my two kids toward our house. We had a tricycle in the driveway and my youngest was learning to ride. I felt a small pain in my side, and I had to sit down. Oddly, after that moment I felt much stronger, and I had more energy than I'd had my whole pregnancy. For the next two days I was back to my old self.

I was surprised then when we went in for my twenty-week exam, the doctor said he couldn't find a heartbeat.

"I'm sorry," he said. "These things sometimes happen."

Over the next few days of loss, I was in shock. I know this because months later, my neighbor, Lisa, told me she had come over and sat with me for hours into the night, but I didn't even remember it.

The grief was strong. Despite learning this naturally happens to a third of pregnancies, despite my relief to feel my physical strength return, I had to find a way to climb out of that grief quickly because my summer intensive for my master's degree was about to begin. Sure, I could have canceled it and put it off another semester. But I'd already put off one semester for my son's birth, eighteen months before, and I'd put off one semester when the house had burned down. I couldn't put off a third one. I felt like everything was trying to stop me from being a writer. Yes, I lost a beautiful baby girl, I reasoned, someone I was so happy to get to know and love, so I couldn't also lose out on finishing my degree.

After only a few days in the hospital and a few hours of grieving, I decided I was going to finish this degree no matter what happened, I would become a writer. Off I went to summer school to stay in the dorm for two weeks.

I don't know where I got the perseverance to pull through the hardest thing I'd ever been through. But I figured the worse things got, the more I should stick to what I knew to be true—to my callings. It had taken me over a year of prayer and inner searching to deicde to get my first degree, and a lot of introspection and prayer to begin a second one. I felt God had called me to be a writer. These obstacles didn't make me give up. They had the opposite effect—they were another reason not to quit.

Ruth is someone in the scriptures who I really related to at that time. I didn't realize how much I'd come back to her attitude of prayer time and time again. Ruth lost a spouse. Loss happens to a lot of us, and sometimes that loss feels like everything. I'm thankful to the writers of scripture for capturing one of the most human life experiences when telling Ruth's story. Her type of prayer has come to mean so much to me, putting one foot in front of the other in faith.

※※※

At first, Ruth has everything:[1] a husband, a brother and sister-in-law, a mother-in-law, and a home. She's from a mixed family. While she was of northern African descent with local spiritual beliefs, her in-laws were Jewish—a family who moved to the region due to famine in their own country. (Some say Moab was more "North Africa," others say it was in the western region of present-day Jordan.) Either way, I often picture Ruth is brown skinned, with peaceful but determined wide eyes.

When Ruth's husband dies (and his brother dies) rather suddenly, two Moabite women and sister-in-laws, Orpah and Ruth, are left without children or husbands.

In that day, women's only provision came from their fathers or husbands. Even land was inherited by men through law. In this story, women connected to that land were often inherited with it or passed on to another relative to be a "wife" of that man if her husband died. I'm guess this was anywhere from being a servant, living in a nursing residence, or actually marrying the head of the household. Ruth has no brother-in-law. Her husband's former lands were far away, and he had no other brothers. Her only option, to go home and live with her parents.

Ruth refuses to go home.[10] The other widowed woman is happy to go back to her parents. But Ruth wants to stay with Naomi, her

---

[1] *Ruth 1-4, NIV*

widowed mother-in-law:

> *Don't urge me to leave you or to turn back from you. Where*
> *you go I will go, and where you stay I will stay. Your peo-*
> *ple will be my people and your God my God. Where you die I*
> *will die, and there I will be buried. May the Lord deal with*
> *me, be it ever so severely, if even death separates you and me.*[2]

I don't advise fast grieving, but I understand Ruth's commitment
to her new family and her new faith. She gets back on her feet and
immediately cares for her mother-in-law, something she wasn't really
obligated to do. Sometimes the more we lose, the more we hang on
to what we have.

Ruth reminds me of myself. She was different in that she held on
to her commitments. She felt called to follow the God of her adopted
family. Unlike the tribal gods of Moab that some say required human
sacrifice, she must have seen the Jewish God as someone very different. Jewish law still believed in sacrifice, but only of the first fruits
of someone's herd: wine and grain, a lamb, a bull, or even pigeons,
which were offered by the very poor.

Somehow in every culture, there was an understanding that a
blood sacrifice was needed to wipe away sin. Ruth must have seen that
the Jewish faith was different. Their God was more of a father who
cared for children, than a desert spirit inspiring fear. Tribal gods were
seen to inhabit large statues or small carved figurines. Their faces were
sometimes grotesque or frightening. The Jewish law said no figures
could be carved of God. His "picture" was seen through the service
and care of his people and his creation.

Jewish law had many protections for women, more than a lot of
other cultures at that time. It was based on a system of justice that
anyone could understand. Maybe over the course of living with this
family of her husband, Ruth had built up a personal relationship with
this God that she began to know. I think this pulled her to join God's
family beyond her already deep sense of loyalty.

Ruth keeps her promise to Naomi. The journey from the Western
Jordan region, where historians believe the Moab people lived some-

---

2   *Ruth 1:16-17, NIV*

what nomadically in the desert, was probably near the Armon River. They walk back to Naomi's home country from Moab to Bethlehem, a distance of 150 kilometers or about 100 miles. The terrain is not soft sand, but basalt rock desert with ancient lava flows that create finger-shaped ravines.

If expert hikers walked for eight hours a day, this journey would take at least four days. However, with an elderly woman and their belongings to carry, the trip may have been slow, up to several weeks. I imagine Ruth helped sell all their household items or had a relative sell them, maybe even sold their livestock. If I were Ruth, I would have kept one camel to load up necessities and Naomi, then led the camel up the river and north around the Dead Sea, on through the beautiful, lush plains of Jericho, then back south past Jerusalem to Bethlehem.

While cooking over a fire and sleeping under the stars, I'm sure they hoped some help could be found in Naomi's hometown. Her family would surely still be around in some form—maybe nephews and nieces. Naomi returned as a refugee into her homeland with her daughter in law. Ruth becomes an immigrant and a convert. Two women, no money, no property. Nothing. What would they find there?

When they returned to Israel, scripture doesn't mention them finding a place to live. I know what it's like. I once moved across country and arrived with fifty dollars to my name then looked for work. Another time I stayed with relatives for three months looking for a job. Moving is hard. You too may easily imagine their predicament. Maybe they sold their camel and lived on the funds, looking for a place to live before the winter frost.

Whatever happened, Ruth kept her promise. She did everything Naomi asked her to do. She went out and gleaned wheat fields for leftover grain—working in the hot sun to gather sheaves (leftovers or scraps set aside for the poor by Jewish law). It wasn't the safest of moves to be homeless gleaning food. They hoped they would "catch the eye" of a landowner who might let them take what they needed. They hoped for respectable farm hands who "wouldn't lay a hand on them." We know it was a hard time because Naomi changed her name to Mara, meaning bitter.[3]

The unusual part of Ruth's story is how incredibly obedient she is. Yet, she has a will of bronze. She wears what Naomi tells her to wear, says what Naomi tells her to say, and even goes through re-enacting an obscure legal precedent. In Jewish law, Naomi's daughter-in-law would still have some legal right to be adopted by "marriage" into the family of the closest male heir. This means they'd become part of the family that owned the land that should have belonged to Ruth's husband. Their family land was still around, owned by another relative. But getting the attention of someone to honor his detail would be tough, if not impossible, for an immigrant and a penniless widow with no power or recent connections. [4]

Thankfully, Ruth is noticed by a landowner. Boaz. He gives "wine" and some attention to Ruth. He tells the men to leave out extra grain for her and makes sure to share part of the food prepared for the paid laborers.

When Ruth comes home with these details, Naomi advises her to keep going back to Boaz's field to glean extra grain, because Ruth will be safe and treated well there. After a few days, Naomi lets Ruth in on important intel. Boaz is one of the male heirs to their former family land. That means he could take Ruth for a wife, and Naomi in turn would get back her family name and honor.

In trying to find a modern-day example, I'd say, imagine that you lost your last name and your bank account and identity. You could only get it back if you lived on your grandparents' farm and agreed to "marry" or serve indefinitely whoever owned it. The plan is an ancient form of social security, even if it seems weird now.

Boaz seems to like Ruth and has noticed her several times, so there is some hope. However, harvest time means the cold season is coming. Being homeless won't be comfortable, the winter chill in the desert air could sometimes get to below freezing. I imagine at this point that Ruth and Naomi are still basically homeless, perhaps living in one of the nearby caves, or in someone's barn (those were usually caves or the "garage" entry level of a stone house). Naomi wants a good home

---

3   *Ruth 1:20, NIV*
4   *Ruth 2:14, NIV*

and family for her daughter-in-law. They both want each other to be well cared for but they have no power to make their situation change.

Naomi shares a plan with Ruth that pushes the decision about the family land to a head. It's risky, but you guessed it: she does it anyway. Following the directions carefully, Ruth goes to the fields in the middle of the night where the second shift is winnowing wheat. Inside an open stone wall set in a circle, the sheaves are thrown up in the air with a huge pitchfork. The straw would blow away leaving those heavy, high protein barley kernels to fall back down on the stone threshing floor. It was a slow but effective way to get the grain separated from the chaff. There they could easily be swept up to make yummy foods like tabouli or ground into flour for flat pocket bread, an amazing winter food.

Nighttime was cooler for this task. Birds who might steal the grain were asleep and possible heavier night breezes may have helped sift the grain. However, this was also the best time to rob a farmer, so guards would be posted during the winnowing. If you were short on money for guards, and you needed a break, you might lie down and sleep with your wheat to keep it safe. Boaz does this.

After a long evening of threshing, Boaz lies down to sleep. Ruth, following Naomi's orders, washes, puts on perfume, and dresses in her best clothes. She sneaks down to the threshing circle by Boaz's fields. Boaz is already asleep in the open air, Ruth goes up next to him, pulls open the cover over his legs or "feet" and lies down next to him.[5]

Sure, this is odd, and takes a lot of audacity, but it also is a cultural symbol. This is a wordless way of telling Boaz that she wants to be his; that she needs his protection. It immediately shows him that legally, he can claim her as his wife. This would have been clear what these actions symbolized to anyone in the culture at that time—as easily as kneeling with a ring would be today. Also, it would be really frowned upon if not illegal to be with a girl overnight and not marry her, so in one sense it's a bit of a power play to force his hand.

There's a problem, however. Boaz is an honest man. He knows that there is another relative who has closer legal rights to Naomi's son's land and property, and that property includes Ruth. Boaz is the kind

---

5 *Ruth 3:1-4, NIV*

of guy who has to do everything the just, right, and legal way. It shows what kind of person he is, but you know it had to be annoying to the women waiting for his answer.

Boaz is kind to Ruth. He doesn't shame her. He even declares he's honored by this "marriage proposal." Those of us that love a cheesy romance story, cheer here. Happily, he doesn't make Ruth wait. He goes to the other relative and explains the situation using the customs of the day to signal the decision with the other claimant. Thankfully for Ruth, the other relative turns her down, along with the lost property.

If I were Ruth, this rejection still might sting. Was it racial or did he think Ruth was unfit? The story says that this land owner didn't want to have more than one heir to fight over his own property. He already had a wife and land. In any case, this small legal incident ended by the rejecting party taking off his sandal and giving it to Boaz. Before fax machines and legal contracts, this was the quick, public way to finish a legal deal. Everyone would remember this "signature."

So, Boaz legally bought all the property. He redeemed the lost property and he redeemed Ruth. Boaz took Ruth as his wife.[6] Everyone witnessed these two migrant women transform. They are raised from refugee to a high position in society. Now they again had land, property, a home, and a name. In one sense, it was an example of how laws used well by honorable people keep the community running. It was their way of taking care of widows and orphans. (Not that I think we should use this method today.)

⬩⬩⬩

A year after the loss of my second daughter, I graduated with my master's degree in writing. I had suffered a lot. But with God's help, I pushed through. He gave me encouragement in those long dark nights when I felt alone and lost. I had two wonderful mentors as my professors that year who let me work through my grief through writing. I decided to do my critical thesis on dreams and the writing process. I kept a dream journal and worked through grief that way. The dream journal was my gleaning. I gleaned insight, I gleaned energy, I gleaned healing. And what is more free to a poor mom in grief, than

---

6   *Deuteronomy 25:5, NIV*

dreaming? Those dreams later became poems, short stories, paintings, prayers, and a critical thesis. I was glad that those teachers adopted me and mentored me when I needed it most.

❧❧❧

Four years later, I sat in my car in my church parking lot, watching my son in his first year of kindergarten soccer. Like Ruth, my life was different and not easy. Four years had brought about the upheaval of my whole life. As a writer, my life was going nowhere fast. My first books accepted by an agent were ultimately rejected. My work was too local, the publishing market was changing, and the new rise of ebooks and the instability of the economy from the recession filled the news.

In those four years, I'd lost my house, my marriage, my job. I was just a single woman without a name, a career, or a reputation. But, I hadn't been praying as much for direction as you might think. Prayer is sometimes thought of as a honey-do list that we give to God and wait for him to check it off. That's not the kind of prayer I had. Instead, my prayer was more of an equal sign. A simple equation that I had dedicated my life to God and his callings on my life and I was just being me. I wasn't looking too hard, thinking too hard, I was just existing with his call on my life. I was trying to glean where I could.

I sat in the car by the soccer field and opened my mail. One envelope looked important, so I read it:

> *Dear Polly,*
> *Your critical thesis, "Doorway to Dreams: Writer's Self Awareness through Dream and Memory" has won the following award from the International Association for the Study of Dreams. Your winning entry was announced at our recent annual conference in Berkeley, California. Here is a check for $500 and we hope it will help you come to our conference this summer at Virginia Beach to share more about your fascinating work.*

I couldn't help crying at this good news. It was the first sign that my persistence at following my dreams to be a writer was the right direction. It was my first sign that my dreams were worth something to anyone other than myself. It was my first sign that this odd backwards person that I was, someone who loved to focus on the interior life of prayer and dreams and reflection, had a place in this busy, loud, utilitarian world. I sat in the car staring at the check and crying for a long time.

Later that summer, when I stood up at the conference to speak, I knew I was a writer. I was glad I persisted with my callings and my dreams. I was glad for the insight I had gleaned through trials.

❧❧❧

That experience changed me. I didn't want to doubt God's callings and plans for my life anymore. I wanted to be persistent like Ruth. Her story grew in my mind. Ruth's prayer was not one of words, but of staying centered in the idea that she was part of God's family. She wouldn't give up. At no point did Ruth have an idea about her future. She did not receive a vision or a word. She was not visited by an angel. She'd lost everything. She had only her commitment and her acts of service to hold onto. Ruth had no proof that any amount of dedication or obedience would pay off. She simply said she would follow God. She would serve her mother-in-law and care for her, and that was it.

Ruth's story came back to mind again when my father died, and my mother became a widow. It was just the two of us taking care of my mom's house in our old hometown at the very north most part of Kansas City, thirty minutes from where my great-grandparents used to have a farm. Yes, it was where I had grown up, but I didn't really remember anyone. I often thought of Ruth and Naomi during these years. We were two women with no money, no prestige, no name, and few connections. Sometimes we would drive to the old farm or to visit the graves in the cemetery. We were strangers in our homeland. Like Ruth and Naomi, we wanted to reconnect. We wanted to take care of each other and be obedient to our callings. We wanted to take care of the family we had left. But nothing could tell us the future.

There were bright moments when something said we were headed in the right direction. But each day was an act of faith. Nothing prepared us for the hardships. We had to take each day at a time and continue to trust and serve. I didn't do any gleaning but one time I went to a single mother's event for Mother's Day. I stood in line with hundreds of women waiting for free haircuts, food, make up, new tires, diapers, and a fancy dinner. I couldn't believe the parking lot with so many women of every age with babies and toddlers clinging to them from every side. When I got to the front of the line everything was gone except for the dinner. I sat alone with a beautiful plate next to fresh cut flowers and wondered that there were so many women who needed daily help, glad that I had my mother to share the daily joys and hardships with me. I decided Ruth's prayer would be my meditation through hard times.

So, what did I do? Each day before my feet touched the floor, I gave my day to God.[11] I wasn't always excited about the day, but I knew that I was dedicated to being committed to my calling and to my family. So, I got up and did that day anyway. If my mother told me to keep writing, or to keep painting, or to go buy a bag of onions. I did what she said. I told myself that this was my prayer like Ruth. To be faithful, to be present, and to trust in God's plan.

Over the last seven years, I've prayed the prayer of Ruth every day. Each day my mom and I have coffee and a prayer or a Bible verse, and each weekend we go over what we are grateful for and how to keep going from here. There was safety in Ruth's type of prayer: The prayer of persistence and loyalty of trust in daily action. From those seven years of morning meditations with my mom, I've been inspired a great deal. She's encouraged me to laugh and play and try new things. To write this book for one, to launch a small press, to make art, and to teach classes in writing and creativity.

Like Ruth and Naomi, my mom and I have been on a journey together to take care of our family. My mom inspires me. Every day she is ready to tackle new problems. Worldwide food shortages, pandemics, homeschool—we've faced it all together. She has helped me raise my two kids. It's been a healing journey, and I hope it has been mutual. I'm thankful for the family God placed me in. All this time, I've meditated on Ruth. From Ruth I learned that prayer does not tell us the future; it gives us strength for each moment. Sometimes prayer is an attitude of knowing that you are in God's family, and he cares for you.

I've studied and been a part of so many faith traditions inside Christianity, and Ruth's prayer is one I think fits in all of them. It's a prayer of daily faith and service.

Despite all the differences inside my faith, and other faiths outside of mine, I've always felt close to God. And each place I've visited, I've found God there: I adore short Catholic homilies, odd books about saints, two-hour long Presbyterian sermons, and the Anglican Common Book of Prayer. I've heard scriptures sung in synagogue that would break the hardest heart. I've sat on the balcony of a mosque while women braided their hair and listened to daily prayers. I've eaten the best kimchi lunch with friends after services in Korean. I've danced at a Messianic Jewish service and have been healed from a lifelong illness in a Pentecostal one. I've followed the Stations of the Cross and partaken of hours of baptisms in swimming pools, streams, rivers and lakes. I've listened to services at a French Coptic Monastery, had tea and discussed faith with Russian Orthodox friends, spoken in tongues with those embracing the Holy Spirit, learned the Rosary, and lived a week on a commune with hippy nuns. I've visited the Mount of Olives, worked through the catechism in a Lutheran church, hung out in a midwestern seminary library for two years, sung in a traveling praise band, attended a Mennonite service that didn't believe in instruments—vocals only, hung out at missionary revival services, and visited refugees in Palestine. I've been best friends with atheists who had my back when I was my loneliest, studied Tibetan Buddhist meditation, I've hung my art about prayer in bars, and met druids and mystics and people with alternative belief of all kinds.

All that to say I have been Ruth in a lot of places, traveling like a refugee looking for a place to call home: In each place, I've been given acceptance when I was in need by people that would never been accepted in a lot of faith communities. I've been cared for and encouraged by people that had to take their faith journey on an open road. I've been fed, housed, and prayed over by diverse groups of believers who might not feel comfortable walking through the doors of each other's places of worship.

God has taken me on such a strange journey both inside and outside my family's faith tradition. I've gotten to know people from every walk of life. Each person is a unique wonder, a treasure. Everyone I meet has told me about how they want to have better spiritual life or a relationship with God.

I hope that this book of life stories and meditations on scriptures and experiences that transformed me will testify that choosing to live a life of prayer can only be a blessing. God can handle the fact we worship him differently, he loves us. So why should we stop and turn on each other when we can turn to him. Let God work out our differences–if there are any left when we are busy looking at his face.

If there is one idea I hold close, it's the Judaeo understanding of a Father-Mother God. I think that is the idea Ruth might have loved the most. She left her family's beliefs in exchange for new ones. When Ruth promised to love and serve God, and to love and serve the family who needed her, her loyalty knew no bounds. She fought homelessness and hunger. She traveled great distances, but nothing could stop her determination and her loyalty to God. She went by faith.

Ruth also experienced that ancient idea of a kinsman redeemer. Her property was redeemed by a kinsman, Boaz. (Yes, it does sound like being rescued by a knight in shining armor but remember Ruth is the heroine of her own story.)

I think it's the idea of a redeemer[7] that is an important part of Ruth's prayer. Nothing changed my life more than the idea that I can be redeemed. That I can start over—fresh, new, wholly alive. I can have a new name and a new sense of purpose. I'm confident I have an inheritance of God's family, his love and protection both now and somehow in eternity.

It would be remiss of me to explain if I haven't already, that my experience is limited to praying with an understanding of Jesus as my "redeemer." I'm living under his name, in his inheritance. I've tried to walk that out in life—sometimes successfully, but more often imperfectly. That is one decision I've never regretted. No matter where I go, and who I am with, no matter what spiritual practices I encounter,

---

7   *"I know that my redeemer lives, and that in the end he will stand on the earth." (Job 19:25, NIV)*

I've taken Jesus with me. I'm never alone. That's how I see myself, as adopted into God's family.

I'm not a theologian. I'm only a woman who decided to go on a journey with God. You could say my faith was tested, a lot. Jesus is that Redeemer who came in and rescued me when I was a small child, when I was a teenager, and who keeps rescuing me. He's real to me. Alive to me. He helps me believe that God loves me and cares for me, helps me find ways to be loyal and loving when it's way beyond my power. It's Jesus who gives me that spirit of comfort and energy. To me, he's that redeemer[8] who answers when I'm facing another dark night. Without that belief of being rescued and transformed, my life of faith becomes impossible.

One thing I can't testify to is how to pray without Jesus in the mix. It's outside my experience. I grew up being taught it was okay to treat Jesus as a best friend, to understand him as the fulfillment of many Jewish prophecies of a Messiah, a suffering servant, a savior. Coming from that faith, I could explore the mystery that Jesus is fully human and also fully God's son, and to understand him as the final sacrifice to end all sacrifices. The last sacrificial lamb who was so perfect, he broke the mold and made death work backwards because when he died, innocent, and came back to life, everything was forever changed. Something he somehow shares with anyone who asks.

From these beginnings, I've discovered a life of faith and prayer that is fulfilling, a God who loves me and is there for me in every little thing. How can the Creator of the universe hear my prayers? It's a mystery. Whether aloud or silent, he hears and answers them. He can hear yours too.

Christians always end their prayers "In Jesus's name, Amen." Amen is just a word that means I agree. And seeing ourselves adopted into God's family means Jesus is like a brother. I guess I think of his name as a direct line, a cable, a stamp on the envelope of God's love letter to me. I know Jesus died, rose again, and never stayed dead. Somehow, he's still alive, and gives us his spirit when we pray. That makes him

---

8   *"This is what the Lord says— your Redeemer, who formed you in the womb: I am the Lord, the Maker of all things, who stretches out the heavens, who spreads out the earth by myself." (Isaiah 44:24, NIV)*

our mediator and advocate, our way to reach God: a bridge.[9]

Many times, I've doubted the story of Jesus. It's one that seemed simple when I was a child, but other times, felt opaque. However, God always brings me back through a small word, a sunrise, the book of Isaiah, a poem, the snuggle of a mysterious barn cat, a rainbow. He's always telling me he loves me while I'm running away. When I do come running back, I see that I've never been alone and that he has a hope and a future for me. I don't have to be afraid. On this journey with God, I've found a hope to get me through every day and every dark night—no matter how many of them there are. I've found a friend in God. He carries me through each struggle and shows me how to love.

I feel like Ruth's prayer was one of the hardest for me to learn, and also a good one to end on. Where I thought love wasn't possible, where I thought traditions were too difficult, or beliefs too foreign— instead I've found friendship, kinship, family. Because I am carrying God with me in my heart, I feel at home wherever I go.[10] Going on a life journey with God creates a beautiful, good, wonderful, exciting adventure, a beatitude life. I'm happy to be walking with a Creator God who loves everyone.

Like Rehab's prayer, God is always my new banner. Like Tabitha's prayer, God is always bringing me back from the dead. And I keep getting closer to being fully alive. With Ruth's prayer, I'm trusting in my life being redeemed from that starved desert. I'm walking from incredible loss and loneliness to a life of being blessed. Each day, I walk in that prayer, and whatever extra I get, I want to pass it on to others that need it.

I don't believe we have to live like spiritual orphans. We can adopt each other into God's family. Sure, like Ruth's situation, it may be risky, embarrassing even. But asking God to redeem us and adopt is the first step. He's already said yes.[11]

It's my experience that there is nothing I've been able to do on my

---

9   *"You may ask me for anything in my name, and I will do it." (John 14:14, NIV)*
10 *"By faith he made his home in the promised land like a stranger in a foreign country; he lived in tents, as did Isaac and Jacob, who were heirs with him of the same promise." (Hebrews 11: 9, NIV)*
11 *" For God so loved the world, that he gave his only begotten Son, that whosoever believeth in him should not perish, but have everlasting life." (John 3:15-16, KJV)*

own to live a life of faith. I've failed at mediation, at forgiveness, at adulting, at peace. To me, Ruth's perfect loyalty and love is impossible without God. But when God rescues me, redeems me, those things become more and more possible. Ruth's prayer didn't work on her own power. What I've managed to hold onto with my faith wasn't possible on my own either. But being redeemed, letting God take the wheel of my life, that is possible. Sure, it's been hard, but it's not over, and I imagine it will keep on going into eternity.

Maybe you are like me, or like Ruth, and you don't know what the future will bring. Maybe the future doesn't look good. But you have a commitment to holding on to your faith. Maybe you don't know where to get that strength. I think Ruth's prayer is one of dedication. Ruth's prayer is one of hope in God no matter how hard the circumstances. Ruth's prayer says God is wiser, and I'm going to let him lead. If we are homeless or refugees, or even if we just feel that way, Ruth's prayer is one of steadfastness and holding onto faith. If I could put it into words, I think Ruth's prayer might sound like this:

Dear Father of lost people and lost places,

I'm lost. I don't have a plan. I don't have a way. I don't have any roots, and I don't belong. I don't fit in. I'm crushed. I'm hurt and I'm destroyed. My hope is small, and my future doesn't even seem to exist. But you have a way for me.[12] You have a plan for me. You have a future for me, and you are making a way even now.[13] You are the God who sees me.[14] You are the God who knows me. You are the God who doesn't overlook even one sparrow. You know how many hairs there are on my head.[15] You knew me before you created me. You put me here in this place where I am right now with these people because you want me to be your hands and

---

12 "We are hard pressed on every side, but not crushed; perplexed, but not in despair." (1 Corinthians 4:8)
13 " I will lead the blind by ways they have not known, along unfamiliar paths I will guide them; I will turn the darkness into light before them and make the rough places smooth. These are the things I will do; I will not forsake them." (Isaiah 42:16, NIV). "Forget the former things; do not dwell on the past. See, I am doing a new thing! Now it springs up; do you not perceive it? I am making a way in the wilderness and streams in the wasteland." (Isaiah 43:18-19, NIV)
14 Genesis 16:14
15 "But the very hairs of your head are all numbered." (Matthew 10:30, KJV)

feet.[16] You want me to be a help and a light and a hope to others. You are my Redeemer.[17] You are giving me a place that is mine, and right now, you are my Home. You will give me a family, and right now you are my People. You will give me safety,[18] and right now, you are my Safety. Everything I have is from you. I can't see the future, but you are my Future. No matter how long my life is, no matter how full it is, I will take each moment to follow your path,[19] one step at a time. And when there is joy, I will celebrate, and when there is food, I will eat it, and when there is work, I will do it. Most of all, I know that you have a hope and a future for me. You have a place for me. You place the lonely into families,[20] and for that I praise you. I praise you with everything I have. Right now, I am your servant. Adopt me into your family and let me be your child. [21]

---

16 *"Just as a body, though one, has many parts, but all its many parts form one body, so it is with Christ. For we were all baptized by one Spirit so as to form one body—whether Jews or Gentiles, slave or free—and we were all given the one Spirit to drink. Even so the body is not made up of one part but of many." (1 Corinthians 1:12-14 NIV)*

17 *"Who forgives all your sins and heals all your diseases, who redeems your life from the pit and crowns you with love and compassion, who satisfies your desires with good things so that your youth is renewed like the eagle's?" (Psalm 103:3-5, NIV)*

18 *"Where does my help come from? My help comes from the Lord, the Maker of heaven and earth." (Psalm 121:2, NIV)*

19 *"He refreshes my soul. He guides me along the right paths for his name's sake." (Psalm 23:3, NIV)*

20 *"God sets the lonely in families, he leads out the prisoners with singing." (Psalm 68:6, NIV)*

21 *"But I tell you, love your enemies and pray for those who persecute you, that you may be children of your Father in heaven. He causes his sun to rise on the evil and the good, and sends rain on the righteous and the unrighteous." (Matthew 5:44-45, NIV)*

Thanks for reading Pray like a Woman. Wow. It's an honor to be part of your prayer life journey. If you enjoyed "Pray Like a Woman"...here is a sneak preview from Polly's next book, PRAY LIKE AN ARTIST... coming soon.

Freedom to Think Poster, Detail, Oil on Birch,

24 x 36 in 2018

Generosity Prayer

Creative Prayer is Generous ~Mary M's Prayer

One of my earliest memories is a dream. (If that sentence doesn't bother you, you are probably an artist too.) I was probably six years old; sometime after my baby brother was born. I lived with my parents in our ranch-style suburban Kansas home. For some reason, they moved me from my cute girly room into the guest bedroom located in the farthest corner of the basement.

Almost a forgotten space, it had once been an office. Cold, dark, full of cupboards, the room had a countertop that was supposed to serve as a desk, but it was covered with boxes. The closet was full of storage, so there was no room for my dresser or toys. I put some of my clothes in one of the drawers and brought down just a few dolls to sit on the windowsill. The bed's coverlet was worn but had to do, a strangely satin-like texture with an odd turquoise color.

There was no way to turn out the basement light except at the top of the stairs. Each night, I climbed down the steps in the pitch dark. Terrified for the first few nights, I kept at it. Once I got to my bedroom, I could turn on the light. I never felt entirely safe in the dark.

No one can quite remember, but it's my guess that my parents had given my bed to my new little brother because it could be rebuilt ı a toddler bed into a crib. Not having another bed, I slept in the guest room. This experience ended a year or so later when we moved. However, it gave me this unusual feeling of being a "guest" in my own house. Old for my years, that feeling of being a guest never left me. I always felt like a traveling visitor, someone in need of a suitcase for adventures. Maybe that's a good metaphor for the artist's heart.

As I said, one of my earliest memories shortly after moving into that room was a dream:

I saw a vast plain with a few smooth trees. The landscape glowed from an unseen light, maybe a setting sun. There, in the darkening sky, I saw a rainbow. Not just any rainbow: it was a beautiful shape held by undulating twists and turns. More than a circle with no end—it is a knot. I shouted for my family to turn and see the amazing rainbow, but they did not. No one else saw the knotted rainbow except me.

Being one of the first and most important remembered dreams in my life, I cherished that memory and thought of it often. I hoped to find others who had what I now call an interior life: people who loved to discuss dreams, imagination, poetry, prayer, and other intangible things.

Just as vivid as my dreams were my imagination about God. In Sunday school I'd heard Jesus was the best friend I could discover more about. One day, the Sunday school teacher in my first-grade class announced if we could memorize the names of the sixty-six books of the Bible in order, we would get an entire Bible to keep.

I said each name over and over, learning them in little groups. I had my parents quiz me. I recited them up and down the stairs. "Ezra, Nehemiah, Esther, Job!" I shouted. Nothing could stop me from getting that Bible.

The very next Sunday, I brought it home, an apple-red cardboard NIV, and I started reading the first page. I don't remember it well, but I must have stuck to reading it many a night there in that quiet room because after reading the creation story, I entered the throes of the Old Testament, with its poetry, songs, and prophets.

In that little room, I felt far away from my parents and my baby brother upstairs. Like my grandma's attic, this room had the same feeling of being a solitary retreat. Here, I read books, played, and spent time daydreaming. Here is where I began practicing prayer at an early age. For me, the dream rainbow was an image similar to one I found in the Bible. It was a promise that a spiritual life was a treasure, something to practice every day. That there was a Creator God who loved people and wanted the world to be full of life.

As a budding young artist who was taking art lessons at the local art gallery, ballet lessons down the street, and playing outside with neighbors and friends, I was sure life was like a rainbow: full of loveliness and color, dancing, and mysterious wonders.

One special night in particular, I was praying before going to sleep and I had the strongest feeling that God loved me. It was like getting a fierce hug from my grandmother. I felt completely safe, completely happy, and full of anticipation. My mother's mother was my favorite person to visit. Grandma Ray's house usually meant Christmas, cookies, Easter eggs, picnics, craft shows, cousins to play with, and other wonderful things. That's how God's love felt that day—like a promise of enduring love, good food, and family celebrations.

You can see better than I did, that even as a kindergartener I was an artist and a poet. I loved rainbows and ballet, I cried at song lyrics to the tune of, "You are My Sunshine, and "The Old Grey Goose." I learned to write in a diary. I marveled over those first words I read in the Bible about a God who was like an artist, creating things one fantastical day at a time, the colors emerging from darkness and stars exploding over rising birds and fish, seeds blooming, and whole people being born out of the earth.

As the dream of that rainbow of seven colors, undulating like a ribbon in the sky, became more important to me, it became more prominent. Looking back, I let it change my life. First, the dream led me to try to remember important dreams and to talk with others about theirs. And of course, dreams led to conversations about all kinds of things like faith, prayer, and spirituality. Second, it led me to recognize the language of dreams and to continue to believe that prayer and imagination were not just an invisible bore. No, they were sacred, tangible spaces I could visit, or be a part of all the time.

My dream also led me to feel open to faith. I hungrily read the nd New Testaments before finishing high school. In the Bible, dreams were an accepted and important form of aid, not only in life decisions but also as emotional and spiritual sustenance. In the Bible, art and creativity were a big deal. There, I found weavers and potters, dreamers and colored coats, giants, and poems.

In my first book, "Pray Like a Woman," I shared ways I found to pursue a life of faith, even when it felt there were few heroes and few considerations for someone who valued creativity over control and people over power. In this book, "Pray Like an Artist," I'm going to share with you how I found ways to keep pursuing the calling to be a creative artist and the calling to be a person of prayer.

In my ideal world, more people would know we are called to be creative. What has been different about my faith journey is that I am an artist. If anyone has ever told you it takes faith to be an artist, they are right. What I've found odd about my life is that my testimony about that beatitude life, the journey of faith with God, has almost been neck and neck with my journey to be an artist.

I mean, is it weird to say I felt called to be an artist? More accurately, I'd say God has never let me choose to be anything else. Finding a way to be an artist has been the same path as finding a way to be a person of faith. I can't separate them out like seeds and watermelon. It would be like trying to separate hydrogen and oxygen out of water: it would just fall apart, or worse, explode. My faith story and the story of how I became an artist is one story, not two.

The life of faith and the life of an artist share a major similarity, a life of prayer. I think all people are called to have faith, all people are called to have prayer, and all people are called to be creative. But no two people are the same kind of creative. As an artist, it's always been apparent to me that there are as many ways to live out a life of faith and prayer as there are types of artists. What we make, what we imagine, is as different as two fingerprints. And our imagination can be a sacred space to know God and find his will for our life.

Now there are many myths about being an artist that are simply untrue. Maybe you are an artist who is finding it hard to prove that you should keep doing art. Maybe you just can't believe you are an artist; you'd like to give up, or you have given up. This book is for you.

Maybe you are someone who's always longed for a deeper spiritual life but those old tenets just aren't accessible to you. I'd like to share my journey on how I became an artist, sometimes against my will, and how I discovered ways to walk a life of faith as someone imperfect and doubtful but who is also called to be creative. I promise it will at least be interesting, at best helpful to find new ways to think about faith, prayer, and the artist's life!

❧ ❧ ❧

It was 2011. My two kids were finally getting a bit older—not babies anymore. It had been about four or five years since I'd truly given any attention to my art. My art was always a visual manifestation of the work I did in my faith: things I read, things I felt strongly about; ways to encourage myself or others. But lately, I had felt my faith was slipping away.

"God, I really want to make art again," I prayed while flipping through some old files of paintings on my computer.

I figured that I'd created roughly ninety-some paintings in my lifetime. I decided I wanted to paint something extraordinary. I set out to make my 100th painting. But I was immediately stumped.

"What should I make art about?" I prayed.

My attitude wasn't hopeful. Why is creativity so hard? I wondered. Why am I always dry with absolutely no ideas? Then another question arose. And where can I find the space to paint something?

"God, I need help." I prayed. "If you want me to start making art again, to be an artist again, I need to find a space to make art…a free space," I reminded him.

Knowing I could never leave the kids alone long enough to make art, or afford a studio, I walked around the house looking for a corner to inspire me with the possibility of a desk.

"Lord, help me to find a creative solution."

Downstairs, my spouse's office filled the basement. The kitchen was small, as was the attached dining room and living room where the kids played. My little girl's room was full of bunk beds and toys. The nursery was a tiny, dark space with a crib and a dresser. The master bedroom was full of bright light and already held a corner for my desk and office space.

You guessed it. When my spouse came home from work, I asked him if we could move our bedroom into the tiny nursery so that the master bedroom could be my art studio.

I was so thankful for that yes.

It wasn't hard to make an art studio. Well not to me, but the family had to adjust.

"We have to get a new kitchen table," I announced. My art table that had been serving all our family meals with a highchair attached to it was going back into service.

When I couldn't wait any longer, I simply moved all the furniture myself without scratching anything too much. Within a few days, my kids shared a room, my spouse and I had the nursery, and the pretty room filled with light became an art studio. Having lost my easel in a previous move, and my paints to a house fire, I started with the only thing I could find to work with—a mostly empty sketchbook.

There in the little studio, I sketched out my novel, submitted stories to editors and agents, and looked for something to paint on. I made charts for my creative time management from an old paper plate that came home decorated from my daughter's preschool.

I unboxed all my art supplies from the closet. A trip to *Goodwill* allowed me to start organizing. A wicker chip-and-dip platter became a basket for my paint. A kitchen spatula holder was ready to receive paintbrushes. An old stool from a garage sale and an extra chair completed the look.

"Now, what am I going to paint on? I need supplies," I prayed.

The next day, one of our neighbors set out some used wood paneling on the side of the road. I picked them up with a, "Thanks, God." I was back in business.

Sure, I painted the worst art I'd ever seen on that paneling—I'd forgotten how to paint. But that didn't matter. I was an artist again. Many times, I went into the studio with the sunlight streaming in through ivory curtains and bouncing off the pale blue walls and admired the light.

"Look at my ugly attempts at art," I wailed half to myself and half as a prayer.

"I'm like the ugly duckling." I laughed at myself. I knew would help me get my art back on its feet. That prompted me to _____ a design of a beautiful swan looking into the water with surprise that she wasn't ugly anymore.

One thing that's nice about prayer: it slows down negative thoughts, makes room for humor, and brings openness to creativity and new ideas. I guess that's because praying is talking to a friend.

Despite momentary glimpses of home, impatience returned most days. Being positive was hard. I'd been making and selling art in a gallery before my kids were born, but now my work looked so childish, and my ideas felt a million years away.

"God, why am I not getting anywhere?"

The more I thought about it, the more I realized I was too hard on myself. I hadn't spent much time painting outside of college, which was a decade ago. And hadn't I learned using oil paints? That's why the acrylics I had now were a mystery to me. I was out of white paint and my brushes were really run down. I reminded myself to get some white paint and a few brushes.

"God, help me find a way to paint something!" I prayed in desperation as I went back to momming, cooking and cleaning.

Sitting in the studio a few months later, I couldn't believe the progress. One Saturday, I was happily painting in the studio. I had found a job as a paint-and-sip teacher at a local storefront. I was paid to teach two-hour painting classes to guests, as well as to paint and design sample paintings for the "paint parties." Each sample came with step-by-step directions written by other artists. I was to paint a sample, then teach the class. With so much practice, painting in acrylic became just as easy as oil painting had been, though a little slower. I'd come so far in just a few months. I was even able to bring small bits of leftover paint home to work with.

"Thank you, God." I prayed. "You're always there for me. I have a studio, and I'm getting paid to learn to paint with acrylic! I never dreamed you'd do so much for me."

All that year, I kept meditating on what my special 100th painting would be. How would I restart my career as an artist after so long away? Finally, I found a dream journal and remembered my special dream about the rainbow. There, on the table, sat my paint palette, a bit like its own rainbow. I knew what to do. I'd honor that childhood dream with a painting.

There are few paintings of rainbows in art history. One I had seen at the National Gallery (and you may have seen it too, at the 2020 US inauguration—it was chosen to hang in the Oval Office). The problem was it was a really small, a partial rainbow. Mine needed to be a full rainbow. How would I paint such a large undulating band of pure color when I'd never seen one like that in real life?

"God, how am I going to paint a large rainbow? I have no money for supplies, and I have nothing to paint on," I prayed in the garage one day. That's when my eyes spotted two small pieces of canvas left over from a mural. The scraps were too small for what I needed so I left off starting the painting for another day.

A few weeks later in the studio, I sat with the sewing machine, mending old clothes. We were so broke that my son didn't have pajamas to sleep in.

"God, my son has no pajamas." I prayed really hard. "There are a lot of things we need. Help me to be creative."

Suddenly I noticed the bag of clothes on the floor my neighbor had given me. There was an extra-large yellow Henley with long sleeves. It didn't fit anyone, and I'd set it aside. It was a duckling yellow color. The arms of the yellow shirt were exactly the same size as the legs of a pair of boys' pajamas. The fabric was warm and thick.

I prayed for my brain to just know what to do. I cut off the arms and began working to join them as legs for pants. As I worked, each piece fit together so perfectly. Miraculously, I sewed an entire pair of pajamas for my toddler, both top and bottom. It looked pretty close to store-bought. That's saying something, considering my craftsmanship for sewing is known to be on the crooked side.

The pajama miracle was huge and felt like an answer to my prayers to be more creative. After years of being a student, a volunteer, and a stay-at-home mom, could it be that my brain was finally waking up? Could I be more creative again? That spirit of creativity was still somewhere inside if I could find it. I had to start making art again. To me, that meant I had to trust God again. I would find a way to paint that rainbow.

Fears immediately began blocking me. What if I did make my rainbow painting, but sharing that painting didn't go well? What if people hated it? What if someone stole the painting or the image? Or what if the opposite was true: what if people went crazy and wanted a million copies? What if they put it on T-shirts? What if someone tried to buy it and I didn't get to keep it? Could I ever let anyone else have my special dream rainbow?

Recognizing my crazy excuses, I knew fear wasn't an option. I pulled out a Bible and looked up the letter to Timothy. "God has not given us a spirit of fear, but of power, and of love and a sound [undivided] mind." It made sense. Fear isn't a God thing. It's the opposite of God. Fear comes from being pulled in two instead of toward love.

On one hand, I wanted to be creative again; on the other hand, I was afraid I couldn't trust my ideas out in the real world. I was being pulled in two directions: worried about being rejected and about success. My circling indecision triggered more fear.

If the only way I could conquer my fear about making a shareable piece of art worth hanging in a gallery was to focus on love then I would do it. I focused on the people who might see my art. People who might buy it, celebrate it, or ignore it. If I focused on loving those people, I could finish my painting. The sewing machine out on the table gave me an idea. Mending. I needed to mend my divided mind. I could put myself back together by meditating on love.

Mending was the answer! I ran to the garage and found the two pieces of canvas. Taking those two scraps, I sewed them together into one. Now they were big enough to paint on and stretch over a frame. The rainbow, the 100th painting, had begun. Carefully I began to paint with my new acrylics. I created a beautiful background of grass, sky, and trees made with figure eights.

Then the work paused. I couldn't find a picture anywhere of that undulating mandala shape for the rainbow. I researched the library and the internet. I found kids' toys that helped draw mandalas, Indian mandalas in every shape, Korean knots, and scientific equations, but nothing worked. I couldn't find the right shape.

I prayed about it, excitedly anticipating the moment when I would snap a picture of the final piece and send out a mass email about my 100th painting. I dreamed about the rebirth of my art studio and the celebration of friends and family: those from my old art groups, my old church, galleries, art buddies, customers. I'd be back as an artist. But when the image I needed still remained elusive after a few days of research, I left the painting unfinished.

"Your timing, God," I prayed. "Please let someone post the shape I need on the internet so that I can find it." Sure, I'd searched thoroughly. Now the only thing left to do was to wait on God's timing. I'd just have to work on other projects and pray that God would bring me the help I needed to finish the painting. I went back to the kitchen to cook supper, leaving the work on my makeshift easel made from a stack of books.

Only God knew how long it would take me, or how much I would have to change to be ready to be an artist again. Sometimes things take time. I try to think of it as God's timing when I get stumped, or doors closed. His timing is mysterious but in his hands.

❈❈❈

My choice to follow my faith and be an artist would have bigger effects than I ever dreamed possible. Two years had passed. Serious prayer, the loss of a job, and the unexpected grace of family and friends prompted me to take some time to return to my roots as an artist more seriously. In just twelve months' time, my life had changed. I found myself a full-time artist getting ready for my first open studio. My studio was now located in the arts district downtown. While touching up the rainbow painting for its first show, I contemplated how far I'd traveled to this moment. Looking around, I had a few other illustrations scattered around and a box of white canvases, and a still mostly empty sketchbook.

As I put on a final coat of fresh paint on the undulating rainbow, the changes in the past years struck me with fresh force. I was a single mom with two small children depending on me, but I had a job and a tiny bit of child support. We lived with my mother and brothers. The kids had a good school and a safe place to live.

Painting the green line, I pushed my thoughts toward gratefulness.

I thought about how my fridge was full for the first time in as long as I could remember—co-living with family meant that being food insecure was over.

As I focused on layering the warm colors, red, yellow, and orange, they reminded me of how creative I felt coming downtown to the art studio every day. The space was comfortable and inviting despite its old warehouse smell and the fact that it was scheduled for demolition at an indeterminate timeline. I had a cheap monthly sublease. The walls were covered with teal and orange paint donated by a friend and painted on rather creatively by my kids. The curtains from my old bedroom graced the high windows to block out the blindingly bright sunlight.

As I painted the blue line I remembered two nights before, I'd been to a local Christian artists group organized by *Transform Arts*, a group connected with *InterVarsity*. The faces were mostly young college students, but there were visual artists of all ages including poets and performers. We sat down to a potluck dinner in the garden of the director's home in Midtown.

"Any praises or prayer requests?" she asked after the lovely dinner of vegetable soup and fresh bread. A few artists mentioned upcoming shows or doing projects.

"I opened an art studio in the Crossroads!" I proudly proclaimed.

"With who?" they asked.

"Well, it's just me in an empty warehouse. It's 12 x 12 feet and all my supplies and paintings."

Everyone laughed.

I never was sure what the laughter meant. Did they think I would fail? Did my studio not count because it was just me? Was the location not good enough? Thinking back, maybe it was because I wasn't in one of the legitimate art spaces. I was a block or two from the main drag for the first Friday gallery walks.

I didn't let the laughter get to me. It was pretty funny that I expected great things from 144 square feet of about-to-be demolished space. And of course, the people from that group became some of my closest friends and contacts. If anything, that laughter, whether in doubt or incredulity, made me more determined. I knew God would help me

ꜛ each small step if I followed his calling. Even if it was only for a few weeks or months, I'd do my best at having an art studio.

All week long I'd filled up the studio. And now I hung art for the open house. As Friday evening approached, I felt nervous. First Friday in the summer meant thousands of people would be walking around downtown, visiting galleries, and looking at art. I reminded myself of the verse I'd found:

> *Wisdom shouts in the streets. She cries out in the public square. She calls to the crowds along the main street, to those gathered in front of the city gate: 'How long…Come and listen to my counsel. I'll share my heart with you and make you wise.'*

My studio was just off the main street. If I stopped worrying and focused on just "sharing my heart," maybe I'd feel at peace. If art was about, sharing my heart, well… that was something I could accomplish.

"Lord, help me share my heart and be honest with this art," I prayed.

I took a step back from the rainbow painting. Wait, it was missing something. What was it? The purple! Why had I left it out? (You can't easily leave one color out of a good rainbow). I painted the last stripe carefully in honor of my dad. He had passed away about a year ago and purple was his favorite color. I knew he'd be proud of me for making art again.

Practice makes perfect, he used to say. And he was right. Painting was much easier now after many months of practice.

With the last finishing touches I added swirls of blue and pink into the sky, some mysterious trees, and twinkling stars on the horizon. The dream landscape was finished. It was beautiful. My hundredth painting, complete.

Walking around the mostly empty warehouse, my fears grew. Would anyone come? Would anyone buy the art? How would I pay the second month's rent if I didn't sell anything? I tried to focus back on being thankful.

"God, you've brought me so far," I prayed. "You listened to my tears to be an artist. I'm going to need help to do this."

I began to think over how far I'd come. I marveled at the changes in the last two years. I had a studio and an art show, and I was about to meet a lot of artists, and maybe finally take part in an art community. I knew the best thing to keep fears at bay was to keep praying; keep telling God about my fears and listening for answers; finding inspiration to keep going.

As I returned to the easel I put on a final clear coat over my rainbow painting and let it dry, I prayed some more. It was becoming a habit, but there were a lot of doubts.

"God why in the world did you bring me to an abandoned warehouse. I'm mostly jobless, dreamless, heartbroken, and now alone in a stinky, dirty, empty building. Will anyone really come here? And will anyone care that I painted my 100th painting?"

As I drove home on Thursday, I was all nerves. Silently, doubts were ever-present ready to drown me. Was being an artist what completely derailed my life or some flaw in my personality? Or were my rejections and failures part of God's direction to be where he called me to be?

To get through each wave of doubt I was going to need help. I decided I needed to find a scripture verse to meditate on. Memorization often escaped me, but I came as close as I could. Searching for any grasp at a Bible verse, I thought of the manager of the building who rented me the studio space. He was a sweet-talking photographer who seemed more like a West Coast movie director than an art dealer—even though I knew we had grown up in the same town. When I paid my first month's rent, he had texted, "Thanks for doing a new thing." Hadn't I just read that phrase somewhere?

At home, I pulled out my Bible. It was a verse from my favorite book, Isaiah. "See, I am doing a new thing! Now it springs up; do you not perceive it? I am making a way in the wilderness and streams in the wasteland." The description seemed to fit that emptiness I felt when I was in the warehouse in the middle of the city. My studio sat on 19th Street, a quiet spot where few businesses or people were hanging out.

Maybe instead of worrying and complaining, I could pray for all the good things, new things, God wanted to do in this place. I didn't know what those things might be. I didn't know what in the world

God would do even if he had a way through the desert, or what I might do. But I prayed for it anyway.

That first week studio was a blur, but I do remember I went home at the end of it, the front door echoing to the empty building behind me, and something changed. Instead of feeling empty, I imagined a spring rising up and hoped that "water" would draw a community together in that Crossroads desert.

Now it didn't happen all at once. That first Friday, it was just a few of my friends who sat around and talked and looked at my studio and paintings. We were a few blocks off the main drag, so almost no one came in. For the second month, I kept going to the empty studio and trying to paint. I had this crazy idea to paint stamp shapes.

I was really stumped on what to paint until another artist moved in. She was from Paris.

"Let's make a paper mâché sculpture to put outside, so people know we are here," she said.

"Okay," I agreed reluctantly. I really needed to paint. But as I wasn't getting anywhere fast. I should be neighborly. I'd been sitting in the warehouse for a month with mostly blank canvases. I'd been trying to paint and not much was coming out. I couldn't afford to stop and play around when I needed a body of work, and I needed it fast. But I couldn't say no. After a few hours of playing with papier mâché, I felt inspired.

I walked back into my studio from the common area and quickly I finished sketching my next painting on canvas. In one day, I had accomplished what had previously taken all month. The answer seemed clear. Now I understood that without community, without play and fun and sharing stories, without collaboration, I really was a desert. I need people! Creatives need each other to create.

Within a month of praying for God to bring streams in the desert, another artist walked through the door. It was the second month I'd host a first Friday open house, and this time I was ready. I was dressed up, I had new work. My Rainbow painting was on an easel. I had a new stamp painting. I'd tried to put out a sign with balloons so people would spot our "gallery."

"God, don't you think it's time this whole artist community thing started. I can't be a community of one." I sighed, worried no one would come.

Suddenly around four o'clock, a new artist whisked in the door.

She barely had a second to introduce herself as Vera, and explain she'd rented the studio down the hall from mine. Immediately, she hung up her art and set up the studio all in an hour. She flitted here and there like a hummingbird.

Soon people arrived to walk through the building. Vera had invited dozens of friends. Including two models. As she began to put them in costume and apply body paint to their face, neck, hands, and feet, they transformed—one into pure gold and one into silver.

The models practiced pantomiming, waving bare tree branches. Wearing only black and white, they looked striking. At least one wore a fedora. I'd never seen performance art in person. Suddenly the art wasn't a painting on a wall. It was action, it was an event. The art wasn't a silent 2D grouping of images, it became people, it became a movement. It became a spectacle that gave the viewer something to ponder, something to wonder about. I watched silently in awe until one of the models, a round-faced guy with curly black hair, came up to me. He had been painted silver.

"Will you help me with this shirt?" I helped him button his shirt so his silver fingers wouldn't get color onto the white cuffs and collar. I couldn't imagine this young guy feeling welcome in my old suburban neighborhood or even my old church. I felt honored he trusted me to help with the performance.

Strange to be out of the cloistered, homogeneous setting of my old world and now into a new one. It was like the world went from black and white to color, for sure. The model quickly took his place to act out his mime. Vera posed him again—giving instructions.

The empty warehouse filled with life. Dozens and dozens of families and couples began pouring in, some with strollers or children in tow. They were all ages, genders, cultures—and no one looked traditional or even stereotypical. The streams in the desert were certainly different than I expected, and they were beautiful.

The smiles on people's faces were unusual too. There was a unique light that came into people's eyes as they came to see the art. They were waking up to thinking about "new things;" about being creative.

They talked about forgotten dreams to decorate cakes, build cabinets, take photographs, or spend time on travel. They seemed more hopeful, more relaxed. A photographer from Sweden had taken a small corner space in the warehouse, so we had four studios for people to walk through. Some of my friends came, some I knew well and some I didn't. People posed for photos with me and some bought prints. No one bought the large paintings. I had worried about losing my personal work too quickly needlessly. First Fridays were about the experience more than taking art home, I gathered. I would probably need a different way to make the next month's rent.

All too soon, everyone was gone. As we closed up that night, we shut off warehouse lights and closed all the loading dock doors, we had to shoo people away.

"You've got to be in this show I'm going to be in," said Vera. "It's called 'Waffles and Booze.' There's loud music. It's crazy, and there's body painting. I sold three pieces last time."

"Sure," I said. "I can bring this one," I pointed to my rainbow. "I'm just trying this artist thing out, I might only be here for the summer," I said "but I'll try anything. I'll come with you."

"Don't worry. You'll fit right in. Your art is good," she said.

I smiled.

Things were really going to change. I was no longer alone in home studio with my quiet reflections on art and faith. No longer stuck only going to church and the grocery store during the week. I was out, in the city, with people. Who knew what might happen. Suddenly my rainbow painting was going to start going places, and people were going to interpret it in a lot of ways I didn't first anticipate. I was going to meet a rainbow of people from all walks of life and my world would be turned upside down.

Over the next week, I was so thankful for more artists in our community space. But just when I thought I was getting the hang of the art studio life, an unexpected feeling arose. Guilt. I felt so guilty taking the time to make art, taking the money to buy supplies. It felt so wasteful. That money could be used for food or clothing or something more important.

On the way to the studio, I had to pass people who looked like they needed food and shelter. How could I justify taking time and money to make art when there were so many people in need? If my prayer was to "make room" for creativity and for God's spirit in my life, my city, my community, why would God choose art to do that? Why would God want there to be "room" for art and artists?

You know, he could have asked me to volunteer at the homeless shelter or let me find a regular job so I could give help to people who needed it. Why was I even here? God could have possibly fixed my marriage or the church ministry I had envisioned, but here I was in the urban core. Why? My mind whirled with all the things that didn't work out.

"God," I prayed, "Why did you call me to spend time being an artist when I'm just *wasting* time and money?" That's what I needed to find out.

I couldn't get the word "wasted" out of my mind. Oil paint was expensive paint. Was I wasting money on oil and canvas? Suddenly, I remembered a line from the musical my roommate used to listen to in college, "Jesus Christ, Super Star." I could hear the angry voice of Judas singing the lines about wasting money on oil "*your fine ointment.. should have been saved for the poor. Why has it been wasted?*"

The lines from Judas in the play were based on the ones in scripture where he basically complains that the poor could have been fed with money fro the sale of the super expensive, fragrant oil. In other words: basically, the oil was poured out for Jesus as performance art rather than for its normal use.

Here I was saying the same excuse over and over, Judas' line. Somehow that guilt washed over me and kept me from pushing forward. To try for a third month in the studio, I needed to somehow stem the flow of guilt.

So, I took time to meditate on that story from the gospels where an unnamed woman is remembered for wasting precious oil. Sometimes she's called Mary. She doesn't use her extremely expensive oil for its regular use (to prepare a body for a funeral). Instead, she interrupts Jesus at a meal in Bethany, to do something unusual with the bottle. I imagine it went something like this:

෯෯෯

It is a nice spring day in Bethany. Everyone sits down, half reclining on the ground on cushions. Their feet out to the side, eating the Roman way. The dinner is served near the floor on a low table. Guests take the usual positions, reclining on the left arm and eating with their feet pointed to the right side. The guest's feet should have been washed as they entered but somehow Jesus comes in and is seated without the typical foot washing.

Jesus doesn't make a fuss. Maybe this lack of hospitality was intentional, but it might have been accidental. Jesus and his merry band of followers could have been a lot of extra people to handle. Or maybe their state of homeless wandering meant they had particularly dirty feet that the server didn't want to wash. We don't know why the oversight occurred.

No matter. Something happened that changed that day from a casual meal to a legend emblazoned in memory.

A woman came and took about a pint of pure nard, an expensive perfumed oil; she poured it on Jesus' feet and wiped his feet with her hair. Some say she washed his feet with her tears. The story was written down for posterity. The writer says no one could forget because the house was filled with the fragrance of the perfume.

In charge of the money for Jesus and his groupies, Judas is the team accountant. When he sees a woman bringing a donation of oil, he's excited about the large amount of cash they can get for the sale. (Rumor says he skimmed money off the top for himself). So when the woman pours out the oil instead of handing it over as a donation, he is personally disappointed, if not incredulous.

Judas makes a comment that if Mary wanted to contribute to the cause, she could sell the oil and donate the money to the poor, or even Jesus' ministry, but what she was doing is a pure waste. Although John the writer, distracts his readers with this bit of foreshadowing, thankfully, he also records what Jesus replies. (And if you've ever listened to Jesus Christ Superstar, the Musical you'll know the tune to this line):

'Leave her alone,' Jesus replied. 'It was intended that she should save this perfume for the day of my burial. You will always have

the poor among you, but you will not always have me. Truly I tell you, wherever the gospel is preached throughout the world, what she has done will also be told, in memory of her.'

spending my 'wealth' on the gifts of my own & others' art — for joy.

To me, the idea of memory is one of the most important things Jesus says in the Bible about artists. And this line is one reason why I was able to continue being an artist, and an artist of faith–despite the needy in the world. Every day when I wanted to quit going to the studio to make art and find something useful to do, something where I could have actual income, enough to help the poor, I continued to keep going to the studio to make art. The job of art is to help us remember. These words are why I continue to this day to keep getting up, keep praying and keep making art. It's why I know I'm called to be creative.

Now I've heard other people tell this story, but they often leave out the explanation that only someone from that culture (or someone in the arts) would notice. This open bottle of perfume is important because scent is always connected to memory. I can almost smell the scent now, woodsy and fragrant and spicy. Jesus says the oil is what has been used to stop and help people remember.

In Matthew's retelling he quotes Jesus as saying:

"Truly I tell you, wherever this gospel is preached throughout the world, what she has done will also be told, in memory of her."

Memory is the key here. Some say this story is about sorrow, repentance, or need for forgiveness. The writers and theologians get distracted and make this story about sin. Looking at the story from an artists' perspective, the key is her memorial act. Her visual way to mark this moment in time both in her memory and in those around her. This is a public performance. This is performance art.

Brilliant

The unnamed woman who breaks open the oil and wastes it is an artist. Why? Because art is about memory. Art brings something invisible to light and strikes a chord so we can move forward from that moment in commemoration, in honor, or relief.

In light of that, I'd connect Judas' comment about the expense of the oil as even more important. Breaking open the oil is a sacrificial act. This is expensive. It will be remembered precisely because it was unusual, it was visual, and it was a drain on the finances, on the reputation. It took guts. Combined with the wonderful smell—Jesus picks up on the most important part of this story. This is about remembrance.

What could you do in today's world to remember something in such a way that it was expensive, visible to a lot of people, and would mark a moment to remember? Hire an artist? What if you threw an enormous party, fed a lot of people, or gave a performance of some kind? Hire an artist. There is hardly a celebration or a memory to be made without an artist. No halftime shows, no galleries, no birthday cake designs, no unusual dinnerware, no new recipes, no interesting haircuts, no beautiful clothes. Without artists, we have no way to remember one day from the next. No way to set an intention, no way to commemorate. No way to imagine. And where would faith be without the ability to commemorate and imagine? It would be lost.

As an art student in college, I once heard a sermon on this story by a visiting artist and theologian, Makoto Fujimura. He said that this story was one that enabled him to be an artist. It gave him the courage to buy expensive pigments and gold leaf for his art. The temptation to call his work a huge waste of money was always present. But he said he realized he had a calling to be an artist and that was not a waste.

Makoto's interpretation of the story came back to me that day. I recalled how exciting it was when a new artist came bounding into Kansas City on 19th Street. It was something I would not forget. Vera came to that empty place full of hope, breaking open all that silver and gold paint and anointing those people, posing them, taking their pictures, bringing in limbs from trees, hanging up paintings. My friends came. I served fresh baked bread and wine. (Good old communion is the base of the art show table). Along with my art hanging on the walls, the owner of the building brought in a musician, and two photographers: one from France and one from Sweden. On that ght in July, that empty building came to life. People came flocking in, families and couples, and crowds of friends walked through. They ate up all the bread and wine, they listened to music.

They said things like:

"Oh, I used to make art but I want to start again."

"I'm not an artist," said one guy with a mustache, but I make cabinets.

"I'm not an artist," said a woman in a ponytail pulling out her phone to show me all her designs, "but I decorate cakes."

"My daughter makes t-shirts," said a third man pointing to a young girl still in school.

"I want a print," said my friend who installed internet wires all over town.

"Tell me about this painting," said a high schooler.

"I have some kids who'd like to color," said a mom as I pulled out some toys and crayons...

We created a night to remember, and the art people took home was a reminder of that wakeful moment where they remembered their dreams, their imagination, their community, their hope.

As I came back for a third month in the studio. I kept working with stamp images and making more paintings about commemoration. Art was about memory, what did I want to remember? As I locked up the warehouse, I remembered to pray, "Dear God, send something new, something good to the desert place, yes something new for the desert in my heart, but also to the place where my studio is too."

That's when he reminded me he already had. I pictured the hundreds of people who had come through that Friday.

"Oh, so that's the stream in the desert?" I asked.

I didn't need an answer in reply.

※ ※ ※

Maybe you have a calling to do something memorable or visual. To mark a moment in your life in some way—to say, today I make this stand. These types of personal events mark our landscape of the world, it's where we get Cathedrals, sculptures, museums, fountains, new restaurants, portraits, and the like. It's even the way someone decides

:chase a tattoo. Certainly, most would say these items and events xpensive, even a waste. All art is if we look at it that way. But the important thing to me about art is memory. What is this piece of art in memorial of? What does it remind us to do? Who does it commemorate? What hope does it inspire?

So, what happened to my 100th painting? It showed many many places, in many places, warehouses, and coffee shops. It hung in nightclubs and churches, clinics and galleries, and schools, including two of my own solo shows. It eventually found an owner.

Over the next seven years, I stayed out in the community making art and meeting people. I kept my practice in prayer and in art. I listened to the stories of everyone who would share with me. In fact, I went on to have 100 art shows. My rainbow painting, a moment of prayer to be an artist, blossomed and grew like a tree with branches. Most importantly, I learned volumes on love, compassion and creativity from community minded artists like Vera, and many more.

So how did I find a way to follow my calling to be creative and to be a person of faith? It began with openness to making room for my own art and space for God's calling in my life. I had to be open to sharing my dreams and my vision with others. That created space for God speak into my life in prayer. Making room for faith and hope in my life allowed me to make room for other people and hear their stories.

Art. It's not just the supplies, the oil, the studio rent, it's all a risk; it's all expensive in every way—but people of faith are sometimes called to be artists too. Remember Jesus said it's worth remembering. Art doesn't work well when it's self-serving, it's a community thing; it helps the community remember what is important. Art humanizes us. Yes, it's our time to play, our time to express joy, to be distracted, to be creative. I guess a Creator God thinks creating is important.

If art helps us remember, the question is, what do we want to remember? We want to remember what we are here for. To open our eyes to his invisible, upside-down Kingdom where servants are greater than kings and strangers become family—where God is a father and a mother, not a judge, to be open to a way we can all take part in the journey together.

I let myself create one painting. Just one visual reminder of
I felt God's presence in my life, and it began to change everything
about my life. By the time I completed the rainbow painting, I had
been through three new art studios, the final one being open to the
public. When I answered that call to make art, art took me out into
my community—creating conversations and relationships. Just that
one simple sacrifice to spend some time creating, something I felt
called to make, became the beginning of a new and more energized,
more focused, and more faithful journey.

Prayer does not help you remember to be a saint; it helps you
remember a God who rescues and saves you. Maybe you are like me
or like the women who broke open the oil, and you want to take
a risk to remember what your callings are, to remember the words
over your life, to remember your story and your place on a journey
of Faith, Prayer, Hope, and Love. I think the the-break-open-the-oil-
prayer from that well-known performance artist who spilled out that
expensive oil might go something like this:

Dear anointed one, King of my life,
    **You rescued me. You taught me. You gave me faith for my jour-
ney. When my life was over, you put it back together. When I had
nothing to live for, you made the world seem alive again. You haven't asked for much, only my listening ear, my attention, and a
little bit of faith, but I want to give you more than that. I want to
have extravagant love. I want to be generous. Give me a generous
heart, a creative heart, and don't ever let me forget you. Don't let
me worry about what I need. Don't let me get overly distracted
by temporary things or by what others think about me. Don't let
me forget who you are to me, and what you've done for me. Don't
let me wander away from you, become stale, or dead inside. Keep
me alive. Keep me in love. Keep me close to your heart, forever.
Amen.** ❋

The Dress I Made Myself ~ Quilted, Hand Dyed Shibori
Collage on Cotton, 8 x 10 in 2018

Frequently Asked Questions

What if I pray and my prayer isn't answered?

Scripture and tradition tell us that this is often because of three basic reasons. One, God's answering but it's a process; he's waiting for his perfect will and timing. (Remember he's outside of time, so really, he's always answering.) Two, he's already answering but in his own perfect way, different from our vision. Three, our closeness to perceive or find God's will or answer is blocked by unforgiveness. That could be for ourselves, someone else, or a group of people. Similarly, I've often wondered if being in a binding legal or spiritual relationship with a person or group blocked by unforgiveness might also make the prayer life more difficult. But this goes farther than I want to say here.

I'll only say that I see forgiveness as the beginning of all creative acts, and all relationships–including prayer. It's what makes being a human that can connect to God possible. God's forgiveness of us makes God accessible to us. Our forgiveness of others makes him accessible to us. It's the core of everything. Blaming someone else for a delayed or unanswered prayer, is the opposite of forgiveness. I remember a friend of mine asked me what I thought about working for a company that had an imprint that sold pornography. I know that's something that causes a lot of pain and division between relationships. Looking back, I might have told them, be mindful of who you are tied to. Your prayer life might be easier if other binding relationships you have are also with someone who believes in love and forgiveness and isn't gaining financially from adding pain and division into the world. Of course, I'd pray about whatever decisions you make, marriages, jobs, partnerships, and the like. God always has a calling for us, he's always guiding us toward his will and his hope and future. To me, prayer is often about finding a way to listen to that calling; to become someone who listens and wants to discern God's path. ❀

What if my prayers are answered?

Prayer is all about praising God and testimony. I used to keep track of answered prayers. But I found that they were all answered. All of them. I'd have a list of let's say thirty things I'd added on a sheet of paper from top to bottom over the course of a month. By the time a few months would go by, all the entries would have a note about how I saw an answer or partial answer to that prayer. Maybe one larger prayer would remain unanswered or have a partial answer.

After a year of this, I stopped writing answers to prayers down because why bother? They were all answered. There were just too many. This includes items as small as, "Lord, I need a new pair of sunglasses," to "Lord, I lost that important thing I borrowed and need to return." This includes prayers for recovery from illness, and direction for jobs, relationships, finances. This includes asking for peace or hope; healing from stage four cancer, healing from the loss of smell; finding a lost ministry; finding a lost pet. This includes single people finding a soul mate, or praying for people to return to their faith; from trauma that is physical, spiritual, or other. This includes the reunion of people who haven't spoken in thirty years. This includes all kinds of prayers. Everything. Everything was always answered.

To me an answer is seeing movement, progress, a good turn, the return of hope. An answer is simply the return of a twinkle in someone's eye, to a full complete miracle. Make sure to keep praying about something even when you think the answer has come. Let's say that new job is certain. Keep praying all the way through that first day, all the way through that first paycheck. All the way through that first paycheck clearing and making into the bank. Don't stop praying.

And don't worry if that answer you see for full health or someone to find a spouse ends up with imperfection later. That's not because prayer isn't strong enough. That is just the imperfect, human world we live in. And if someone experienced a few more years of health or family, that is a good answer to prayer. We live in a temporary world. That's why I think it's good advice to keep praying.

That's what we have to do. We live in a broken world where there always seems to be something that tries to stop, slow down, or thwart what's good. So, keep praying. Just like a doctor stays t until a baby is born and breathing, until the parents are holding the child with a sigh of relief; that's how long you must pray through–to the end.

And if that's how long we have to pray, then how long should we praise? Let people know, as you feel led, and you feel comfortable, that you've prayed for them. Let them know you are having faith for something you've prayed about, so that when they see an answer, they see God working. Prayer holds hands with testimony. Prayer holds hands with praise. Praising and thanking God, reflecting on grace and thankfulness is at least half of a healthy prayer life. I bet if we searched scripture and had time to list it all here, we could say that up to ninety percent or more of our prayer life should be thankfulness and praise.

God reaches out to us and blesses us, why not thank him? Now you may wonder why we should thank an all-powerful God; I mean it wasn't truly hard on God's end, was it? Or you may wonder why we should keep praising God and telling everyone how great he is and how many prayers we see answered, how many miracles and daily blessings. Why do that at all? Some people insist praise is like a magical guarantee: if you tell people God will answer your prayer then your prayer will be answered so God can save face. Well, that's one philosophy. So, you may wonder, does God has a big head? Do we have to keep talking about him because of his ego? What's the deal?

No. I don't think that's it. It's not his ego, it's not God's need for praise in the way we understand it. No, this is about our understanding, not his need to be made a big deal of. It's more about his identity. God is all about love and God's natural state is one of praise. It's something the human mind has a hard time understanding. But think of it this way: the natural state of a tree is to have its arms raised to the sun. Even a flower follows the sun with its center during the day, following its motion from morning to evening. Even the earth is pulled around the sun by gravity. But God made the sun, and the sun is a small star, just one in an infinite universe; one of the many that he thew up with his hands at the beginning of time because he was so full of joy over making a space for love, a space for us. We naturally lean toward God. And imagine the pull of a God so big that the universe is small enough to fit in his hand. Praise is like our gravity. That's why we need to praise and thank God. It's our natural state.

Have you ever hit the side of a water glass and seen the water shake? Even the glass reverberates with a note of sound. People are the same way. We are mostly water, and our natural state is one of reverberation. In our natural state, that is a note of praise. Prayer and praise to humans is like singing for birds. It's what we are meant for. So much so, that it is the opposite of what everyone nowadays feels is our natural state–the state of worry and panic. Prayer is a satisfying way to keep fighting against that fearful anxiety. Scripture says thankfulness fights anxiety. It's good medicine. So why not use it? Sharing the good news of reaching out to God and hearing an answer, feeling peace, finding love and acceptance is good news. People may balk and complain if you share theology with them or tell them what to believe. But hardly anyone minds hearing about a good personal testimony that your prayer is answered. ❋

What do I do with inner promptings?

What should I do with feelings or intuitions I sense during prayer? What about those promptings from God's inaudible voice? It's hard to know what to do with promptings you feel from prayer. Are you being led to quit your job, or avoid a certain highway on your commute? Are you being prompted to go visit a friend or are you just wishing to see them?

This is where trying the common recommendation, to be discerning by looking for a Bible verse that relates to your intuition, may feel overwhelming. Imagine when you are praying you get the idea to start a small group, a company, a church, a preschool, or a weekly game night for friends to reconnect. They all sound great. Most people say that in order to see if the intuition you felt during prayer was the will of God, you should check with friends to see if they feel spiritually led in the same way.

Sure, this works, especially for smaller issues. However, I think one reason a lot of us don't want to pray is because we know this isn't accurate. We are filled with confusing feelings of guilt and impatience as we wonder if the ideas we get during prayer should be acted upon, especially ones that seem helpful or positive. The truth is, if we acted on every prompting, we'd be exhausted, especially those of us who are idea people.

And when we consider bigger issues, that fact that friends tend to agree anyway, this doesn't feel right. What about the fact that cults or heresies are built out of like-minded agreement around a rule or Bible verse taken out of context? Truths that are twisted or used to manipulate or control people makes us wonder if we should even try to pray at all.

Let's start here. The "Bible verse check" (the idea from Jesus's words that two or three need to agree to know if something is God's will "For where two or three gather in my name, there am I with them,"[1]) is not a failsafe to decide how to proceed on ideas we feel we've "heard" or thought of during prayer. Why? Aren't we following scripture when we do that? Kind of, but I'd say, the Bible is not a magic eight ball, or a set of dice. Even a friend's agreement is not a failsafe. Even a pastor's agreement is not a failsafe. Despite this common practice, of checking our leadings from prayer with two to three friends, I've seen many examples of this not working, myself included. Someone will be trying to make a decision, trying to be prayerful and wise, but feeling later they were misled. What then? Should we just say that most of the time, our intuitions in prayer are false, or probably won't work out?

I don't think so. Complete inaction from fear is not a God thing either. If you have an idea and confirm it in scripture that might not be a good idea either? Well, think about it. Some scriptures do not easily apply to culture right now, like stoning people who are "sinners," or stepping on snakes, smiting the enemy. Those verses taken out of context and put into your home on a Tuesday when the doorbell rings with a delivery of a package are not going to be a safe interpretation of God's leading through scripture. It would be crazy to throw snakes or stones at your mailperson. That one might be easy for most of us, but there are other ideas maybe we shouldn't pursue. So, if our friends aren't the answer, and every scripture verse isn't always helpful to each situation, then what about common sense? Leaning towards our common sense to interpret every emotion and prompting during prayer

---

1 *Mat 18: 20, NIV*

may not work either. We have to admit that sometimes we aren't that
sensible. So, how do we decide what to do with ideas we find during
prayer, intuitive leanings that prompt us to consider new actions?

Let's look at it this way. The scriptures were written by dozens and
dozens of diverse writers over a long period of time. Let's say at least
3,000 years or more. Are those words holy? Yes. Inspired? Yes. Life
changing? Yes. Sustaining? Yes. Alive and Active? Yes. Am I always
certain which apply to me today or if I understand the context of
the ancient culture they are from with its different views of time and
place? No. I'm the one whose fallible. It's the same with prayer. We all
have diverse imaginations, so how do we handle that vast ocean that is
an invisible in audible conversation?

What can we do? I handle it this way. God didn't promise me a
perfect life. I'm an imperfect human with a lot of failing. I'm trying
to follow his will. So, in the little things, if I have an intuitive feeling
during prayer, a prompting, a leading, or an inaudible voice, I write it
down and I pray about it. I meditate on it. I look up scripture on that
leading. Because I've paired reading scripture and prayer for so long,
most of my intuitive moments or "hearing from God during prayer"
are being reminded of scripture anyway. I honor those feelings by
calling them a part of the process of prayer. Sometimes in prayer, I'm
reminded of songs or poems or biographies, sometimes important life
events. I consider those promptings an answers to prayer.

In decisions, I talk about how I feel led in prayer with people I
trust. They often pray for me, and we pray together. I wait to have
that prompting again. I ask for, direction, confirmation. That's my
process. Now that I'm older I'm more likely, I hope, to listen to those
people who say I might be going down the wrong bunny trail with an
idea. Today, I still take action on things, that really aren't my responsibility, that probably aren't God's will. But I keep praying and looking
for ways to figure out what his best is for me and how I can be a better
listener and be more discerning.

The answer is that prayer is a relationship. It's not a magical set of
dice, it's not a set of programmed responses. It's a conversation. So,
it's more than idea. I hope the chapters in this book show examples of
that long relationship over time about how decisions and new things

are part of a prayer life, that you travel with God. It's a journey which means it's new all the time.

As an artist, ideas I get during may mean I have something to meditate on later visually in my work. As a writer, I also have more outlet for exploring my thoughts from prayer. So, find ways you think prayer could be a part of your daily life. When I paint a mural, I pray for everyone who works in that company and for all the people they meet. I don't need to discern anything about action. Maybe you work at a bank or as a forklift driver, you have a lot of time to pray for people or the place you live and work. Any leadings you feel might be more internal about your personal relationships or understanding of how much God loves you. That's okay. Prayer doesn't always have to be about action, a to-do list for God, or interceding for others. It can just be a conversation to pass the time, or a chance to bless others. ✖

How often should I pray?

I'd say somewhere between daily and all the time. I like to pray at night before bed. Morning is good. Before the sun sets is a good time. Meals can be a good reminder to pause and pray. Entering or exiting in and out of doorways, cars, trains, planes, or buildings is a good reminder to pray. Crossing rivers, state lines, territories is a good time to pray.

Any time. Yes, any time. All the time. Normally, praying all the time is a rare gift attributed to saints like Brother Lawrence, an early seventeenth century soldier who after a war injury became a chef in a monastery in Paris at the age of 26. A collection of sixteen of his letters became the book titled, "The Practice of the Presence of God." His informal way of all day, every day prayer became legend, but I think it's possible for most of us to turn our inner dialogue into a state of constant prayer.

When I'm praying in inner dialogue, maybe even something so humble as my complaint over my birthday not being perfect, for example, and then a pink sunrise blooms in my favorite color over the horizon, I feel like that's an answer to prayer. The silent call and the response of life continuing is like a love letter, a note, that says God sees me and loves me. It's much better than sharing those complaints aloud. People have often said I seemed so calm and peaceful. Not true, my inner dialog is as messy as anyone's, it's just turned into silent prayer. And the good things I see in my life are woven into a conversation of relationship, the beatitude life, the journey with God. ❋

What if I'm worried I'll see angels?

What if I'm worried, I'll see, or won't see angels when I pray? What if my prayers attract some sort of demonic attack, bad luck, or some kind of "push back?" I remember as a kid I prayed I'd be able to see angels like Abraham did in the Bible story I'd heard at Sunday school. I was sad when I hung out between two trees like Abram's Oaks of Mamre. I even brought some snacks, but the angels never arrived. Well to be clear, I never saw them.

Angels are usually invisible. The Bible says to treat everyone as Angels in disguise and I take that seriously and I always have. So much so that one particularly bad day, someone brought me some oranges. She was smiling with white hair. When she left, I told my preschooler in a stunned voice, I think we were visited by an angel. Then I peeked out the window and saw her get into a van and park two houses down. It was our neighbor I'd hardly ever seen her so I didn't recognize her. It's an ancient tradition to treat visitors as you would a guest from heaven, and I think treating everyone as spiritually important can only be a good thing.

As an adult, I went to a church one Sunday where the testimony was from a woman who often saw angels. Somehow, this terrified me. My mind had changed since I was young, and I definitely didn't want to see any angels. A few times I've had the sense that I might have seen an angel or felt a presence, but I don't think that's what's important about reaching out to God. I'm going to cite St. Augustine and his fifth century writings on the topic for this one. I wish more people agreed with him today. Angels are God's messengers, and we don't have to worry about them, talk to them, pray for them, help them, or avoid them. Angels are God's helpers, and they are focused on loving, worshiping, and serving God. Seeing or not seeing them doesn't help our relationship with God. That's still up to us. And angels aren't gods to be worshiped. It's like if we went into a tall skyscraper and worshipped the elevator instead of taking it up. Our focus should be getting close to God, not worrying about his system of helpers.

Sometimes, when I feel like someone is in the direst situation possible, and I can't think of a prayer that would help them, I'll pray for God to send angels to help them. Prayer is about reaching out in relationship to God. Remember, God is all knowing, all powerful, and all loving and all just. God created us. He knows how we work. So, God can hear your prayers if you are silent or aloud. He can hear thought, and he can hear the desires of the heart that aren't even in words. God is outside of time, so he knows your future prayers, and what you mean even when you don't say it.

Angels, however, cannot hear thoughts or prayers. I assume they can hear just fine when they visit in person whether visible or not visible. I'm more a student of prayer than of the supernatural. I'm hoping I'm never in a situation where I need a visit from one of God's glowing messengers, and the ones I've met in dreams probably don't count, but they were always hard to look at directly and they were always there to teach me a word or phrase they wanted me to memorize. Not very exciting, but I did find those words helpful in mediation.

As a human we are "a little lower than angels" but as part of God's family you are with Christ, and everything is "under his feet." When God adopts you into his family and you accept Jesus, he becomes like a brother to you. So, you don't need to fear evil spirits or take note of them. He lifts you up to be above those spirits both light and dark. Remember that any evil wandering spirit in the air won't hear your thoughts unless you say them aloud, and in many places it's unlikely you have them wandering through.

Again, I agree with Augustine, one of the most influential founding church fathers, on this one. Leave spirits alone, don't mess with them, talk to them, invite them, try to attract them. If you do run into them, will you successfully discern a good spirit from a bad one? That seems like too much work. An evil spirit's goal is to make you think they have power, make you afraid, distract you from what your life should be about. Make you think they are interesting or important. Make you think they are a ghost that's got an exciting history etc. Or make you delve into genealogies and past lives of people they've met to make you feel important. Fear and distraction are their only programming. All of those things just make you forget about God and his will for your life and his love for you.

There's historical precedence of people allowing evil spirits to be a guide, and since they are known to be ruled by the "father of lies" it's just not going to be good company. You can't trust them. Simply pray that God would send any evil spirits away, play some praise music, burn sage. Whatever you want to do to cleanse your space then you can get back to your life. Don't worry about it, focus on God. If you find yourself thinking, talking, or researching demons a lot, they've successfully distracted you. Even I love a good Korean TV series with people fighting demons etc. It's great drama. But I think I probably have to admit, if I'm craving something like that, it's because my spiritual life is dull and lifeless. Stories can be fun and energizing, but I know when it's time to put my focus back to my own spiritual life.

That being said, I have noticed some spiritual push back when I pray intercessory prayers for others. In fact, this has bothered me some. But not enough to write about. It would be a boring chapter and that's a good thing. I've blamed evil spirits for my car trouble, my smoke alarms going off, and appliances not working—although spiritual friends have told me that's "giving the enemy too much credit." All that to say is that I hope you remember that with an all-knowing God, your prayer closet, or a private place to pray, is a great way to pray especially if you want to pray intercessory or prayer for others. A prayer closet, or silent prayer is what Jesus recommended. "But when you pray, go into your room, close the door and pray to your Father, who is unseen. Then your Father, who sees what is done in secret, will reward you." [2]

When I'm doing something new: going into a new territory of space where I've never prayed before—or never had family or friends praying for me—I walk around or drive around a bit to pray. And especially on those types of days where I start a new job, a new ministry, a new class, a new project, I have come to the practice of praying beforehand. If I'm about to do something that influences others, and I'm bringing God's spirit with me, there might be "push back." Gen-

2   Matthew 5:6, NIV

erally, that's car trouble, an undeserved traffic ticket, a closed road, that kind of thing. One verse from Revelation has been my go-to prayer for these situations. I pray aloud in the morning before my feet touch the floor. "Dear Lord, cover this day with the blood of the lamb and the word of our testimony."

This prayer said aloud reminds me (and any listening ears) my intention to trust God and to focus on being a light. It reminds me to focus on being grateful for my story and God's help in the past. This verse helps me remember that there are two things (and they are the best things) to fight off spiritual push back that might keep me from praying big prayers or continuing to pray. The first is Jesus, and his perfect sacrifice that broke down evil, unlocked the gates of hell, and made death work backwards, besides saving those who believe in God by bringing them into God's family and closing that gap between his perfection (holiness) and our imperfection.

The other part of the verse spoken aloud reminds me that my true strength against fear and doubt and any spiritual attack, is my testimony. This book is my testimony shared in small pieces. On a daily basis, my testimony is God's goodness, his provision, and the close and sweet bond I have with Jesus as my best friend and his spirit as my comfort. My testimony is my story about how God has shaped my life and remade my heart.

So, to avoid some of the minor irritating spiritual push back like colds, smoke alarms going off, flat tires, the medium sized issues like missing payments, extra bills or random lawsuits, or the big ones like breaking out in hives, car accidents, or bouts of fear or panic, I use this verse as my guide for where to put my focus. I block out distractions that come to stop me from following my calling or having faith. Now of course, I am not the best at this. Fifty percent of the time, I forget to follow my own advice. So, I also make sure if I'm going to pray a big prayer for a whole people group, region, country, neighborhood, denomination, or business that I have some other people cover me in prayer first. And I pray those big prayers silently or in a group.

Really and truly, most importantly, I try to pray God's will and not mine, I think that's what makes prayer work, and makes it easier.

His timing is perfect. I want to even pray for his will in his time and in his way.

This is a space where I'm still learning, just like you. One thing that's always hard to discern is whether a problem you are having is just random; is a spiritual attack because you are trying to follow God's will or is a block because it's not God's will to do that thing or go that direction. I'd again say, prayer is how to decide. For example, one day I felt ill before it was time to go to church, so I went to bed. A handful of other times, I've felt a headache or weakness come on, and I knew I needed to go to that church or other community event. As soon as I left the house, I'd feel fine. The illness was a temporary mirage to keep me from going and receiving something great, a good work, a friendship, or a new opportunity. Sometimes I'd pray to feel really awake if God wanted me to go to an event some evening, and surprisingly I would feel so alert, I'd have to put away my constant shyness to attend. We are all human doing the best we can. Thankfully God loves us and wants us to partner with him. ✻

What about praying against things?

What if we accidentally curse someone when we pray? Or what if we pray for something but that causes bad things to happen? Praying against something is simply saying "I pray against ..." It's a common folk tradition. Even movie stars, say "Get behind me, Satan." They may not always know they are quoting Jesus who was trying to stop Peter from disrupting the last supper with his reverse egomania (being humble to get attention). So, let's look at this. I think we can all agree, we should be careful to approach prayer, not as a weapon against other people, but as a way to pray blessings and truth into their life.

For me, the key is to remember that prayer is a relationship with God, not a way to control others. That means that before we pray for someone, we need to think about what God would want for them, and how scripture would help us to look at a situation. For example, many, if not all of us, at some point have, prayed against someone. It's a natural human feeling that when we feel trapped or stumped in a problem that we wish that problem away. So, if you feel drawn to pray for someone who is causing you duress to quit their job or move away, so you don't have to deal with them anymore, that's natural. However, that's praying against someone, praying harm for them.

Praying against someone is caused by fear and fear is not from God. God is love and his spirit is one of love. For example, let's say there is a parent who is afraid of a big change. Maybe they might pray that their family members break up with their significant other. They don't want them to get married because they aren't right for each other. That's an example of praying against someone, and it is more of a curse than a prayer. Praying for someone to leave, get out of the way, or stop showing up, is a sign that you are nearing the end zone of prayer. You are leaning toward praying for someone to be harmed rather than praying for a blessing. If you feel tempted to pray they get hurt so they can't play a sport, get sick so you don't have to see them that day, or even die so you never have to see them again—those are curses. You have left the prayer zone.

I want to be sure to say that praying against people, this is not okay. This is one reason prayer is dangerous. Not that God will let a curse happen, or that your prayer will work like magic and harm someone. That's unlikely. The harm is to yourself, building up a heart of fear rather than love, or even leaning your soul toward hate. Whatever the situation, we don't want to pray against people or assume we know what is best for them, or God's will for them. That is a spirit of control/ pride, i.e., magic. And as we know, control is the opposite of prayer. Of course, praying in Jesus' name or for God's will is one way to make sure those accidental controlling words don't go out into the world. You are in the end, submitting to God's will—God's will is always first centered in love. We shouldn't mistake our job to pray for justice that is some sort of revenge or retribution. God's justice is paired with righteousness, it makes everything the most fair and right.

So, when those little agonies of fear cause you to slip up, give them back to God instead. I've found that when I find myself exiting the prayer zone and heading toward being controlling or hateful, there is an easy way around this natural feeling. And this redirection is something I love about prayer the most because I have to give over that fear to God and tell him I have no idea what to pray, I'm at the end of my rope. This is when I feel God changing my heart and I'm so grateful.

Go back to imagining you are the parent praying for your adult child to quit their job, their relationship, their church, or their school, for example. Your reason is because they aren't ready for it, because it's not "right" for them, because you don't want to be connected with that person or group. Okay, those are natural feelings, but praying against is not praying for. What if you flip that prayer on its head and change direction back to the prayer zone–back to love instead of fear?

Imagine that you are in God's shoes, and you love that person very much. What would God want for them? God places the lonely in families, he satisfies our desires with good things, he cares for us. He's the provider. Pretty soon, God will move your heart to have empathy and compassion for that person. You can pray for them to have the best job that is just right for them, one that suits their needs and their callings. You can pray for them to have a strong relationship, one that is satisfying or healing; one that makes them a family that invites others in, a family from which good things come.

You don't know which relationship or job God wants that loved one to have, but if you pray for the blessing, and for God's will, then whatever happens you know it's in God's hands. So, whether they take that job or not, whether they get married to this partner or the next, you've bathed it in prayer and in blessing. You've bathed that prayer in God's will and in the spirit of love. You've let go of your will for that person and prayed God's will by imagining his best for them. You don't have to fill in everything, just pray around their needs in a circle. Pray blessings on that school or future spouse or business. If you feel worried about that person keep praying until you feel you've prayed for them from every angle you can think of. For me this just takes a few minutes anywhere from two to twenty minutes at most.

Now you can use your natural inkling to pray against things by praying against evil: pray against harm, pray against accidents, miscommunications; pray against greed, against vices and addictions; pray against confusion–spiritual deafness or dumbness. I'd be wary about praying for people to "get it" to "wake up" to "learn from their mistakes." Instead, pray for them to hear God's voice and then practice listening to God's will for your life.

Let me give you an example: If I were a tree covered in ivy vines. Would I want someone to leave those beautiful vines up? No, they would choke the tree (me) until I died. If I was a tree covered in poison ivy vines, would you want to help hack off that poison? No. the vines feed birds in the winter and don't harm the tree. Just like knowing what is helpful and what is harmful, only a knowledgeable, careful, and experienced gardener would know which vines were harming the life of a tree. Prayer lets us partner with God as our gardener. He carefully removes what hurts us, and leaves what is helpful to our self, and if we ask him, in our community as well. We may not be able to tell what things in our lives are "strongholds" lies that will ultimately kill our calling and ministries, if not our spirits. Strongholds are those misguided ideas in our reasoning that may be causing huge injustice to ourselves and others, but only God can root them out. We may have some beautiful valuable traits or beliefs we admire that are slowly choking the life out of us.

We have God work in others. I think the idea of focusing on prayer as a battle is dangerous. I've seen actual prayer journals with guns and bullseyes in them. This metaphor if taken the wrong way, might make us think to take the axe to someone spiritually. Maybe we think their attitude or belief is a poison that needs to be choked out. We think they are spreading a huge problem in the world. But in prayer, we can't swing axes or other invisible weapons at God's other kids. I think in prayer we should be more like children than soldiers. In prayer, we have to consider all sides. We must love rather than accuse.

Let's say we pray again someone. What if we are mistaken? And what if their belief is natural and harmless? Can we really play God and say we know everything that is right in every situation? In any case, we can never be as wise as God. So, before we hack at a neighbor or a business or a law, trying to make it perfect to our own ideals and understandings, I'd say prayer is the first step and that prayer should be in love. Why not meditate on what God's will is? Why not pray for someone rather than attack them?

When we pray, we are not battling each other. Even the most heinous villain, we can pray for him to have a change of heart. We can pray that the world would be protected from his evil decisions; that someone who will do God's will take his position; that people will rise up to speak out against those evil practices; that the new person to take their place would be safe and sustained and strong enough to keep working. We could pray that this villain would somehow do God's will anyway or by accident, but our job is not to pray against people for them to be hurt or killed or suffer because we are all people and God loves all of us.

If I feel my heart being hateful, I imagine the mother of that person. I ask myself, what would she want me to pray for that person? That works almost every time. But if I still find myself leaving the prayer zone, fearful of war or famine or serious abuse, and I still find myself wanting to pray against someone, then I pray for that person to feel convicted. I do this sparingly. I can't imagine anything worse than being a part of bringing a lot of evil to the world and then being able to see and know how much evil I'd done. That must be the worst thing imaginable.

I don't think, in prayer, it's our job to change other people. So, in following the Lord's prayer, we pray against evil, but not against people. Prayer changes us and allows us to learn to love. As for my ability to cope with an imperfect world and huge injustices even by my own culture, my own denomination, my own church, my own friends who pray, myself, I've decided to handle it this way: I pray to be in God's will, so I am. It's a process. That path may meander. That path may be for me to help someone else while may dreams are on hold, or it may mean that one thing that seemed like a failure led to another thing God needed to happen for his best will. It means I learn things, regret things, and find ways to change bad habits, to fend off inner and outer lies about myself. I place any failures, problems, surprises, missteps in God's hands. To me, that is what prayer is for, to keep asking God to keep me on his plan, on his path, to help me listen, become loving enough, strong enough; to become someone who can be on that journey with God. Surprisingly, this makes me more and more open to others, not closed.

With prayer, we should begin with gentleness. One example I can think of easily is when California had a drought of several years. I, and many others, prayed for rain. Soon after, I heard that California received rain and their aquifers had been refilled, but mudslides had caused serious damage. This reminds me that in prayer we must be considerate. And if we need to be considerate for rain or trees, how much more so for people? Now, I always pray for gentle soaking rain, and I pray against drought and flood. It's the same way with people. Only God is big enough to know what the earth perfectly needs, and he is also the only person who knows what a person's heart or soul perfectly needs. So, rather than force our ideas, let's gently pray for God's hand to move in and help, and for our hands to know their calling and to do good work, and to bless. ✳

What if I have negative self-talk when I pray?

What if I hear voices when I pray, negative self-talk or worse. What if I'm worried I'll hear voices? Hearing the audible voice of God is going to be super rare. Jesus heard God speaking to him only three times, and that was Jesus! To other people it sounded like thunder.

I may have heard God's audible voice once, but no one around me seemed to hear anything, and it was simply a scripture verse being said aloud by a teacher. Suddenly I couldn't hear the teacher, I heard a loud thundering voice that seemed to reverberate both in my mind and to my ears. Conveniently, it happened during stormy weather. It sounded very thundery to me, so I asked the other people with me if they'd heard anything, and no one answered me or paid me any mind. They acted like they hadn't heard anything, not even thunder, so I left it at that. What did I hear? A verse from Hebrews, "Never will I leave you, never will I forsake you."

The common teaching is that we should pray about what we receive in prayer and confirm any decisions with two or three other people who are praying as well. I've also heard to make sure any leadings you have in prayer match up with scripture. With the help of scripture search engines that's a lot easier nowadays, but you can also use a concordance. It's like a dictionary which is an analog way to look up one word and find all the scriptures in the Bible that have that word. (As you might guess, I love playing in the concordance and having fun finding out how many times the word "heart" is in the Bible, for example, or seek out other fun word searches).

Sometimes, while praying or preparing for something new, like a ministry, a class, or a project you feel called to do, you may hear negative voices-your own interior dialogue, but not audible. These worries that confront you, that may give you a panic attack or stop you in your tracks, can be painful. This can be confounding.

For example, right before doing a new small group, you are suddenly full of doubts. "You aren't good enough to teach this group." "You'll never make a difference." "Your space isn't right for entertaining." "People won't feel comfortable." "You should cancel." "You feel a headache coming on."

Don't worry. This is not an attack by an evil spirit who has somehow entered your brain. Frankly, that's unusual and unlikely that there's a spare demon lying around who has the time and inclination and is suddenly able to read minds. For one, demons can't put thoughts into the heads of people trying to serve God and praying for his will. No one can read thoughts, only God. Only God can hear our inner thoughts. No, if we hear negative inner thoughts, this is normal human doubt.

However, if it seems more than that, or the negative thoughts are stopping you from continuing, consider combatting this anxiety in another way. Realize how hard you've worked to get ready to build community and share love and hope with people in your upcoming ministry or project. Then instead, turn that inner destructive language around by thinking about the other people involved in your group. Those feelings that "you are not good enough" for example are the words that the people who want to come visit with you, may be hearing. That negative self-talk is your inside information as to what to pray about for others. Other people are feeling these same inhibitions. Turn this painful panic attack experience around. Make it something for good by realizing its insight on how to pray for them. Praying will help you all come together, able, and hopeful to do the things you are called to do— whether it's just to have breakfast together or start a new ministry. Any time I've felt, or actually been, flat on the floor in panic, the only thing that seems to help is to think of someone who might be feeling the same as I am and pray for them. This has always helped.

Now many times over, I have just lain down on the floor and let the negative thoughts hold me back. So, believe me, I understand it's hard. When praying over these negative thoughts, there's something that doesn't work for me. If I just wish to feel better or for something to get better, it doesn't work so well. To me this is the definition of " warm thoughts." They are just wishes. I still may still feel anxious and unrooted.

On my best day in this kind of situation, here is what I would do. Sit up. Write down those pesky "you" statements that are cutting you down inside. Then find a scripture verse to negate each one. You can do this ahead of time before your next moment of anxiety—You can also plan this the morning or evening before that next event where you expect anxiety or to feel blocked. It may evolve into a thing where it's generally helpful to pray these verses ahead and during the times you are doing something outgoing. Prayers with scripture are stronger, sharper, more realizable prayers.

All that to say: those "you-are-not-enough-statements" are felt by everyone, all of us. So, pray for the other people who are most likely feeling this way. It's the surest and quickest way to feel better. And ask others to pray with you and help you find scripture that combat lies and bring truth—verses that show you are loved that you are part of God's family, that you have a hope and a future. Pray for others and yourself.

Now, on the other hand, if you are having visions that are confusing or frightening or hear audible voices in the second person that take on personality, and the voices are accusatory in nature, that's usually a sign of schizophrenic affect. It comes from stress, medication reaction, a hit on the head, or illness. At least one out of every million people suffer from a chemical imbalance that can occur naturally around the age of seventeen or from a trauma. The effect is a daily struggle with audible accusatory voices, even confusion between dreams and reality or books or movies or news that you read and reality. If you are worried about these types of voices, doctors are the most helpful paired with healing prayer. Talking to many other families with this genetic illness, these types of accusatory voices seem to be physical and chemical rather than spiritual. So, treat your body, soul, and mind and be patient with yourself. Pray to be able to hear God's voice and know it above all others. If you have trouble with voices, find a friend or family member to help you weigh things carefully before making decisions. Remember those inner voices sometimes represent real concerns in your real life that you can address with help from family, friends, faith, and good counselors.

I'm tempted to say it's unlikely, if you are seeking God and filled with his Spirit, that you'll have to deal with audible voices from an evil spirit. In all my life experience this has been true for myself and those I know well, so far. Think of how two magnets can't be pressed together. I imagine what it is like to try to put evil with something that is close to God. However, that is out of my realm of experience and knowledge. So, I suggest that there are a lot of helpful studies on that topic. The main temptation to avoid is to get caught up in the interesting "fear factor" of it all and neglect what our real faith is all about.

Here's what I think is most important: Jesus taught that he had authority over any and all spirits and his power keeps them under his feet. That's true. His teaching was that we can be a part of that authority, so we don't have to suffer from situations like that whether they are just annoying or frightening or affecting our everyday life. I once enjoyed reading a fiction writer compare evil spirits to a small flea, which is a good metaphor. A flea can cause a lot of fear, but it's so small and easily overcome. I like that image of the idea that we have authority with Christ over evil and goes with the idea of evil and death being "under our feet." We simply use our authority in Christ to clean out any shadows of darkness that bother our home or families with clear and confident words and prayers, and consider it done.

My caution: If you are having trouble in this area, I'd recommend getting teaching and training on dealing with evil spirits before going out and learning the hard way by experience only. From what I've overheard second hand, the only thing I can say, is I'd recommend having a strong able-bodied friend with you, if possible before attempting to deliver someone suffering from the appearance of an evil spirit, make sure that person is not just suffering from mental illness, and I'd have the scriptures on the topic of authority and God's deliverance and power,[12] memorized well ahead of time.

My last thought on this. The spiritual world is mostly invisible to us. Whether an illness starts out physical or genetic and becomes spiritual or vice versa is hard to say. Whether something is part physical, a mental illness or chemical imbalance and part spiritual is hard to say. It could be one or either or both. It could change between the two over time. I've seen a lot of partial healing when praying for mental illness. So, my thought is to trust God with everything, keep praying, and pair prayer and faith with the best medical care you have access to. We are mind, body, soul, and spirit. God gifts us with all type of healers, doctors, and medicines of every kind. I think praying for wisdom and asking people for help is a wise way to address worries about these issues. ✖

What about dreams and visions?

What about seeing visions or dreams during prayer or in response to prayer? Sometimes I've heard a voice right upon waking, something simple. This is not uncommon among people who remember dreams. I consider those dreams that are directed from my subconscious and probably also a leading from God to help me consider my true feelings. I've studied all the leading philosophers on dreams from the ancient Greeks to Freud, Jung, and newer voices. When paired with the dreamwork done by people in the scripture, it's clear to me that dreams are another way God helps us discern our true emotions. Dreams give us healing insight through images that often have word play.

Dreams are indirect, so when I have a dream about a friend, I may call them up and ask how they are doing or pray for them. But more likely, I'll ask myself who that friend represents to me, and what emotions am I dealing with personally that I can pray about. I've heard voices in dreams from "angelic figures" with or without wings, which I see as the same kind of thing–something to journal and pray about to gain energy, insight, and direction, not usually for impulsive action.

If you are worried about hearing God's voice when you pray, if you are having dreams or thinking of images while praying that scare or bewilder you, I was taught to pray a special prayer that always helps me. It's a prayer for imagination. I pray for a hedge of protection around my imagination–that God would use it for good and keep out anything that could harm or mislead me. That, to me feels safe, like locking a door to a house–one that's bigger on the inside. Remember, our imagination is a gift and a tool to help us pray. It's how we connect with an invisible God.

To me, a wandering imagination during prayer is the same as a dream. Those images are helpful to meditate on. For several years, some of my church friends practiced a prayerful meditation that used visualization. This became frustrating to me. What was I going to do with these images of golden mansions, Jesus passing out bags of candy bars, or seashells at the bottom of the ocean? It took a lot of years, but I researched how the imagination and dreams work and now I see those visualization meditations as something playful, a place full of healing metaphors, homonyms, and archetypes. A whole other personal language that takes a lifetime to learn, and in some ways remains mysterious.

If you feel nervous about prayer because of your imagination, images, or dreams (waking or sleeping), be patient with yourself and pray how is most comfortable to you. My favorite types of prayer are singing praise songs with the guitar or praying in words rather than visualizations. I leave those to my dreams. I hope to write a book on dreams and prayer someday. ✵

How can I pray with others I disagree with?

How can I pray when I know prayerful people who are part of injustices or oppressing the poor or innocent? How can I pray when I know people are praying the opposite to my heart? Does that mean they cancel each other out? No. Prayer is not magic or a universal light and dark side with a balance to hold. Prayer is a relationship with God, so it's never wasted.

The heart of this question is a serious one–why we misunderstand or ignore God's voice. Because if there are disagreements, so much that we can't pray together, then someone must be in the wrong. Someone has misunderstood what God has called them to do. And if a lifetime of prayer and Bible study still leaves some of us careless of the poor, still leaves some of us abusers, still leaves some of us rooting for power and control then how much effect can prayer have? If we are objective and look at all the evil in the world done by human hands, even hands that pray, then we'd have to say prayer does very little, we'd have to doubt we are really being changed by God. We may say that change is so small, it's not enough to make the world or ourselves that much better. Why does prayer seem like such a weak thing?

Well, that's a dark road, but one we have to address. I don't think this line of reasoning is accurate. It's easy to say when we miss God on the small things (his will, his values, his likeness) it's because we are human. We've all "gone astray" and "in our own way."

For the large things, we have to accept we are part of a broken system. Some of us then quickly point out that there is no reason to spend time in relationship with a God who invented a broken system. He's at fault, he's not fixing it; he lets evil happen. Don't most of us at one time think to ourselves, no one can be that great if they let evil into the world. Then we reason there is no point in prayer. Or, if we can't help praying because we are idealists in nature, we'll only pray with those people we find the least unjust, the least abhorrent; the people that agree with us.

So how can we trust God to speak to us in prayer when we see so many people who say they follow God, but we don't agree with their actions or associations. This seems compelling if we look at the large scale: look at how Christians handled slavery, the holocaust, the crusades? Many were on the side of those injustices and found ways to bend scriptures to back up their practices of dehumanizing, enslaving, relocating, or murdering others. So, scripture alone cannot be the only way to gauge how we feel lead in prayer. And people's actions are definitely not a good basis who we pray with or how we pray.

This certainty makes us want to give up, or to accuse God of having very little power, when we see all the issues we have today with Christians being known for their hate, for their racism, for their xenophobia, for their oppression and marginalizing or stomping out of diversity. When instead we should be known by our love.

We must know then, in our hearts, that prayerful Christians can be misled, even take part in serious wrongs in the community. But let's turn around and look at our own hearts. If I ask myself, how many times have people decided I was not a great friend, or sister, or co-worker? Plenty. I'm imperfect, I've dropped the ball on being compassionate or understanding or observant many times. What about larger issues? How many times has my country, my community, or my ancestors been unjust, even to the point of atrocity? How many times has my culture not taken care of widows, orphans, wildlife, or the planet? How many times have we skipped out on sharing our faith, hope or love well? The answer is: all the time.

Does that mean we should just let it all go to hell? There's a great prophecy that says God will make a new earth someday. Does that mean we shouldn't worry if this one is trashed? No. I don't think that this verse lets us off the hook. This applies to people as well. They may only be in our lives for a moment, but they are important and have value.

Not to make light of it, but prayerful people continue and begin new injustices, both small and large every day. It might be as small as voting to give less money to the bus system that our blind neighbor needs to commute to work. It might be as small as a spouse who never allows their significant other to choose the movie or the restaurant. It might mean we avoid slow fashion and accidentally support sweatshops or child slavery with the clothes we wear. There are a million opportunities to be unjust—with intention or without. We can walk and talk the faith, preach, and teach and pray with our mouths, while somehow causing injustice in the same step. None of us have been able to stop perpetuating the evil in the world. Sometimes we disagree on what is evil so much, we are ready to excommunicate each other, or worse. So, even if we hear God's leading, silent, or aloud, can we ever trust that we can understand, let alone follow it well?

Should we give up then? Is prayer useless? If getting closer to God in prayer doesn't make us perfect, should we stop praying? No, it's the opposite. Prayer is how we daily walk away from injustice and into communion with God and each other. It's how we learn to identify those "strongholds " that harm us, those things we may not even know we value, but somehow, we've embraced lies twisted around our root understandings. We all have blind spots and often more than one. A prayer life is the best way to carefully find paths to stop being unjust and to pull out roots of bitterness; to take apart personal or cultural lies that we've been using to hurt others.

God is there for us. Prayer is not for the faint of heart. It takes a lifetime. Prayer is dangerous, it changes us, and it changes the world.

When we pray, we are battling the distance we feel from God; fighting our human nature to run away from him; our nature to believe lies about him. And if we lose the battle, we become someone else. Losing means, we turn more and more selfish over time until we reject God and others completely–a simple definition of hell, ultimate aloneness.

What I want to say is that, praying against people, pushing them away is not the right direction. But praying with them won't hurt. Praying for them will help. I promise. So, pray for people to come into a place of peace, of health, of blessing. Pray for families to be reunited, for homes and businesses to be built, for children to be safe and to learn they are loved. For faith to spring up where there isn't any. For God's spirit and Jesus' heart to enter dark places and bring light.

When we pray for blessing, when we pray for instead of against, that allows us to accept each other with all our flaws. When we can pray together, take communion together, love God together, then we have a strong enough relationship to talk through the areas where we see each other as unjust. And hopefully, the heart to listen and change. Spiritually, we are all partly blind and we need each other to find our vision. Likewise, we are all partly deaf. Together, not apart, we have a chance to hear and see better God's vision for our own path, and for the "new thing" he's always pushing us toward. ✳

What about the masculine pronouns of God?

The Trinity can be confusing. How strange is it that God is fully one God, but also in three parts, or three relationships to himself? That he is like Neapolitan ice cream, or a three-leaf clover in some way. That God is somehow all God, and yet all son to himself. That the Spirit of God is somehow the spirit of the son and that's what we need the most to connect to God in heaven? If you think about it, you can get worse than an ice cream headache.

What I think many of us find hard is the masculine aspect of the Trinity. Maybe you've been in a tradition that emphasize one aspect more than the others. Your faith only allows room for one part of the Trinity. That's very common. I think in every subculture of every tradition, we have a preferred way to think about God and what we feel comfortable with. What's sad is when our own comfort is keeping faith and joy, hope and peace from so many people.

It might be hard to pray if you visualize God as a man, or a father. Finding Jesus might be that much harder if you see him as a single young man or a tiny infant. As for the Holy Spirit, often pictured as a dove, I think that's inaccessible to all of us not saturated in a doctorate in the ancient story of Noah. So, does that make God as the trinity a men's only club? Maybe you've been in an abusive or hurtful relationship with someone with masculine pronouns or hurt by a father figure. That makes prayer incredibly hard. It's amazing the power of a pronoun to hurt our feelings or get in the way of our visualizing God. And prayer is visualizing God.

Let's go back to the truth here. Remember God is neither male nor female. The word Yahweh is a combination of the ending sounds for male and female combined. So, God is the "I am, the I was, the I will be, and the She is, the She was and the She will be and the He was, the He is and the He will be). You can see why they didn't want to spell out the name (that's a Bible joke). He's the first person to agree with you that pronouns are misleading.

The truth, and scripture backs us up here, you can use any pronoun to refer to God: he, she or they. They are all accurate. For example, the word Shakina is a name for more feminine aspect of God's spirit. God has many names in scripture and in the original writing, their name wasn't fully written as it was too powerful to spell out completely. What gets me through the pronoun issue the most, is my favorite Bible verse that relates to God as a mother bird.

In Andrei Rublev's fifteenth century icon of the Holy Trinity, arguably the most famous orthodox icon painting ever painted, he shows three figures seated at the table with a chalice of wine. The Father wears a multicolored robe and a halo. The Son wears traditional red and blue with a symbolic tree behind him. The Holy Spirit wears softer shades and has a mountain behind her. (Only her hand touches the table of communion because she is present with us on earth.)Although historians of every stripe refer to this famous artwork as three male figures, it's clear that they are beardless feminine images. In long dress robes, they have long curled hair. Fan art painted of this icon also traditionally depicts three women at the table. These figures look more like angels, with wings that touch each other showing a reference to the angels that visited Abraham. Somehow these three winged women are the favorite icon of the Trinity despite their gender.

Historians note that the seated figures in the painting have carefully painted bare feet set on flat doors. Common interpretation says they are "chillaxin" on top of something that looks like rectangular slabs, thought of as the doors to hell, smashed open when Christ trampled on death and "delivered humanity from its dominion forever."

That means that though the Latin and English-speaking precedent is to only refer to God as masculine, artists have always been able to show the long history behind the original languages of scripture. God is neither male nor female. One of the earliest things mentioned about God in scripture.

So, what else can you do? Besides ordering a gender inclusive Bible available for sale at online retailers, or reading your scriptures in ancient Hebrew and Greek? While growing up reading the scripture always referring to men instead of women, I was able to usually include myself in the idea that the word man meant mankind. But the older I became, the harder it was to do this. Meditating on scriptures that leave out the feminine gender are hard. The things that have helped me the most in this area are studying saints and meditating on feminine aspects of God and the women in the Bible–which became this book you are reading here.

At times, when that was not enough, I finally allowed myself to picture the Holy Spirit as feminine. Really, I feel this saved my life, my sanity, and my faith. To me, in my imagination, where I picture God and pray and meditate and visualize, that makes the trinity into a family of father, son...and mother—instead of "men's only club with bird."

I haven't studied the theology or extra Biblical texts on this, I imagine there are a few in Jewish scripture and beyond that support that this meditation is acceptable. More and more people are calling for a return to the original feminine and plural pronouns. The Episcopal Church in America has recently been reported to be in the process of changing the common book of prayer (in print since 1549) so that it no longer uses masculine pronouns to refer to God. Regardless, imagining the Holy Spirit as feminine was one way that I was able to keep my faith and continue to pray when I felt the most hurt about pronouns. It has worked for me. I believe that in prayer; we do have freedom to approach God in whatever visualization method we need to reach out to them.

Acknowledging the feminine aspects of God may be the door that finally opens for you to enter a life of faith, prayer, and relationship with God that you've always dreamed of. Give it a try, let God reach out to you, hold you, share their heart with you. Let God prove themself. I love the traditional Salvation message-the "Billy Graham style of accepting God in a moment through Christ. But I haven't emphasized that "salvation" message here. I do believe it. This worked for me, but when this message becomes a stumbling block to many people because it's forced into a conglomerate of ideas that suggest women are less than people, that they are objects to be owned or controlled, we need to pause what has become such tired language as to become unintelligible and consider how best to move forward in faith and prayer as a community.

My best answer: What if we took a small break from fighting, hating, and holding perfectly respectable and reasonable grudges with each other (and maybe let go as much as we can those grudges with the male-centric authors of scripture, they are only human). What if we stopped and refocused on the fact that God loves us?

I want to reach out to God and connect with them. If that means I have to forgive Paul's comments about women that don't fit my

21st century life, I'll have to do that. If it means I must forgive my faith tradition, my family, my friends, my church, and my culture for making me feel less than, I'll do it. Why? Because I need God. I have to reach out to God and find that spiritual life they are offering me. I can't. No, I won't let anything get in the way anymore.

> *These three things remain, Faith, Hope and Love, but the greatest of these is Love.*

Let's think about what we do have. What do we have besides our disagreements and our failures and our imperfection? What do we have that tells us about God? We have creation, Life, Jesus, God's Word, God's Spirit, Saints, saintly people, tradition, experience, stories, the people around us, our own testimony. All of these shout out that God is a parent, our creator, who loves us.

So, what if we do it? Let's embrace love. In prayer, let's ask God to speak for themself. Then let's step back and see what happens. Let's nestle back closely to God in her nest, under her feathers where we are safe and protected and listen to her heart. Let's draw near to God. I have done this through prayer, and I've never regretted it a single day. ✳

Store Window on Mainstreet, Kansas City, Buttonwood Art Space

Acknowledgments

Thank you to my 2021 summer intern from Greenville University Ashely Anderson who helped me to have courage and dedication to start the spiritual imprint of Flying Ketchup Press, Light Shine Books and her advisor Alexandria LaFaye who inspired me to continue growing in publishing. Thank you to my friend Roberta Coons who lent me her beautiful home as a writers retreat. Thank you to Melinda who inspired me to keep writing and publishing and carefully read every page of this book twice! Thank you most of all to my mother who has given me time and space to start a publishing company and to write and make art, my aunt Barb Ellison who has encouraged me in everything, and my sister Christa Miller who bought copious amounts of art to help me keep going as an artist/writer. Thanks to my prayer team who prayed with me through the launch of this book: Rachel Duewer Schwartz, Alyssa Benjamin, Susan Mason, Julia Dell Otterness, Debbie Kirchner, Cheryl Moran, Tina Joy Cochran, Vicky Lanning Feliciano, Ris Ng, Esther Manyeo, Dawn Sachet, Poet t.l. Sanders, Josh Baum, and Diane Boyum, (and the friends from Roberta's prayer group and her cousin, Kim.) Thanks to my friends from my college, university, and Bethel Seminary friends who helped me on this journey. Thanks to my local church Northland Cathedral who supported me with divorce care classes, music lessons, artist group, and prayer team over the last several years, thank you. Thanks also to the Grantham BIC church which hosted my art show to celebrate the launch of this book and curator Geoff Isley. Thanks to the many local visitors to my studio at InterUrban ArtHouse in 2018 who first gave me the advice on how to finish my *Battle Dress* series of art, and the woman who said I should write my own story on the dress because "We all have our own battles, don't we?" That became this book. Thanks to my kids who gave me lots of time to write and are so easy going and supportive.

We aren't the same person every day, so why should prayer
be the same every day?

About the Author

Polly Alice McCann, author, artist, poet, mother of two began writing after a trip to the desert where she slept under the stars with only a book for a pillow. She won the 2014 Ernest Hartmann award from the International Association for the Study of Dreams from Berkeley, CA for research on the subconscious writing process. She is the founder of Ketchupedia Poetry Radio and the managing editor of Flying Ketchup Press. Her soft sculptural paintings are created with imperfect stitching, "I want my work to help share the beauty of imperfection meeting God's grace that mends the broken hearted." She lives in Kansas City with her family. Find her at PollyMcCann.com.

Endnotes

1   ***St. Patrick's Breastplate Prayer***

I bind unto myself today
The strong Name of the Trinity,
By invocation of the same
The Three in One and One in Three.

I bind this today to me forever
By power of faith, Christ's incarnation;
His baptism in Jordan river,
His death on Cross for my salvation;
His bursting from the spicèd tomb,
His riding up the heavenly way,
His coming at the day of doom
I bind unto myself today.
I bind unto myself the power
Of the great love of cherubim;
The sweet 'Well done' in judgment hour,
The service of the seraphim, Confessors' faith,
Apostles' word, The Patriarchs' prayers, the prophets' scrolls,
All good deeds done unto the Lord And purity of virgin souls.

I bind unto myself today
The virtues of the star lit heaven,
The glorious sun's life giving ray,
The whiteness of the moon at even,
The flashing of the lightning free,
The whirling wind's tempestuous shocks,
The stable earth, the deep salt sea
Around the old eternal rocks.

I bind unto myself today
The power of God to hold and lead,
His eye to watch, His might to stay,
His ear to hearken to my need.
The wisdom of my God to teach,
His hand to guide, His shield to ward;
The word of God to give me speech,
His heavenly host to be my guard.

Against the demon snares of sin,
The vice that gives temptation force,
The natural lusts that war within,
The hostile men that mar my course;
Or few or many, far or nigh,
In every place and in all hours,
Against their fierce hostility
I bind to me these holy powers.

Against all Satan's spells and wiles,
Against false words of heresy,
Against the knowledge that defiles,
Against the heart's idolatry,
Against the wizard's evil craft,
Against the death wound and the burning,
The choking wave, the poisoned shaft,
Protect me, Christ, till Thy returning.

Christ be with me, Christ within me,
Christ behind me, Christ before me,
Christ beside me, Christ to win me,
Christ to comfort and restore me.
Christ beneath me, Christ above me,
Christ in quiet, Christ in danger,
Christ in hearts of all that love me,
Christ in mouth of friend and stranger.

I bind unto myself the Name,
The strong Name of the Trinity,
By invocation of the same,
The Three in One and One in Three.
By Whom all nature hath creation,
Eternal Father, Spirit, Word:
Praise to the Lord of my salvation,
Salvation is of Christ the Lord.-

2   **The Lord's Prayer, Jesus' Prayer** *(Matt. 6: 9-13, NIV)*

Our Father which art in heaven, Hallowed be thy name.
Thy kingdom come, Thy will be done in earth, as it is in heaven.
Give us this day our daily bread.
And forgive us our debts, as we forgive our debtors.
And lead us not into temptation, but deliver us from evil:
For thine is the kingdom, and the power, and the glory, for ever. Amen.

3   **Beatitudes, Jesus' Prayer** *(Matt 5:3-12, NIV)*

"Blessed are the poor in spirit,
* for theirs is the kingdom of heaven.*
Blessed are those who mourn,
for they will be comforted.
Blessed are the meek,
* for they will inherit the earth.*
Blessed are those who hunger and thirst for justice,
* for they will have their fill.*
Blessed are the merciful,
* for they will obtain mercy.*
Blessed are the pure of heart, for they will see God.
Blessed are the peacemakers,
* for they will be called children of God.*
Blessed are those who are persecuted in the cause of justice,
* for theirs is the kingdom of heaven.*
"Blessed are you when people insult you and persecute you

and utter all kinds of calumnies against you for my sake.
Rejoice and be glad, for your reward will be great in heaven.
In the same manner, they persecuted the prophets who preceded you.

4   **Kay's Travel Prayer**
Dear God,
Thanks for being with us on this journey.
Help me to drive safely, help others around me
drive safely. Protect us on all sides. Thanks for
protecting us on this trip. In Jesus name, Amen.

5   **Hannah's Prayer** (1 Samuel 2:1-10,CJB)
"My heart exults in Adonai!
My dignity has been restored by Adonai!
I can gloat over my enemies,
because of my joy at your saving me.
"No one is as holy as Adonai,
because there is none to compare with you,
no rock like our God.
"Stop your proud boasting!
Don't let arrogance come from your mouth!
For Adonai is a God of knowledge,
and he appraises actions.
The bows of the mighty are broken,
while the feeble are armed with strength.
The well-fed hire themselves for bread,
while those who were hungry hunger no more.
The barren woman has borne seven,
while the mother of many wastes away.
"Adonai kills and makes alive;
he brings down to the grave, and he brings up.
Adonai makes poor, and he makes rich;
he humbles, and he exalts.
He raises the poor from the dust,
lifts up the needy from the trash pile;

he gives them a place with leaders
and assigns them seats of honor.
"For the earth's pillars belong to Adonai;
on them he has placed the world.
He will guard the steps of his faithful,
but the wicked will be silenced in darkness.
For it is not by strength that a person prevails —
those who fight Adonai will be shattered;
he will thunder against them in heaven —
Adonai will judge the ends of the earth.
He will strengthen his king
and enhance the power of his anointed."

6   ***A time for Everything*** (Ecclesiastes 3:1-8, NIV)
There is a time for everything,
and a season for every activity under the heavens:
a time to be born and a time to die,
a time to plant and a time to uproot,
a time to kill and a time to heal,
a time to tear down and a time to build,
a time to weep and a time to laugh,
a time to mourn and a time to dance,
a time to scatter stones and a time to gather them,
a time to embrace and a time to refrain from embracing,
a time to search and a time to give up,
a time to keep and a time to throw away,
a time to tear and a time to mend,
a time to be silent and a time to speak,
a time to love and a time to hate,
a time for war and a time for peace.

7 Names describing God

Abba	Daddy, Mark 14:36, Rom 8:15, Gal 4:6
Adonai	Master or Lord, Ex 4:10, 13
Elohim	God, They Create, Gen 1:1,
El Elyon	the most high God, Gen 14:18)
El Olam	the Everlasting God, Gen 21:33
El Shaddai	Almighty Breasted One, Gen 35:11
Jehovah	God of Redemption
Jehovah Jireh	the LORD will provide, Gens 22:14
Jehovah Nissi	the LORD our banner, Ex 17:8-15
Jehovah Roi	the LORD who sees me, Gen 16:13
Jehobah Raah	the Lord is my Shepherd, Psalm 23:1
Jehovah Tsidkenu	the LORD our righteousness Jer 23:6
Jehovah Shamma	the LORD that heals you Ezek 48:35
Jehovah Shalom	the LORD our peace Judges 6:23-24
Jehovah Sabbaoth	the LORD of hosts I Samuel 1:3
Sophia/ Logos	Her Wisdom Witness, Proverbs 8:22-23
Shakina	She dwells, Exodus 13:21
Yahweh	The he-she-is-was-will be, Exodus 3

8 Polly's Bedtime Prayer (Psalm 4:8, NLV, NKJV)

I will lie down and sleep in peace. You alone, Oh Lord, keep me safe. I will lie down and sleep in peace. You alone, Oh Lord, make me dwell in safety.

I'm bursting with God-news;
　I'm dancing the song of my Savior God.
God took one good look at me, and look what happened—
　I'm the most fortunate woman on earth!
What God has done for me will never be forgotten,
　the God whose very name is holy, set apart from all others.
His mercy flows in wave after wave
　on those who are in awe before him.
He bared his arm and showed his strength,
　scattered the bluffing braggarts.
He knocked tyrants off their high horses,
　pulled victims out of the mud.
The starving poor sat down to a banquet;
　the callous rich were left out in the cold.
He embraced his chosen child, Israel;
　he remembered and piled on the mercies, piled them high.
It's exactly what he promised,
　beginning with Abraham and right up to now.

10   **Ruth's Prayer** *(Ruth 1:16-18, NIV)*
"Don't force me to leave you;
don't make me go home.
Where you go, I go;
and where you live, I'll live.
Your people are my people,
your God is my God; where you die,
I'll die, and that's where I'll be buried,
so help me God—not even death itself
is going to come between us!"

11   **Polly's Prayer**
Dear God of majesty, of rainbows and rivers, of mysteries and everyday things,

Cover this day with an understanding of Jesus as my redeemer, a lamb who made the ultimate sacrifice for me; God's son, still here and alive and with me in Spirit. Let this day be covered and surrounded with the protection of that knowledge. Let this day be covered with my testimony, my remembrance that you are here with me, you save me, and you have plan for me, a hope and a future. You bring big harvest of joy where we've planted in tears. Before my feet touch the ground, and aloud, let me say that you are my God and I have a story to share that I'm a part of you and you are a part of me. What can anyone do to me if you are with me. Thank you for redeeming me, thank you for being my friend. Give me your strength for this day because my weakness is your strength.

Finally, be strong in the Lord and in the strength of His might. Put on the full armor of God, so that you will be able to stand firm against the schemes of the devil. For our struggle is not against flesh and blood, but against the rulers, against the powers, against the world forces of this darkness, against the spiritual forces of wickedness in the heavenly places. Therefore, take up the full armor of God, so that you will be able to resist on the evil day, and having done everything, to stand firm.

Stand firm therefore, having belted your waist with truth, and having put on the breastplate of righteousness, and having strapped on your feet the preparation of the gospel of peace; in addition to all, taking up the shield of faith with which you will be able to extinguish all the flaming arrows of the evil one. And take the helmet of salvation and the sword of the Spirit, which is the word of God.

With every prayer and request, [pray at all times in the Spirit, and with this in view, be alert with all perseverance and every request for all the saints, and pray in my behalf, that speech may be given to me in the opening of my mouth, to make known with boldness the mystery of the gospel, for which I am an ambassador in [chains; that]in proclaiming it I may speak boldly, as I ought to speak.

Index

Made in United States
Orlando, FL
12 August 2022

20932629R00171